Postfemininities in Popular Culture

Also by Stéphanie Genz

GOTHIC STUDIES 9/2 (*co-edited*)

POSTFEMINISM: Cultural Texts and Theories (*co-authored*)

POSTFEMINIST GOTHIC: Critical Interventions in Contemporary Culture (*co-edited*)

Postfemininities in Popular Culture

Stéphanie Genz
Edge Hill University, UK

First published 2009 by
PALGRAVE MACMILLAN

Palgrave Macmillan in the UK is an imprint of Macmillan Publishers Limited, registered in England, company number 785998, of Houndmills, Basingstoke, Hampshire RG21 6XS.

Palgrave Macmillan in the US is a division of St Martin's Press LLC, 175 Fifth Avenue, New York, NY 10010.

Palgrave Macmillan is the global academic imprint of the above companies and has companies and representatives throughout the world.

Palgrave® and Macmillan® are registered trademarks in the United States, the United Kingdom, Europe and other countries.

ISBN-13: 978–0–230–55150–3 hardback
ISBN-10: 0–230–55150–5 hardback

This book is printed on paper suitable for recycling and made from fully managed and sustained forest sources. Logging, pulping and manufacturing processes are expected to conform to the environmental regulations of the country of origin.

A catalogue record for this book is available from the British Library.

Library of Congress Cataloging-in-Publication Data
Genz, Stéphanie, 1976–
   Postfemininities in popular culture / Stephanie Genz.
      p.   cm.
   Includes bibliographical references and index.
   ISBN 978–0–230–55150–3
   1. Feminist theory.   2. Popular culture.   3. Sex role.   4. Mass media and women.   I. Title.
   HQ1190.G4764 2009
   305.4201—dc22   2008041045

10   9   8   7   6   5   4   3   2   1
18   17   16   15   14   13   12   11   10   09

Printed and bound in Great Britain by
CPI Antony Rowe, Chippenham and Eastbourne

Contents

Acknowledgements

Although by itself a solitary task, writing a book is always a communal effort as well and so I am obliged to a number of people. I want to thank my editors at Palgrave for their belief in this project and their patience. Also, I want to thank my colleagues at Napier and Edge Hill University for their support through all stages of this project. As time is often the most precious commodity, I want to express my gratitude to Carol Poole for clearing my timetable so that I could concentrate on this book. A special thank you goes to my family, who continually help and encourage me. As always, this book is for Ben, without whom it simply would not have been written.

Introduction: The "f-Words"

I do my own laundry. I clean, iron and cook (occasionally). I also like to wear make-up and sometimes a short skirt. I love my husband and hope to have children. I work full-time and I enjoy teaching my students. I am a member of a feminist association and I have a weakness for shopping and celebrity magazines. What does this make me? A housewife, narcissist, wife and (potential) mother, worker, feminist, consumer? A schizophrenic?

If I have given away too much of myself and stepped beyond the confines of academic appropriateness, I apologize for my indiscretion. Yet, it only seems fair that my readers should be aware of *my* social and cultural situation and *my* sexual positioning as a Western, white, heterosexual, middle-class feminist. Born in the mid-1970s, I am too young to have witnessed the political excitement and activism of feminism's second wave. Instead, I grew up in the backlash-ridden 1980s when "feminism" became a dirty word and terms like "equality" and "emancipation" lost their innovative appeal and became part of our everyday vocabulary. As we witnessed more women going out to work and becoming economically independent, feminism seemed to have achieved the status of popular common sense, so much so that obituaries for feminism appeared in some political and media quarters, announcing if not the death but at least the redundancy of feminism.[1] In the 1990s, another "f-word" re-entered our cultural arena as "Girl Power" heralded femininity and sexual forwardness as signs of female freedom and progress. "Pink-packaged femininity" made a substantial and lucrative comeback in fashion, style and the publishing industry (evidenced by countless, pastel-covered chick lit paperbacks). As Jennifer Baumgardner's and Amy Richards' Girlie Manifesto proclaimed, "Girlie culture is a rebellion against the false impression that since women don't

1

want to be sexually exploited, they don't want to be sexual;...against the anachronistic belief that...girls and power don't mix" (137). The Girlies' feisty attitude was dampened somewhat by simultaneous claims that professional single women were in danger of lifelong solitude and unhappiness. It appeared that, once they had to move into the work-force, young women's confidence (bolstered by Girlie assertions) was doomed to hit rock bottom. This, we were told, was indicative of a postfeminist moment of female disorientation and anxiety (Dickerson; Whelehan, *Feminist Bestseller*). The 1990s woman was seen to be in dan-ger of serious mental and physical damage – of ending up "all alone, half-eaten by an Alsatian", as one well-known fictional *singleton* put it (Fielding, *Bridget Jones's Diary* 33). This in turn caused a counter-attack by feminist journalists and academics who lambasted these depictions as media distortions and appropriations that neutralize feminism's radical potential (Faludi; Jones, "Post-Feminism").

It is fair to say that the last decades of the twentieth century were char-acterized by analytical turmoil and popular disagreements regarding the conditions of feminism and femininity. For many of us coming of age around this time, the sheer amount of possible interpretations and alle-giances was confounding and downright confusing. While we wanted to remain loyal to second wave feminists who had fought hard for the per-sonal, professional and academic freedoms that we were now enjoying and almost taking for granted, there was no denying that the political and cultural climate had changed and "we [were] no longer in a second wave of feminism" (Gillis and Munford, "Harvesting" 2). This awareness of feminist change resulted in a number of bitter ownership battles and wrangling, often cast in generational/familial terms as mother–daughter conflicts.[2] These arguments were at times no more than personal attacks on what was perceived as young women's ungratefulness (on the one hand) and established feminists' rigidity (on the other). Yet, they also underlined the fact that "sisterhood" was becoming an elusive, even mythical quality and feminists (young and old) could not hope for a straightforward narrative of progress or a beeline future direction for their feminist impulses. Now that we have entered a new millennium, confusion is still rife about the nature of post–second wave feminism and femininity. At the same time, however, there is also a sense of intel-lectual fatigue and exhaustion as we seem to have run out of steam debating the state of women in twenty-first-century culture and soci-ety. Are we past the "post" and/or riding a new feminist wave? Have we arrived in a brave new world or are we doomed to repeat the patterns of the last century?

As my admittedly personal and self-indulgent confession at the beginning indicates, a woman's life continues to be circumscribed by markers of femininity, feminism and femaleness that measure her respective strengths and failings in these categories. Moreover, we tend to view some of the characteristics inherent in these categories as somewhat incompatible and even contradictory. For example, a successful businesswoman is often perceived to have shortcomings as a mother/wife and vice versa.[3] A feminist academic wearing a miniskirt and make-up might not raise eyebrows, but what if she wore a T-shirt with the words "Porn Star" emblazoned on it or she decided to have a breast augmentation? Or indeed, what if a woman decided to abandon femininity and relinquish its markers (fashion, hairstyle or even through a breast reduction) – would she still be considered a woman? Feminism, femininity and femaleness are thus linked in a cultural framework that is in a process of constant realignment. While the connection between femaleness and femininity has historically been seen in deductive terms (that is, reversibly, "I am a woman, therefore I am feminine"), the relationship between feminism and femininity has been more strained to the extent that, as Joanne Hollows notes, feminist critiques have often been "dependent on creating an opposition between 'bad' feminine identities and 'good' feminist identities" (9).[4] To this end, these categories have given rise to distinct cultural identities that metonymically come to represent the category as a whole and demarcate how far a woman can swerve.

Such distinctions are by no means exclusionary and fixed – indeed, how could they be considering that the majority of Western women today take up most (or at least some) of the roles I highlighted earlier. The subject positions that women adopt in contemporary society are multifarious and varied; some of them are assumed consciously and more or less voluntarily (like our choice of work, although admittedly there is always a degree of economic necessity); some of these roles are deemed "natural", fulfilling a basic human desire for companionship and procreation; others are instilled in us from a range of sources, some linked to our individual situation (our familial/social backgrounds) while others are historically, culturally and educationally "learned". Borrowing Patricia Mann's words, there is no doubt that today we are "conflicted actors" occupying "multiple agency positions" (4, 160). As Mann explains,

> [w]e may be described, without undue exaggeration, as operating within a tangle of motivations, responsibilities, rewards, and forms of

recognition unmoored from traditional male and female, public and private identities. Given the chaotic state of individual motivations and responsibilities in this scenario, it may be wholly unrealistic to expect anyone to worry very much about establishing firm social identities – feminist, feminine, maternal, or otherwise.

(115)

The question of "what makes a woman?" has never had so many different and competing answers and women of the new millennium have been the subjects/objects of countless enquiries (fictional, political, media and academic alike) that have come to a number of conclusions: the "new women" of the bimillenary are hapless "singletons" looking for Mr Right; confident "chicks" who wear their lipstick with pride; political eye candy ("Blair's Babes"); "power feminists"; third wave feminists who relish difference and diversity; postfeminist traitors/saviours (depending on your viewpoint). Indeed, we seem to be trapped in a labyrinth of (re)significations and we can no longer say with confidence and certainty what it means to be female, feminine and feminist in the twenty-first century.

This book endeavours to take stock of women's contemporary situation and representation by looking at a range of theoretical and popular texts that have influenced and formed our understanding of the modern female self since the emergence of second wave feminism in the late 1960s. It aims to address the interplay between feminist polemical writing and popular culture in order to provide a representational history of femininity spanning the past 40 years – from second wave notions of "the feminine mystique" to 1980s accounts of the "superwoman", to a postfeminist re-embrace of girly femininity. Offering both a backward glance and a forward-looking perspective, the book marks an important cross-generational moment in feminist thinking that challenges us to re-evaluate previous conceptions of feminism, femininity and femaleness. These "f-words" demarcate the conceptual framework of this analysis, charting their developments as they have gone in and out of academic and popular fashion. It is a founding premise of this investigation that all of the above "f-words" are variable and therefore have to be recognized as areas of change. While this may be evident and well documented as far as feminism (and its diverse strands) is concerned, femininity in particular has been hampered by negative associations of female oppression and inferiority that stubbornly cling to its descriptions and expressions. Of course, femaleness itself has also been the subject of recent theoretical investigations that question the sex/gender (nature/culture) distinction and argue that sex "ha[s] been gender all along" (Butler, *Gender Trouble* 8).[5] In our "age of uncertainty", these terms can no longer be taken for granted as "natural" or right states of woman and, instead, they come to be interrogated, appropriated and resignified.[6]

While the indeterminacy and multiplicity of the categories of "Woman" and "feminist" have been discussed at length by other commentators, I will concentrate specifically on the changing depictions of white, heterosexual femininity and its shifting relationships with feminism and concepts of female victimization.[7] I am well aware that this is an improbable and highly controversial site for the exploration of feminine complexity because in a sense this is where patriarchal femininity is defined in the most seductive as well as limited terms: white women can gain substantial social power by conforming to the disciplinary regimes of whiteness, heterosexuality and gender – power that might not be readily available to women from other ethnic and "racial" backgrounds and with other sexual preferences. Audre Lorde writes of the "patriarchal invitation to power" whereby "white women face the pitfall of being seduced into joining the oppressor under the pretense of sharing power" (118). The "pitfall" of this logic, Lorde continues, is that "it is easier for white women to believe the dangerous fantasy that if you are good enough, pretty enough, sweet enough, quiet enough, teach the children to behave, hate the right people, and marry the right men, then you will be allowed to co-exist with patriarchy in relative peace" (119). White, Western, heterosexual women are seen to be most susceptible to patriarchal myths of femininity because they stand to gain most social advantages by becoming patriarchally defined but nonetheless admired objects of reverence. This has brought with it charges of conformity, false consciousness and collusion, of "sleeping with the enemy". This privileged position implies that white, heterosexual women "suffer from an excess of visibility" that places them at the heart of traditional Western notions of female beauty and comportment (Whelehan, *Overloaded* 156). Any (re)articulation of white femininity always has to contend with this historically entrenched link between sexual objectification and white female agency. My task then is not only to render visible the structures of discipline and domination that set up this "imaginary feminine" – the ideal body-subject of femininity – but also to imagine alternative modes of identity formation for white, heterosexual femininity (Brook 67). It is here, at the centre of white, Western, heteronormative hegemony, that femininity is the most fought over, contentious and contradictory.

Taking into account the differences between women and the plurality of identities, it is now a theoretical given to think of femininity in the plural. Following sustained critical interventions by a number of schools of thought (including poststructuralism, psychoanalysis, sociology, feminism, film and cultural theory), femininity has been exposed as a social and cultural construct that acts as a norm for women's (self-)definition.[8] As Myra Macdonald notes, "femininity is not a fixed identity...but a constantly renegotiated set of alliances and identifications" (22). Femininity is not an origin in itself but always an outcome of a historically, culturally and socially distinct process of gendering. Moreover, acquiring femininity does not need to imply being passively moulded by a set of external forces. Following Judith Butler, acquiring gender involves "an incessant project, a daily act of reconstruction and interpretation...an impulsive yet mindful process of interpreting a cultural reality laden with sanctions, taboos and prescriptions" ("Variations" 131). As I will discuss later, the notion of femininity as a mutable cultural construction has produced a range of reinterpretations that stress its *performative* dimensions. However, while we have clearly been able to deconstruct and de-essentialize femininity from various critical perspectives, *changing* it has proven more difficult and there has been a great amount of resistance (in particular from feminist theorists) to the possibility of a reformed, reconfigured femininity. Macdonald maintains that while "the myths of femininity have been modified in the course of this century in a variety of ways, what is disturbing is their tenaciousness", concluding that "the 'mode of femininity' has been tinkered with, not redrafted" (220).

The baggage that accompanies femininity is such that it continues to be haunted by a spectre of cultural misogyny that asserts its devaluing and demeaning aspects. Though there is now no denying that we can perform or "do gender" (as Butler names it) to help create our subjectivity and self-presentation, there appears to be a definitional stasis in the sense that any attempt to propose an altered script of femininity has been undermined and overpowered by its bleaker interpretations that emphasize oppression rather than resistance. Unable to shake off its residual negativity, femininity largely remains unquestioned as an anachronistic, patriarchal leftover – a "nostalgic tradition of imposed limitations" and "a rigid code of appearance and behaviour defined by do's and don't-do's" (Brownmiller 2). Feminism owes its *raison d'être* in part to the counter-cultural role it plays in resisting feminine victimization and imagining an alternative future of gender. Feminist activists and academics (past and present) stand almost unanimously in a critical relation to social and cultural constructions of femininity that, in the words of Beverly Skeggs, is doomed to be experienced by women as an "almost impossible", "uninhabitable" identity position (102). Indeed, it was this "uninhabitable" quality of femininity that acted as a political impetus to the emerging Women's Liberation Movement in the late 1960s and that Betty Friedan described so vividly as "the feminine mystique" finding "fulfilment only in sexual passivity, male domination, and nurturing maternal love" (38). This negative inflection of femininity acts as a kind of ideological fire wall to guard off more diverse readings that depict femininity not only as habitable but also as potentially emancipatory.

In this book, I do not seek to make out a case for a new, "antivictimization" femininity that presumes women's already-achieved professional and sexual gains and inverts male-defined notions of feminine submissiveness (Ouellette 323). I am engaged, however, in what Charlotte Brunsdon has described as "the search for feminine agency" that takes into account diverse definitions of femininity (27). The contradictions surrounding modern-day femininity are such that it can no longer be defined in singular terms and instead is characterized by hybrid qualities. Contemporary femininity allows for multiple layers of signification and female identification that go beyond the dualities of subject and object, perpetrator and victim, power and powerlessness. While I am not disclaiming the existence and historical relevance of femininity as an oppressive social discourse, I am disputing the definition of femininity as a straightjacket for women, a gendered prison-house built on restraint and restriction. Over the past 40 years, femininity has acquired different and even oppositional meanings in popular/feminist consciousness that vary widely in their relationship to concepts of female victimization and agency. Rather than providing a uniform, monosemic answer to the feminine conundrum, each decade has added other levels of meaning that further highlight the constructedness and plurality of femininity.

In her *genealogical* analysis of femininity, Alison Stone emphasizes the advantages of such an approach:

> Through this reworking, each woman becomes located within a historical chain comprised of all those (women) who have successfully reinterpreted the meaning of femininity.... [A]ny reinterpretation of femininity must overlap in content with the interpretation that it modifies, shedding some elements of that pre-existing interpretation while preserving others.... Over time ... successive modifications in meaning necessarily build upon one another so that determinate

historical patterns of interpretation of femininity emerge.... As this branching occurs... quite separate cultures of femininity emerge, within which different women become located.[9]

(92–3)

Following this genealogical method, femininity appears as a complex, multi-layered puzzle that is dynamic in its capacity to change and absorb cultural messages, without being amnesiac and forgetful about previous versions of femininity. In this model, women are connected in intricate and variable ways – both inter- and intra-generationally – through historical chains of overlapping understandings of femininity. As Stone writes, "[t]here is no unitary meaning of femininity on which all women agree: although all women may identify with femininity, their femininity invariably differs in content" (92). The meaning of femininity is thus less stable and consistent than one might suppose; rather it is characterized by mutability and vulnerability that expose its cultural/social/personal construction. While this process of attrition reworks pre-existing patterns of interpretation, it does not provide femininity with instant new meanings that wipe out previous significations. Diverse meanings of femininity intersect whereby "any reinterpretation of femininity must overlap in content with the interpretation that it modifies, shedding some elements of that pre-existing interpretation while preserving others" (93). In what follows, I argue against the creation of a neo-femininity that constructs a new dream of feminine self-actualization. Instead, contemporary femininity continues to be haunted by echoes of the past that stress its subordinating, oppressive elements.[10]

Femininity

In recent years there have been a number of calls for a modernization of femininity and the construction of a "new femininity" organized around sexual confidence and autonomy. Signified by the cultural trope of "Girl Power" especially during the 1990s, femininity came to be seen as part of young women's "right" to individualism, liberty and sexual self-expression. While the intricacies of Girl Power will be explored in Chapter 4, the emergence of newer, more assertive models of femininity highlights the changes that feminine ideology and iconography have undergone. When at the beginning of the twentieth century, various thinkers – from psychoanalytic greats like Sigmund Freud and Joan Riviere to feminist forerunners like Simone de Beauvoir – were "knock[ing] their heads against the riddle of the nature of femininity", by the end of the century (and certainly by the start of the new millennium) femininity had somehow become "unriddled" and resolved as "only one of many choices that a woman can make in creating her subjectivity and self-presentation" (Freud, "Femininity" 113; Inness, "Pretty Tough" 127). Indeed, it appears that contemporary femininity has been reinvented to the extent that it is now "just one technique amongst many, and an amusing, lightweight one at that" (Gauntlett 11). As David Gauntlett writes in his introduction to *Media, Gender and Identity* (2002),

> Modern women are not generally bothered about fitting their identity within the idea of 'femininity', perhaps because feminists never really sought to *revise* femininity, preferring to dispose of the fluffy, passive concept altogether. Femininity is not a core value for women today. Instead, being 'feminine' is just one of the performances that women can choose to employ in everyday life – perhaps for pleasure, or to achieve a particular goal.
>
> (10; emphasis in original)

Gauntlett continues to say that "whilst seen as a 'nice' thing for women traditionally", femininity is "increasingly irrelevant today"; in fact, "the sensible woman of today has little enthusiasm for these traits, and so the meaning of 'femininity' now is just a swishy kind of glamour" (12). Indeed, if one ever happens to come across a (male) representation of women that could be seen as reinforcing normative versions of femininity, Gauntlett is adamant that in this case one should assume that it is "genuine" irony rather than sexism that motivates these images (168).[11]

There are several points that are noteworthy: Gauntlett draws attention to the strained relationship between feminism and femininity, implicitly setting up an opposition between the two whereby feminists are seen to be anti-feminine. Moreover, there is an implied distinction between an old-style, submissive femininity – when the concept was "traditionally loaded, by the unsubtle patriarchs of yesteryear", with weak qualities like reticence, subservience and timidity (12) – and a newer, younger version that has achieved a more broadly "optional" role (10). While traditional femininity is no longer popular because "virtually everybody wants young women to be successful" (10), new femininity is a performance, ideally "just a masquerade" utilized by "a confident woman who knows *exactly* what she is doing" (12; emphasis in original). Gauntlett underpins his discussion with a range of cultural examples, from falling Barbie doll sales to the pop icon Madonna, whose various impersonations epitomize femininity as an inessential, cultural construction. Subjugating and potentially sexist depictions of femininity can thus be played down as an ironic "joke" shared by women and men alike, and critics who object to these portrayals just "don't get it" and they are not sophisticated enough to read through the irony (168).

Some caveats are in order here: Gauntlett rightly identifies the problematic links between feminism (or rather, the second wave) and femininity but he facilely construes the relationship in terms of an analytical reluctance or laziness on the part of feminist theorists to revisit and reinterpret femininity. There is also the suggestion of a definite rift between old, passive femininity and young, performative femininity that can be employed by wily, knowing women in their quest for success and pleasure. This is based on an assumption that the social and cultural contexts have improved enough for women to make redundant traditional femininity and its inherently demeaning characteristics. In fact, normative, "old femininity" appears only as an ironic leftover, a self-conscious "over-performance" of a set of discourses and subjectivities that are already "obsolete" (168). While Gauntlett highlights the transition from an essential, naturalized femininity to an inessential, constructionist one ("not a core value"), his description of contemporary femininity as "a mere performance" or "just a masquerade" belies the complexity of these theories that have gained a lot of critical attention over the last century or so (10). In this way, Gauntlett not only oversimplifies the critical concepts that he refers to but also presupposes a more egalitarian, clearly codified society in which old is separated from new, feminist from feminine, irony from sexism, false from enlightened consciousness.

Contrastingly, I believe that femininity and contemporary culture in which it appears are more complex and contradictory than Gauntlett makes out. While we have clearly witnessed a number of important cultural, social, theoretical and political changes – including the deconstruction of gendered concepts, the diversification and mainstreaming of the feminist movement, the increased emphasis on "choice" and "self-empowerment" in neo-liberal rhetoric and the appearance of a more assertive, sexually autonomous femininity – these transformations do not amount to an innovative, playful culture of ironic performances where femininity can be staged according to one's will and desires. I agree with Myra Macdonald that "in relation to myths of femininity, in particular, with their long cultural history, traditions of seeing and responding cannot be so magically overturned" (12). We cannot simply proclaim the redundancy and irrelevance of "traditional" femininity that has been the subject of so many investigations, including psychoanalysis and feminism. At the same time, we need to accommodate diverse femininities that, as Joanne Hollows notes, "are not 'feminist' but do not conform to 'traditional' forms of feminine subjectivity either" (196). Furthermore, we cannot assume that women (and men) are now blessed with a sufficient amount of "knowingness" to allow for a reinvention of femininity that is significantly different from its pre-feminist, patriarchal counterpart. While Gauntlett is convinced that contemporary uses of irony do not provide a "get-out clause" against criticism (168), other commentators have stressed that this is a "catch-all device" that means "never having to say you are sorry" (Gill, *Gender and the Media* 110).[12] Indeed, in some cases, the promotion of a "new" femininity camouflages the return to conventional modes of feminine behaviour and appearance that support the principles of "vulnerability, the need for protection, the formalities of compliance and the avoidance of conflict" (Brownmiller 4).[13]

Gauntlett's references to feminine performance and masquerade are key here but, in contrast to his suggestions of analytical simplicity and triviality – femininity as a "swishy kind of glamour" – I want to highlight the double-edged potential of these concepts that enable us to interpret femininity as a multifaceted and contradictory construct. The notion of femininity as masquerade first appeared in psychoanalytic circles and then in theories of female spectatorship in the cinema. The concept (premised on the Freudian perception that the libido is male [Freud, "Three Essays"]) is based on the idea that femininity is a dissimulation of female unconscious masculinity. Psychoanalyst Joan Riviere pioneered the conception of "womanliness as a masquerade" in her 1929 essay where she examined femininity as "a charade of power" whereby women compensate for their theft of masculine subjectivity by disguising themselves as objects of male desire and "masquerading as guiltless and innocent", "merely a castrated woman" (38). Riviere analysed the behaviour of three educated and professional American women who "wish for masculinity [and] put on a mask of womanliness to avert anxiety and the retribution feared from men" (35). Riviere described how one female lecturer exhibited compulsive flirtation and coquetry after a public exhibition of intellectual proficiency in order to pre-empt and propitiate paternal punishment and gain reassurance through flattery of those members of her audience she perceived as father figures. Riviere argued that the patient's successful performance in public "signified an exhibition of herself in possession of the father's penis, having castrated him", so that "the coquetting" can be understood as "an unconscious attempt to ward off the anxiety which would ensue on account of the reprisals she anticipated from the father-figures" (37). In flashing her femininity, Riviere's patient sought to "evoke friendly feelings toward her in the man" and chiefly "make sure of safety" by signalling that she was not really threatening (38, 41).

Femininity thus comes to be seen as a disarming impersonation and a defence mechanism, defusing patriarchal anger and deflecting attention from women's pursuit of male control and authority through the construction of a non-threatening/non-phallic and sexualized image. As Riviere famously declared,

> womanliness therefore could be assumed and worn as a mask, both to hide the possession of masculinity and to avert the reprisals expected if she was found to possess it – much as a thief will turn out his pockets and ask to be searched to prove that he has not the stolen goods.
>
> (38)

For Riviere the display of femininity hides an unconscious masculinity and it is a sign of female disempowerment resulting from a woman's social subjugation, a "compulsive reversal of her intellectual performance" (38). In a similar manner, film theorist Mary Ann Doane asserts that the masquerade is not employed to illuminate female autonomy and creativity "but to designate a mode of being for the other – the sheer objectification or reification of representation" (*Femmes Fatales* 33). By adopting the feminine mask, Riviere's patient renounces her subject status in order to conceal her illicit assumption of masculine power. In this account, the masquerade is theorized as a joyless compensatory gesture, "a device for avoiding anxiety" and "the very antithesis of spectatorship/subjectivity", specifying a norm of femininity but "not a way out" (Riviere 38; Doane, *Femmes Fatales* 33). The concept of masquerade upholds a gender hierarchy that makes femininity dependent on masculinity as a frame of reference for its very definition. The masquerade presupposes a system dictated by a dualistic logic that subordinates feminine passivity to masculine activity and thus it remains tied to a set of binary oppositions that masculinize female agency and desire.

While, on the face of it, the concept of masquerade facilitates an understanding of woman as a passive spectacle rather than an active subject, it has also been discussed as an empowering strategy capable of undermining phallocratic dichotomies. In fact, Riviere's theory has been

re-conceived in challenging and subversive ways that allow for a reinterpretation of femininity. This innovative potential is lodged within the
notion of masquerade that deconstructs the idea of an essential, authentic femininity and instead represents it as a resignifiable construct.
Riviere emphasizes that she does not make a distinction between "genuine womanliness and the masquerade", highlighting that "whether
radical or superficial, they are the same thing" (38). Mary Ann Doane
develops and expands this psychoanalytic account of femininity, suggesting that the masquerade's resistance to patriarchal positioning lies in
its denial of femininity as "immediacy, or proximity-to-self", as precisely
"imagistic" (*Femmes Fatales* 37; "Film and the Masquerade" 235). As she
reveals, the patriarchal conception of femininity is one of nearness and
over-presence, hence lacking the distance between "oneself and one's
image" (235). For a woman to embrace this stance of feminine closeness
is to accept her place within patriarchy and to affirm her own disempowerment in the cultural arena. In flaunting womanliness as a mask
that can be worn or removed, the masquerade challenges this patriarchal idea as it delineates femininity as a culturally assigned site. It marks
an internal contradiction that attributes to the woman a signifying gap
for redeploying femininity and reading it differently. In Doane's words,

> to claim that femininity is a function of the mask is to dismantle
> the question of essentialism before it can even be posed. In a theory
> which stipulates a claustrophobic closeness of the woman in relation
> to her own body, the concept of masquerade suggests a "glitch" in
> the system.
>
> (*Femmes Fatales* 37)

Doane concludes that "the effectivity of masquerade lies precisely in
its potential to manufacture a distance from the image, to generate a
problematic within which the image is manipulable, producible, and
readable by the woman" ("Film and the Masquerade" 240).

Riviere's and Doane's insights have been reworked in contemporary
theories of gender parody that take up the idea that there is no essential
femininity in order to advance the notion of the performative status and
the imitative structure of the feminine construct. The influential theorist
Judith Butler has been instrumental in the formulation of gender *performativity* whereby femininity and masculinity come into being when a
body performs or "does gender" in a stylized reiteration of conventions
that eventually become naturalized and consolidated. As Butler writes,
gender is "an identity tenuously constituted in time" and "instituted

through the stylisation of the body" ("Performative Acts" 402). The gendered body is performative in the sense that it has "no ontological status apart from the various acts which constitute its reality" and thus gender "can be neither true nor false, neither real nor apparent, neither original nor derived" (*Gender Trouble* 136, 141). Instead, "gender is always a doing", a "performance that relies on a certain practice of repetition" that retroactively produces the effect of identity and the illusion that there is an inner gender core (*Gender Trouble* 25; "Lana's Imitation" 2). Hence, "all gendering is a kind of impersonation and approximation", an "imitation for which there is no original" but rather the idea of an imaginary or fantasized origin ("Imitation" 313).[14]

While the everyday performativity of gender resides in unacknowledged acts of citation that produce the female body as feminine, Butler's particular interest lies in disrupting this appearance of natural continuity and making "gender trouble". By exposing gender as a reiterative mechanism and a performative achievement, Butler explores the potential of an unfaithful or critical repetition that might displace the very constructs by which it is mobilized. As she notes,

> if the ground of gender is the stylised repetition of acts through time, and not a seemingly seamless identity, then the possibilities of gender transformation are to be found in the arbitrary relation between such acts, in the possibility of a different sort of repeating, in the breaking or subversive repetition of that style.
>
> ("Performative Acts" 402)

In other words, femininity becomes available for a deconstructive practice that uses simulation in ways that challenge the stable notion of gender as the edifice of sexual difference. Rather than being a homogeneous structure, the gender template is opened up to a more complex and fragmented set of signposts that allow the individual to disengage from the roles of an apparently naturalized femininity/masculinity. Yet, at the same time as proclaiming that gender can "be rendered thoroughly and radically *incredible*", Butler also stresses that this form of parodic imitation should not be confused with a voluntarist stance whereby subjects choose their various identities much as they would select their clothes (*Gender Trouble* 141; emphasis in original). She is adamant that "gender performativity is not a question of instrumentally deploying a 'masquerade' " for such a construal of performativity presupposes an intentional subject *behind* the deed ("For a Careful Reading" 136). On the contrary, gender is an involuntary and imposed production within a culturally restricted space and it is always "put on" under constraint as a compulsory performance that acts in line with heteronormative conventions.[15] In this way, femininity is "not the product of a choice, but the forcible citation of a norm, one whose complex historicity is indissociable from relations of discipline, regulation, punishment" (*Bodies* 232).

With this in mind, performativity can be discussed in terms of both transgression and normativity, empowerment and limitation. Butler admits that "there is no guarantee that exposing the naturalized status of heterosexuality will lead to its subversion" as the gender meanings taken up in these parodic styles remain "part of hegemonic, misogynist culture" (*Bodies* 231; *Gender Trouble* 138). Like the masquerade, Butler's notion of gender parody accommodates a disruptive potential that cannot be summed up by a dichotomous logic as *either* a powerful and self-conscious protest *or* a disempowering and unconscious placation. As Véronique Machelidon concludes,

> the subversiveness of masquerade [and gender parody] can probably never be calculated, for its actors as well as its spectators… are themselves located within the power they are hoping to expose. But neither should the possibility of subversion ever be underestimated because power always generates contradictions and because 'subjects' will respond idiosyncratically to its multiple, complex, and at times inconsistent cultural imperatives.
>
> (116)

Ultimately, the importance of such concepts as masquerade and gender parody lies in their transgressive doubleness, an inscription of alternative wishes that both undermine and reinforce patriarchal representations of womanliness, blurring the opposition between activity and passivity, subject and object.

It is precisely this coexistence of power/powerlessness that has come to the fore in twenty-first-century versions of femininity that mingle old and new, tradition and innovation. Critics have sought to discuss contemporary forms of feminine subjectivity by producing a number of oxymoronic formulations that combine previously opposed and historically conflicting concepts and positions: Western women who take up femininity today have been discussed as "double agents" intertwining "complicity and subversion" in their appropriation of a "liberating discipline" (Lockford 52, 48); they are said to espouse variously a "complicitous critique", an "enlightened false consciousness" or an "enlightened conformity" (Hutcheon, *Politics of Postmodernism*;

Dubrofsky 280; Roberts 83).[16] Rosalind Gill notes in her examination of gender representations in the media that nowadays women have undergone a "shift from sexual objectification to sexual subjectification" whereby they are not "straightforwardly objectified but are presented as active, desiring sexual subjects who choose to present themselves in a seemingly objectified manner because it suits their liberated interests to do so" (*Gender and the Media* 258). Gill continues to say that contemporary femininity is now predominantly seen as a bodily property (rather than a social structural or psychological one) and it includes a "new 'technology of sexiness' in which sexual knowledge and sexual practice are central" (255, 258).[17] Other commentators have re-examined the long-standing opposition between feminism and femininity, emphasizing that modern-day femininity is formed in relation to feminism, while not necessarily being identified or defined as "feminist". For example, Angela McRobbie suggests that "[w]e need to look at what emerges between feminism and femininity and we have to attend to the inventiveness of women as they create new social categories" (*Postmodernism* 8).

Analyses such as these attempt to break down well-established dichotomies between feminist and feminine identities; subject and object; victim and perpetrator; complicity and critique; false and enlightened consciousness. Critical concepts such as "sexual subjectification" highlight the complex identity positions that women adopt in contemporary society, both as a conscious and as an unconscious "choice" and interpellation. It appears that many women of the new millennium reside in a strangely unsettled, blurry in-between space where, as Ien Ang says, they are "free and yet bounded", inhabiting a contradictory site that is simultaneously constraining and liberating, productive and oppressive (165). Yet, the varying degrees of "freedom" and "boundedness" remain open to debate and most critics are hesitant and wary as to where this precarious balance lies. Gill, for instance, is sceptical about the liberating potential of sexual subjecthood, warning that "subjectification" might just be "how we 'do' objectification today" (111). As she points out, the shift from sexual object to desiring sexual subject also represents a move to "a new 'higher' form of exploitation": "a shift from an external, male judging gaze to a self-policing narcissistic gaze" (90, 258). In this way, "sexual objectification can be presented not as something done to women by some men, but as the freely chosen wish of active…female subjects" ("From Sexual Objectification" 104). The focus on femininity as an avenue to self-determination is interpreted as a malicious cover-up that obscures a deeper exploitation than objectification. This, Gill argues, is representative of a neo-liberal society that constructs individuals as autonomous and free ("New Femininities?"; see also Genz, "Third Way/ve").

Moreover, we also need to be careful that in the attempt to celebrate the creativity and innovation of a "new femininity", we do not dismiss previous feminine forms that connote female powerlessness and submission – in a sense perform a similar intellectual and conceptual severance that David Gauntlett hinted at in his description of contemporary femininity that I quoted at the beginning of this section. Gill insists that "it is important not to lose sight of the fact that many things have ... stayed the same" – new stereotypes may not have necessarily "displaced older ones but may coexist alongside these" (111). Similarly, Joanne Hollows admonishes that in the process of depolarizing conventional dualities "there is a tendency to create a new opposition which allows the new femininities (not feminist, but informed by feminism) to be privileged over 'traditional femininity' which operates as a homogeneous, non-contradictory 'other' " (196). Here "new" is given preference over "old", present over past, novelty over tradition, approval over critique.

Rather than adopting a model of feminine discontinuity and hiatus, I prefer to retain the notion of historically and generationally overlapping interpretations of femininity. While each appropriation of feminine standards holds the promise of a more or less subtle modification of their meanings – "gender identity", as Butler reminds us, is "a personal/cultural history of received meanings subject to a set of imitative practices" (*Gender Trouble* 138) – these significations are not exclusionary or exclusive but always refer to other possible meanings. We cannot simply disconnect contemporary forms of feminine assertiveness from previous modes of feminine subjugation – in a way, to paraphrase controversial American writer Naomi Wolf, create a dichotomy between "power femininity" and "victim femininity".[18] In what follows, I use the term "postfemininity" to depict the paradoxes of contemporary femininity that references both traditional narratives of feminine passivity and more progressive scripts of feminine agency. I deliberately choose to enlist the double-edged and often denigrated 'post-' prefix in my discussion in order to bring attention to the manifold layers of feminine meanings. Postfemininity is not "new" in the sense that it no longer bears any resemblance to conventional and culturally dominant forms of feminine behaviour and appearance; nor is it an old-fashioned, retrograde re-embrace of phallocentric femininity. By contrast, postfemininity carries echoes of past, present and future femininities – in much the same way that, as I argue, postfeminism encapsulates a range of possible relations towards feminism. Indeed,

I suggest that postfemininity is best understood as part of a postfeminist frame of analysis that urges us to rethink issues that still remain unresolved: Does femininity always entail victimization? Can femininity and feminism coexist? Can femininity be described as a feminist subject position?

Post-ing feminism/femininity

Before I go on to discuss the intricacies of a postfeminist femininity or postfemininity, we need to address the semantic confusion surrounding a "post-ing" of feminism/femininity. While the 'post-' prefix has long been the subject of academic and theoretical analyses (in particular, in its expression as postmodernism, poststructuralism and postcolonialism), it has achieved particular notoriety and ferocity ever since it attached itself to the social and political phenomenon that is feminism. Although the term "postfeminism" made its debut as early as the 1920s, it was only in the latter half of the twentieth century that it became a widely spread and controversial concept permeating academia and popular media.[19] As soon as it reappeared in popular consciousness in the early 1980s, postfeminism caused a furore among commentators who debated its potential meanings and uses.[20] While early critics were almost unanimous in their interpretation of postfeminism as "anti-feminism", the list of significations keeps expanding: Girl Power, "do-me" feminism, "power feminism", poststructuralist feminism, popular feminism. A simple definition has proven elusive, with proponents as well as detractors vying for their respective take on how a "post-ing" of feminism can be effected and understood. What these debates centre on is exactly what this prefixation accomplishes (if anything), what happens to feminist perspectives and goals in the process and what the strange hybrid of "post-feminism" entails. I choose to leave out the hyphen in my spelling of "postfeminism" in order to avoid any predetermined readings of the term that imply a semantic rift between feminism and postfeminism, instantly casting the latter as a negation and sabotage of the former. Also, in my eyes the affixation draws attention to the fact that postfeminism has achieved a certain cultural independence and now exists as a conceptual entity in its own right.

Regardless of our spelling, it is not so much the hyphen but the prefix itself that has been the focus of critical attention and examination. As Misha Kavka observes, the question that has haunted – or enlivened, depending on your point of view – the discussions can be summarized as "how can we make sense of the 'post' in 'postfeminism'" (31).

Even though the structure of postfeminism seems to invoke a narrative of progression insisting on a time "after" feminism, the directionality and meaning of the "post-" prefix are far from settled. "Post-" can be employed to point to a complete rupture, for, as Amelia Jones declares, "what is post but the signification of a kind of termination – a temporal designation of whatever it prefaces as ended, done with, obsolete" (8). In this prescriptive sense, postfeminism acquires deadly and even murderous connotations as it proclaims the passing of feminism – feminism as "homeless and groundless", "gone, departed, dead" (Hawkesworth 969). Diametrically opposed to this conception is the idea that the prefix denotes a genealogy that entails revision or strong family resemblance. In this case, "post-" signifies reliance and continuity, an approach that has been favoured by advocates of another "post" derivative, postmodernism. More problematically, "post" can also occupy a precarious middle ground, signalling a contradictory dependence on and independence from the term that follows it. This is the viewpoint taken by Linda Hutcheon, who detects a paradox at the heart of the "post" whereby "it marks neither a simple and radical break from [the term that follows] nor a straightforward continuity with it; it is both and neither" (*A Poetics of Postmodernism* 17).[21]

Adding to this interpretative struggle is the fact that the root of postfeminism, feminism itself, has never had a universally agreed agenda and definition against which one could measure the benefits and/or failings of its "post-" derivative. As Geraldine Harris emphasizes, feminism has never had "a single, clearly defined, common ideology" or been constituted around "a political party or a central organization or leaders or an agreed policy or manifesto, or even been based upon an agreed principle of collective action" (9). Instead, feminism at best can be said to have working definitions that are always relative to particular contexts, specific issues and personal practices. The assumption that there was – or is – a monolith easily (and continuously) identifiable as "feminism" belies its competing understandings, its different social and political programmes sharply separated by issues of race, sexuality, class and other systems of social differentiation.[22] Thus, we cannot simply "hark back" to a welcome past when feminism supposedly had a stable signification and unity, a mythical time prior to "the introduction of a particular vigorous and invasive weed [postfeminism] into the otherwise healthy garden of feminism" (Elam 55). From this perspective, the attempt to fix *the* meaning of postfeminism looks even more futile and misguided as each articulation is by itself a definitional act that (re)constructs the meaning of feminism and its own relation to it. There is no *original* or *authentic* postfeminism that holds the key to its definition. Nor is there a secure and unified origin from which this genuine postfeminism could be fashioned. Instead, I understand postfeminism in terms of a network of possible relations that allows for a variety of permutations and readings.

Jane Kalbfleisch's discussion of the feminism–postfeminism coupling is useful in this respect as she analyses a number of rhetorical positions that underlie different articulations of postfeminism. Kalbfleisch describes how the "rhetoric of opposition" effects a polarization of feminism and postfeminism that is based on the assumption that the two are fully distinguishable and distinct. In this sense, "postfeminist" denotes a non-feminist stance that can be read as a term of negation. This rupture can be interpreted positively as liberation from old and constraining conditions and an affirmation of new developments; or, it can be read as a deplorable regression and a loss of traditional values and certainties. The rhetoric of opposition thus takes the form of both anti- and pro-postfeminism, either rejecting the term as an opportunistic move on the part of patriarchy or embracing it and thereby denouncing earlier feminist movements.

On the pro-postfeminist side of the debate, there is a group of young women who appear to speak from somewhere outside and above feminism. The term "postfeminism" is used to suggest that the project of feminism has ended, either because it has been completed or because it has failed and is no longer valid. The most prominent advocates of this standpoint – Naomi Wolf, Katie Roiphe, Natasha Walter and Rene Denfeld – support an individualistic and liberal agenda that relies on a mantra of choice and assumes that the political demands of first and second wave feminism have now been met (enfranchisement, equal pay, sexual liberation etc.).[23] It is argued that "all ha[s] been achieved, in fact over-achieved" to the extent that "feminism has...become irrelevant to the lives of young women today" (Coppock 3; Sonnet 170). Accordingly, Rene Denfeld starts her book *The New Victorians* (1995) with the observation that "[f]or women of my generation, feminism is our birthright....We know what it is to live without excessive confinement. We are the first generation to grow up expecting equal opportunity and equal education, as well as the freedom to express our sexuality" (2). The implicit assumption is that feminism no longer needs to be enforced politically as it is now up to individual women and their personal choices to reinforce those fundamental societal changes. In this case, the meaning of "post-" becomes equivalent to both "anti" and "after": "postfeminism is that which both comes after and rejects...earlier feminism – it is the successor 'feminism' to a now surpassed, and now unnecessary, prior feminism" (Braithwaite 24).

Contrastingly, anti-postfeminist critics define postfeminism as a sexist, politically conservative and media-inspired ploy that guts the underlying principles of the feminist movement. This position, taken up by writers such as Susan Faludi and Marilyn French, implicates the work of younger feminists (Wolf, Roiphe, etc.) in a backlash against feminism. Quoting an article from the *Guardian*, Faludi is adamant that "post-feminism is the backlash. Any movement or philosophy which defines itself as post whatever came before is bound to be reactive. In most cases it is also reactionary" (15). Rather than being a full-blown attack on feminism, "[t]he backlash is at once sophisticated and banal, deceptively 'progressive' and proudly backward" (12). It does not reject women's rights and equality outright but redefines them in terms of a liberal individualist politics that centres around lifestyle choices and personal consumer pleasures.[24] This "free market feminism" sells women an illusion of progress by appropriating and co-opting feminist notions of empowerment and choice (Whelehan, *Overloaded* 100). In this instance, the prefix "post-" occupies an uneasy position suggesting an infiltration and appropriation, a "parasite riding on the back of the original movement which benefits from the ground it has won but uses this for its own means" (Kastelein 5). As Ann Braithwaite describes this process, "feminism is 'written in' precisely so it can be 'written out'; it is included and excluded, acknowledged and paid tribute to, and accepted and refuted, all at the same time" (25).[25] Ultimately, however, we are advised to be wary of this supposedly trendy wolf in sheep's clothing as "texts…in proclaiming…the advent of postfeminism, are actually engaged in negating the critiques and undermining the goals of feminism, in effect, delivering us back into a prefeminist world" (Modleski 3).

Rather than situating feminism and postfeminism antithetically, the second rhetorical position that Kalbfleisch identifies, "the rhetoric of inclusion", relies on a polarization of a different kind to eradicate the overlap between feminism and postfeminism. In this case, postfeminism is pitted against some "Other" (for example, postmodernism and poststructuralism) in a move that allows for the presumed commonalities among feminists and postfeminists while effectively erasing their potential differences (258).[26] The critical tension within the (post)feminism coupling is defused in this way as the two terms are conflated into one and incorporated into another discursive project. Academic circles in particular have adopted this theoretical approach, discussing postfeminism as "a pluralistic epistemology dedicated to disrupting universalising patterns of thought" (Gamble 50). The absorption of postfeminism into what could broadly be conceived as postmodernist cultural critique runs the risk of repressing its importance in other domains, specifically its place in the public debate on feminism and the modern woman. In my understanding, postfeminism exists both as a descriptive popular category and as an academic theoretical tendency and, even within these situated contexts, it does not necessarily aim for coherence. Indeed, most critical analyses tend to discuss postfeminism as a bifurcated term that consists of two distinct and competing strands, one defined as mainstream feminism and the other as post-modern feminism.[27] As I have discussed elsewhere, I argue against the establishment of two disparate and disconnected postfeminist versions and locations (academia and the media) that runs the risk of recreating an artificial dichotomy between the academic ivory power and popular culture.[28]

My own usage and understanding of postfeminism are less motivated by an attempt to determine and fix its meaning than by an effort to acknowledge its plurality and liminality. Postfeminism is a more com-plex – and, I maintain, productive – concept than many of its common usages suggest. The fact that postfeminism cannot be contained in a series of well-defined boxes (academia and media; Girl Power and back-lash; popular feminism and poststructuralist anti-essentialism) points towards its *interdiscursivity* and *intercontextuality* that inevitably takes the form of boundary-crossing.[29] Postfeminism elicits a number of different signifieds that defy monological decoding of a comprehensive mean-ing. Adopting Kalbfleisch's terminology, I seek to interpret postfeminism through the lens of a "rhetoric of anxiety" that foregrounds "conflict, contradiction and ambiguity" (259). Rather than simply marking that which comes "after" (or is "anti"), the prefix "post-" establishes a num-ber of relations to feminism that constitute a link with – rather than a break from – it. In this way, postfeminism is indicative of the diversity of contemporary feminisms and the changes in feminist thinking, activism and politics over the last 40 years. This is what Ann Brooks implies in her re-articulation of postfeminism as "feminism's 'coming of age,' its maturity into a confident body of theory and politics, representing pluralism and difference" (1). Similarly, Ann Braithwaite argues for an alternative understanding of postfeminism that takes into account that "the breadth of feminist issues is now much broader than ever before, across a range of political, social and cultural issues, and intersecting with a variety of theories about gender, race and ethnicity, sexuality, class, and even corporeality" (27).

Mid-twentieth-century feminism has undoubtedly undergone a range of significant transformations since its second wave heyday in the 1960s and 1970s: discursive and conceptual shifts "from debates around equality to a focus on debates around difference"; a move away from a collective structure and activism; an increasing mainstreaming and incorporation of feminism into popular culture; and, inevitably as time goes by, the emergence of a new generation of women entering the feminist movement and redefining its goals and identity (Brooks 4). These intergenerational relations are characterized not only by connection but also, necessarily, by discontinuity and divergence as women (including myself) – becoming conscious of feminism and coming to the movement in the 1980s and 1990s – are embedded in an altered social, cultural and political location and climate. Nancy Whittier explains that "just as the links between political generations grow from structural and social relations . . . so, too, are the differences grounded in the changing social structures and cultural contexts that organize the lives of women at different times" (235–6). Not surprisingly, Whittier adds, this "postfeminist generation" has different experiences and outlooks than "longtime feminists" who "acquired a sense of the world and themselves in a different era" (226). Postfeminism's interrogative stance could thus be construed as a healthy rewriting of feminism, a sign that the women's movement is continuously in process/progress. Accordingly, the adoption of a postfeminist position need not imply abandoning the feminist project altogether but jettisoning a certain kind of feminist identity linked to the second wave.

I am slightly less optimistic about this interpretation of postfeminism as a new stage in the evolution of feminisms. While I agree that there is a need to expand the definition of postfeminism, I maintain that postfeminism's appropriation of its feminist origins is more complicated and insidious than a modernization or rejuvenation. As Lynne Alice notes, "[i]n the end postfeminism is always more than a criticism of feminism and a caricaturing of individual feminists" (25). In its various manifestations, postfeminism exhibits a number of relations to feminism ranging from complacency to hostility, admiration to repudiation. In its most denunciatory expressions, postfeminism clearly misreads and classifies feminism as a monolithic movement that is archaic, binaristic and unproductive for the experiences of contemporary women. In order to position themselves in opposition to a supposedly unified and old-fashioned feminist entity, some postfeminists end up distorting and reducing feminism's multiplicity.[30] In my opinion, postfeminism cannot be read as an alternative to feminism and its social and political agenda. Importantly, my analysis of postfeminism does not intend to supersede feminism as a political movement that continues to strive for social change throughout the world. I believe that postfeminism has to be located within a highly situated framework that is specific to a time, place and even class. Postfeminism can clearly be located in a late-twentieth- and early-twenty-first-century context and period in Western Europe and the United States that emphasizes consumerist, middle-class values.[31] This is not to say that postfeminism is apolitical – indeed, I have examined postfeminism's doubly coded politics elsewhere.[32] Postfeminism responds to the changing qualities of female/feminine/feminist experiences in the context of a late liberal society in which feminist concerns have entered the mainstream and are articulated in a politically contradictory manner. In this postfeminist cultural moment, women are starting to re-address traditional trappings of femininity – beauty and body practices, sexiness, domesticity – and engage with them in complex and often paradoxical ways.[33]

For me, the problem surrounding postfeminism is not so much to choose between its various appropriations than it is to adopt a postfeminist framework that allows for polysemy or multiple meanings. Postfeminism is not a "new feminism" in the sense that it represents something radically revolutionary and ground-breaking that transcends the feminist past.[34] Indeed, my intention here is not to argue the case of postfeminism as either a new utopia or the trap of nostalgia but it is to discover a postfeminist liminality that "moves us from the exclusionary logic of either/or to the inclusionary logic of both/and" (Rutland 74). Postfeminism (and, by extension, postfemininity) is both "retro-" and "neo-" in its outlook and hence irrevocably "post-". It is neither a simple rebirth of feminism nor a straightforward abortion (excuse the imagery) but a complex resignification that harbours within itself the threat of backlash as well as the potential for innovation.[35] This double movement is at the root of the difficulty of attributing *a* meaning to postfeminism and containing it within a definitional straightjacket; a futile endeavour in my view that ultimately serves only as a critical shortcut. It is important for me to avoid this definitional trap that might provide us with some appealing conclusions and neat answers at the expense of more complex and thought-provoking questions. Regardless of how the term has been (ab)used, postfeminism's changeable life indicates a move away from easy categorizations and binaries, including the dualistic patterns of (male) power and (female) oppression on which much feminist thought and politics are built.

Thus, postfeminism does not refer to a denial (or worse, death) of feminism but to an altered stage of gendered conflicts and transformations. Patricia Mann offers a useful description by identifying postfeminism as a "frontier discourse" that "bring[s] us to the edge of what we know, and encourages us to go beyond" (208). In a similar manner, Ann Braithwaite describes postfeminism as a "point of conjecture between a number of often competing interests and agendas" (28).[36] I am particularly interested in one such point of conjecture, namely the shifting relationships between femininity, feminism and concepts of female victimization. I suggest that adopting a postfeminist frame allows us to rework the existing balance between these positions by setting up a negotiating space that re-assembles them in a non-dichotomous way. The renewed emphasis on traditional (white, heterosexual, middle-class) femininity in the late twentieth and early twenty-first century has been the focus of critical debates on postfeminism that engage with its progressive and/or retrogressive dimensions. The characteristics and meanings of contemporary femininity have been discussed along much the same lines as postfeminism: suspicious of this historically effective strategy of female appeasement and submission, some critics insist that postfeminism's reclamation of femininity diminishes the accomplishments of the feminist movement and women in general. Women are seen to be seduced (again) into accepting feminine images and roles that, as Marshment laments, "appear to offer solutions to their material problems" (126).[37] Others argue for the emergence of a "'new femininity' in which sexual and social confidence, aspiration, and career ambition increasingly figure" (Tincknell et al. 47). For these critics, femininity is no longer the terrain of female oppression but it is now paired with expressions of female power and agency.

I maintain that the contradictions surrounding contemporary Western femininity go beyond the binary logic of progress and backlash: femininity is pulled in a number of competing directions by, what McNay calls, "the detraditionalizing forces" that break down "fixed gender narratives" and expose women to individualistic values expressed in notions of "lifestyle choice" (112). This move is not straightforwardly liberatory as "the stabilising pull" of conventional narratives of femininity continues to exert its power, offering "coherence to an identity that might otherwise seem fractured and unstable" (Thornham 81, 76). I put forward the term "postfemininity" to describe the paradoxes of modern-day femininity that has become the subject/object of modernization and emancipation, beyond the established parameters of patriarchal, pre-feminist discourses. Postfemininity differs from earlier feminine modes that were the locus of second wave feminist commentary and action by displaying an internal reflexivity and awareness of feminist values and principles. In contemporary Western society and culture, a space has opened up for the articulation of a postfeminist feminine stance that allows for a complexity of interpretation that has been missing in previous conflations of femininity with anti-feminism. As Lisa Adkins notes, contemporary invocations of femininity now "reflexively reference and incorporate previous forms of feminist critique of that very object" (433). In Ann Braithwaite's words, what we have now is "a feminism with and of femininity", a feminism that engages with femininity in a number of different – even opposing – ways (31). Postfemininity cannot be conceptualized along a sharp split between feminism and femininity, agency and victimization. I argue that postfemininity does not simply reverse the victimization/agency diametric – that is, femininity is pro-agency and anti-victimization – as the process of transforming and resignifying femininity continually threatens to re-impose phallocentricity and heteronormativity. Postfeminist femininity presents multiple layers of female identification that oscillate between subject and object, victim and perpetrator. Post-ing femininity (like post-ing feminism) thus involves an amount of rethinking, not a reversal of well-established dualisms, but a process of resignification that is capable of re-inscribing what it also transposes.

Postfemininity

Of course, the changeable life of contemporary femininity puts a certain analytical pressure and strain on critics who try to pin down its defining features, ideological positioning and political orientation. There is no doubt that we have to account for femininity's cultural embeddedness and its sedimented meanings as a patriarchal heritage. At the same time, there is also a need to "unsettle" femininity and re-negotiate its place in a changed social and cultural context. Our critical predicament is intensified even further when we choose to focus on white, heterosexual femininity that has traditionally been seen as a stronghold of patriarchal manipulation and objectification of women. Aimee Rowe and Samantha Lindsey observe that "white femininity's contemporary cultural production" revolves around "the central question of her 'loyalties' ": "to what, or whom, is she being asked to remain loyal? And what, or whom, is competing for her loyalties?" (183). I maintain that the loyalties of modern-day femininity can no longer be confirmed or taken for granted as it is now a fiercely contested terrain where the line between complicity and critique gets increasingly blurred. Femininity has become "unruly" and it can no longer simply be put in the service of an overarching master discourse that sets up a feminine rule book – what Susan Brownmiller calls the "road blocks and detours that say, 'For Femininity, Turn Here,' or 'For Femininity, Turn Back' " (182). Femininity is read simultaneously by dominant cultures, counter-cultural narratives and individual women who seek to understand and change it as at once a symptom of previous inequalities and as a sign, good and bad, of things to come. Contemporary women no longer perform femininity only as a subterfuge but also as a method for contesting and subverting problematic cultural and feminist norms. Nowadays, the feminine feminist is not an oxymoronic, hypothetical subject position but a postfeminist possibility that demands our critical attention and analysis. This is also a challenge that critics themselves face: at the same time as investigating the changing significations and uses of femininity in the second half of the twentieth century, I also want to re-examine the critical categories and standpoints from which we judge these feminine images and expressions. Our discussions of postfeminist femininity are guided and driven to some extent by our own critical/feminist commitments. In this sense, our loyalties are as much at stake in this postfeminist/postfeminine reclamation as are the content and meanings of femininity itself.

In this book, I want to problematize critical frameworks and patterns that oversimplify the polysemy and diversity of contemporary femininity and govern debates from a safe analytical viewpoint. While there is an obvious temptation to steer interpretation in a predetermined critical direction, I believe that it has now become imperative to take further our enquiries towards a more pluralistic understanding of femininity. When such a complexity around interpretation is missing, femininity can only be read as offering "more of the same" rather than a new script characterized by hybrid qualities. I want to address the triangular relationships between feminism, femininity and concepts of female victimization by revisiting some seminal twentieth- and twenty-first-century criticism, fiction and films that have influenced and formed our views on Western women's positions and portrayals. I am not asking readers to endanger or forget their feminist loyalties but rather open their minds to the possibility of change and the ongoing transformations in the fields of feminism, femininity, critical analysis and popular representations of women.

In what follows, I seek to provide a representational history of femininity in both feminist polemical writing and popular culture, exploring the interchanges and differences in the depictions and perceptions of femininity. I focus on the second half of the twentieth century that has seen a significant number of changes in the lives and images of women: from the post-war "cult of femininity" to the emergence of second wave politics and activism in the late 1960s and 1970s; the 1980s backlash against feminism from conservative politicians and the media to a highly contentious postfeminist present when "feminist" and "feminine" are intermingled in female expressions of self-determination and choice. This has been an extremely "busy" and rapidly changing period in late modernity when feminism and femininity have been variously embraced, rejected and reinvigorated in the guise of a number of controversial "post-ings". These latter versions encompass the tensions and conflicts that have come to symbolize the state of contemporary feminisms and femininities. Throughout this book, I endeavour to explore the potentialities inherent in these "post" positions rather than assuming a predetermined frame of reference. For me, the prefix "post" signals an interrogation and active rethinking of feminist/feminine definitions, viewpoints and interpretations. It opens up – rather than forecloses – a range of possibilities that release feminism and femininity into a future of multiple significations.

Moreover, to some extent, this book is also an examination of how feminism has impacted on the popular realm (and vice versa); how it has been used, incorporated and appropriated. As many critics have acknowledged, feminism is now part of the cultural field and its meanings are increasingly mediated. Joanne Hollows and Rachel Moseley note that "most people become conscious of feminism through the way it is represented in popular culture" and "for many women of our generation, formative understandings of, and identifications with, feminist ideas have been almost exclusively within popular culture" (2). Similarly, in her attempt to settle the question "what is feminism?" Rosalind Delmar suggests that "it is, in practice, impossible to discuss feminism without discussing the image of feminism and feminists" (8). Delmar's comment points to the practical impossibility of experiencing and identifying an authentic feminism, unadulterated by the often conservative forces of cultural representation. Feminist discourses cannot be seen as simply being outside and independent critical voices and instead they are part of the media landscape. This gives rise to many different explanations and discussions about incorporation and recuperation while also prompting other questions about the nature of the media itself and the role of the feminist cultural critic. In her book *Gender and the Media* (2007), Rosalind Gill asks whether the media have been "transformed by feminism" and "become – in significant ways – feminist" (41). She also debates the function and responsibilities of feminist critics who can either celebrate women's choices, look for strands of resistance or formulate alternative representational strategies. As Gill rightly says, in an increasingly diverse media culture saturated by information and communication technologies, "the 'obviousness' of what it means to do feminist intellectual work breaks down" and we are left with a "messy contradictoriness", a clear sign that gender relations and media representations – as well as the feminist frameworks used to comprehend and critique them – are constantly changing in contemporary Western societies (22, 2).

Situating its examination in a still unresolved contemporary arena, this book provides both a glimpse of past femininity and its critical/popular reception as well as a progressive, forward-looking perspective into the modern female/feminist/feminine self. In Part I, I analyse the developments and meanings of femininity in a range of feminist, backlash and postfeminist writings since the 1960s. Starting with Betty Friedan's landmark text *The Feminine Mystique* (1963), I move through the succeeding decades to trace the development and images of femininity. According to Friedan, the 15 years after the Second World War were characterized by a major shift in the popular media and the emergence of a "mystique of feminine fulfilment" that encouraged women to give up their career aspirations and adopt the "Occupation: Housewife" (16). This, Friedan argued, results in a "progressive dehumanization" of women who adopt "the pretty lie of the feminine mystique" and their imprisonment in the "comfortable concentration camp" of the home (180, 245). Friedan's exposure of femininity as an oppressive female subject position aligns her with other feminist critics, most notably Simone de Beauvoir and Germaine Greer, for whom femininity is equivalent to slavery. In her uncovering of "the problem that has no name", Friedan's book played an important part in the emergence of the Women's Liberation Movement and its task of raising women's consciousness about their subjugated status in society.

I then examine the most mythical and pertinent icon of second wave feminism: the bra-burner. Born out of the protest against sexism staged at the Miss America Pageant in Atlantic City in 1968, the image of the bra-burning, mannish and fanatic feminist has dominated popular representations of feminism and "the women's libber". This mythologizing of feminism performs an apparently definitive rupture between feminism and femininity that, paradoxically, has been propagated both by an unsympathetic mass media and by the radical feminist writings of the 1970s. As Mary Daly suggested in her influential book *Gyn/Ecology* (1978), women have to throw off socially constructed notions of femininity in order to discover the "wild woman" within. Kate Millett's *Sexual Politics* (1970) and Shulamith Firestone's *The Dialectic of Sex* (1972) followed similar lines of argument by discussing biology as a defence for the ideological domination of men over women and demanding the elimination of sexual roles. These radical and confrontational forms of feminist thought were instrumental in the polarization of feminist critic and feminine victim and they were the main focus of the backlash against feminism in the 1980s which I discuss in the following chapter. The assault on feminism in media discourses in the 1980s has famously been described by Susan Faludi in her international bestseller *Backlash: The Undeclared War against Women* (1992). The backlash propagates the idea that female identity is troubled and tormented by feminism's excessive demands to become "superwomen" who want to "have it all". It cautions women that in their "unnatural struggle for self-determination" they are jeopardizing "their natural femininity" and even their sanity (490). Feminism is represented as "women's own worst enemy" that leads them astray from the path of feminine fulfilment (2). It is the domain of "hard-faced" "macho feminists" who have to be tamed and made aware of their aberrant behaviour (277–8). As I will examine, the backlash goes hand in hand with a "new traditionalist" impulse that resignifies domesticity and femininity as the domains of female autonomy and agency (Probyn).

While the backlash is clearly fuelled by a conservative media, it also exemplifies the increasing diversification of the feminist movement and the disappearance of the illusion of feminist unity. In *The Second Stage* (1982), second wave veteran Betty Friedan acknowledges that something is "*off*", "out of focus" and "going wrong" within the women's movement and she locates the problem in the "feminist denial of the importance of family, of women's own needs to give and get love and nurture, tender loving care" (15, 22; emphasis in original). According to Friedan, feminism is in danger of breeding its own "problem that has no name" – a *feminist* mystique – unless it takes into account "the life-serving core of feminine identity" (32). In this way, femininity is brought back into the feminist picture, not as an old enemy but as an integral part of women's existence. This move is taken further in the 1990s with the emergence of postfeminism that allows for the construction of femininity as a feminist subject position.

The final section of Part I pinpoints the renegotiation and realignment of feminism and femininity in postfeminist discourses of the 1990s.

Postfeminism establishes a new signifying link that no longer understands female power as compromised by femininity. It highlights the postfeminist woman's "choice" to adopt feminine values and appearance as a sign of her freedom and independence. This stance finds its most obvious expression in the 1990s phenomenon of "Girl Power", which asserts sexual subjecthood and the right to "pink things of stereotypical girlhood" (Baumgardner and Richards 136). Girlies are adamant that they can re-infuse the symbols of feminine enculturation (Barbie dolls, make-up, fashion magazines) with new meanings. Late-twentieth-century versions of femininity thus undergo a resignifying process that attempts to sever its traditional associations with female victimization and subordination. However, I argue that the postfeminist link between feminism and femininity is highly contentious and variable as it signifies in a number of contradictory ways. The "pink-packaged" power of sexual subjecthood always entails a simultaneous objectification as postfeminist femininity achieves a state of polysemy, of historically and culturally overlapping meanings. In fact, postfemininity is at its core a paradoxical construction that effects a double movement of empowerment and subordination, creating a subject position that has been described by Judith Butler as a "subjectivation", implying "both the becoming of the subject and the process of subjection" (*Psychic Life* 83).

Part II focuses on textual analyses of popular cinema, television and literary narratives within the feminist, cultural and theoretical frameworks discussed in Part I. Each chapter is dedicated to a specific feminine/feminist subject position whose signification and status have been debated in popular media, feminist and postfeminist discourses. Rather than privileging one definition of femininity over another, I suggest that postfeminist femininities demarcate a site of contest that brings various layers of feminine meanings into contact and conflict. First, I discuss the figure of the housewife who has been held up as an emblem of female oppression in feminist debates of the 1960s and 1970s. Betty Friedan cemented into feminism the "unhappy housewife myth" that defines housewifery as pathology and the female homemaker as a political prisoner restricted to the traditional triangle of *Kinder, Küche, Kirche* (children, kitchen, church). The housewife has received renewed attention in recent years but this time as the site of "mystique chic", with *Cosmopolitan* magazine announcing in 2000 that young women have become the "New Housewife Wannabes" (Kingston; Dutton). I will access this shift in the representation of the housewife and women's domestic role by juxtaposing feminist classics, such as Sue Kaufman's *Diary of a Mad Housewife* (1967) and Marilyn French's *The Women's Room*

(1977), with a range of backlash and postfeminist texts, including the television series *Scarecrow and Mrs. King* (1983–1987), the Hollywood film *The Long Kiss Goodnight* (1996) and Sophie Kinsella's best-selling *The Undomestic Goddess* (2005). As this chapter reveals, the postfeminist housewife occupies a controversial position that re-negotiates the meanings of domestic postfemininity.

Then I discuss the female/feminist icon of the "Superwoman" who emerges in the 1980s as a foil for the feminine housewife and whose feminist promise of "Having It All" becomes translated in backlash narratives into an imperative of "Doing It All". The feminist movement's advances that allowed women access to the workplace are depicted in popular 1980s texts to be responsible for a range of female crises, from unhappiness and dissatisfaction to burnout and psychosis. The backlash's stigmatization of working womanhood is accompanied by a revival of domesticity that centralizes and idealizes woman's apparently fully knowledgeable choice to abstain from paid work in favour of family values. According to backlash rhetoric, the workplace has switched places with the home front as the source of female frustration and now the corporation is presented as the same prison for women that the suburban home had once been. The "Superwoman syndrome" will be examined in relation to the films *Fatal Attraction* (1987) and *Baby Boom* (1987) and the best-selling novels *Having It All* (1991) and *I Don't Know How She Does It* (2003).

The tensions between feminism and femininity, domesticity and careerism, that the Superwoman experiences are further intensified in the representation of the Singleton who emerges in the 1990s as the figurehead of a new generation of women struggling to unite their demands for heterosexual romance and professional achievement. Young, unattached and mostly city-dwelling, the Singleton has been credited with summoning the *zeitgeist* of a particularly postfeminist moment of female disorientation and experimentation. Caught between the lure of feminist politics (and the accompanying promise of public empowerment) and a desire for feminine beauty and heterosexual coupledom, the Singleton re-negotiates her position in a social terrain of shifting roles and changing images of womanhood. I will investigate the figure of the Singleton, from her emergence in the 1960s in *Sex and the Single Girl* (1962) to her heyday in the 1990s serial dramas *Ally McBeal* (1997–2002) and *Sex and the City* (1998–2004) and the best-selling *Bridget Jones's Diary* (1996) and *Bridget Jones: The Edge of Reason* (1999).

In the final chapter, I discuss the 1990s figure of the "Supergirl", the female action adventure hero, whose appearance in popular culture can be read as a response to both the worn-out Superwoman and the anxious Singleton. Fuelled by the notion of "Girl Power", the Supergirl engages with the complexities of modern female subjectivity by reclaiming and resignifying once disparaged images and elements of femininity and reconstructing them as expressions of choice and power. The Supergirl thus depolarizes the dichotomy between feminism and femininity that has been held up by feminist and media discourses alike. She emerges in both filmic and literary works as, for example, Helen Fielding's *Olivia Joules* (2003), *Miss Congeniality* (2000) and, most famously, the television series *Buffy the Vampire Slayer* (1997–2003). As I argue, the Supergirl is a complexly composite persona who inhabits a problematic social and emotional space and whose identifications involve a continuous play between passivity and activity, vulnerability and strength, individualism and communality.

In tracing the representations and meanings of femininity in feminist theory and popular culture since the 1960s, my main aim is to highlight the changes that it has undergone and the complexity of "new" feminine identities that are marked by their own distinct characteristics and concerns, yet not without a strong historical link to "older", more conventional versions. I advance the notion of postfemininity to account for the diverse and often conflicting ways in which femininity figures in modern women's lives and participates in their cultural experiences. By adopting the controversial "post-" prefix, I want to draw attention to the complicated entanglements between the categories of "feminism" and "femininity" that are characterized not only by disagreement and opposition but also by overlapping meanings, vocabularies and frameworks. As it affixes itself to both feminism and femininity, the "post" does not mark a simple chronology that implies a temporal sequence in which these two "f-words" have been transcended, occluded and overcome. Rather, the contemporary context and cultural condition are more problematic and difficult to grasp: as Patricia Mann explains, the old "game board is still visible beneath our feet, yet there are new players, new moves, and new rules to be negotiated. It is an old game and a new one at once" (5). Mann is convinced that women who adopt feminine behaviour and appearance "need not identify with or submit to sexist images of women" as they have "the capacity to be self-conscious social actors now rather than traditional passive objects of the patriarchal gaze" (87). The reference points for postfemininity include the stereotypes of womanhood propagated by a misogynist, patriarchal culture but also a feminist "raised" consciousness and critique of these images, a postmodern awareness of gender deconstruction as well as a neo-liberal belief in the autonomous individual. In Mann's words, what typifies the present historical moment is a certain "conceptual strangeness" of various social situations and relationships (206); others have described our age as one of uncertainty and confusion where the "Good-God-Gold standards" no longer apply (Ang; Fekete 17). This is especially testing but also exciting for feminist cultural critics investigating feminine images and representations, in the sense that a less than denunciatory attitude to these historically subjugating modes could be interpreted as a defeat of their feminist principles. However, as Shelley Budgeon reminds us, it is important to remember that "the continued goal for the project of feminism is to learn to practise conflict constructively" ("Emergent Feminist (?) Identities" 25). To say that female identities may be postfeminist or postfeminine is productive insofar as it is understood as a critical interrogation of feminist/feminine norms and the multiple ways of inhabiting feminism and/or femininity. Postfemininity thus presents us with a challenge and an opportunity to rework our systems of signification and critical frameworks to better articulate the complex social, cultural and theoretical categories that characterize contemporary feminism and femininity. Postfemininity encourages us to live "the woman question" and confront the contradictions that we face.

Part I

From "Feminine Mystique" to "Girl Power"

1
The Problem That Has a Name: The Feminine Concentration Camp

"Feminist consciousness is consciousness of *victimization*", Sandra Lee Bartky notes in her examination of the phenomenology of oppression, explaining that "to come to see oneself as victim" is to have "an altered perception of oneself and one's society" (15; emphasis in original). She is convinced that for women such consciousness of victimization is "immediate and revelatory", allowing us to "discover what social reality is really like" and gain knowledge of, in Bartky's words, "an alien and hostile force outside of oneself" that creates and perpetuates "the blatantly unjust treatment of women" and enforces "a stifling and oppressive system of sex-role differentiation" (15–16). While feminists have debated at length what exactly this "hostile power" refers to – "society" and "patriarchy" for some; for others, it is simply men – the recognition of women's victim status is inexorably linked to the awakening of a feminist awareness, on a personal as well as collective level. Some proto-feminist treatises are well aware of women's disadvantaged social position and their exclusion from "man-kind" – indeed modern feminism begins with Mary Wollstonecraft's famous *Vindication* (1792), in which she examines how social constructions of femininity misdirect women away from the "first object of laudable ambition", that is, "to obtain a character as a human being, regardless of the distinction of sex" – yet it was only in the latter half of the twentieth century and with the advent of second wave feminism that women's individual and combined victimization became the focus of a sustained women-centred politics and activism. According to many second wave feminist writers and campaigners, the key to women's disempowerment lies in their immersion in and (often unconscious) dependence on, what Simone de Beauvoir calls, "that mysterious and threatened reality known as femininity" (13). To be feminine in appearance, behaviour and activity is described as an "essential" component of both woman's sense of self and the sexual and material subjugation that she encounters in many parts of her life. One of the most well known and characteristically second wave strategies – consciousness-raising (CR) – directly draws on women's everyday experiences of feminine victimization to politicize their personal outlooks and pave the way for a wider politics of engagement.[1] In this way, the argument goes, "consciousness of weakness" ultimately enables "consciousness of strength" as women's understanding of and exposure to social and individual injury can be converted into "a joyous consciousness of one's own power" and "the release of energy long suppressed" (Bartky 16).

In this chapter, I want to address the trialectic of feminism, femininity and female victimization that has been the subject of a wide range of second wave feminist texts, critical as well as fictional.[2] I want to concentrate on early second wave accounts and critiques of femininity that are rooted in a liberal feminist tradition that fights for women's equality of opportunity in the public sphere. This tradition, represented by writers such as Betty Friedan in her foundational text *The Feminine Mystique* (1963), is in marked contrast to the later, more radical feminist viewpoints that draw attention to the institutionalized oppression of women and the underlying "sexual politics", to borrow Kate Millett's phrase. What characterizes the liberal stage of feminist theorizing is that equality is constituted within a set of terms that disparage things female or feminine in favour of masculinity. Christine di Stefano designates this "the rationalist position" that uses a minimalist notion of gender difference and suggests that women have been unfairly treated on the basis of the assumption that they are less rational and more natural than men (67). "Difference" therefore must be repudiated if women are to assume their rightful place in society as the non-differentiated equals of men. As di Stefano notes, "in the rationalist framework, *she* dissolves into *he* as gender differences are collapsed into the (masculine) figure of the Everyman" (77; emphasis in original).[3] In a similar manner, Joanne Hollows also distinguishes a particular strain of feminist criticism that conceptualizes femininity as inferior to masculinity; that is, "equality between men and women might be achieved if women rejected feminine values and behaviour in favour of masculine values and behaviour" (10).

In order to pursue the ideal of equality, feminists in the early 1960s were keen to abolish markers of difference – such as femininity – that they saw as fundamental to understanding women's oppression. It was during this period in Western history – after the tumultuous years of war had opened millions of jobs to women, and in response to the post-war backlash that saw industry, government and media converge to force a female retreat[4] – that the relationships between feminism and femininity were formulated and theorized, predominantly in terms of a binary division, with "victimization" heavily leaning towards the feminine side of the dualism. In years to come, it was this equation of femininity with victimization, and the supposedly factual and static description of the victimized *femme*, that was going to be challenged by a new wave of (post)feminist critics who saw this enforced polarity as an oversimplification of the complex power structures linking feminism and femininity. However, as I will elaborate in later chapters, some of these post–second wavers have ended up creating a similar, albeit inverted, binary – with feminism now criticized as a victimizing position that "urges women to identify with powerlessness" and invents "the very same morally pure yet helplessly martyred role that women suffered from a century ago" (Wolf, *Fire with Fire* 148; Denfeld 10).

Women's feminist awakening and their "raised" consciousness are thus intimately connected with an acceptance of victimization and a growing awareness of alienation, both from society and from one's self. Second wave feminist critics highlight that women are oppressed not only from the outside by institutional, political, societal and cultural directives and norms, but more insidiously they are also victims of their personal beliefs and convictions, caught in "the prison of their own minds" (Friedan, *Feminine Mystique* 265). We often find descriptions of "truncated" selves; women facing inner conflicts and a "schizophrenic split" (Bartky 25; Friedan 9).[5] Women have to confront not only their gendered Otherness in relationship to men – as Beauvoir famously put it, "humanity is male and men defines woman not in herself but as relative to him .... He is the Subject, he is the Absolute – she is the Other" (16) – but also an internalized alterity that works to subjugate them and circumscribe their limits. As Bartky reveals, "feminist consciousness is the consciousness of being radically alienated from her world and often divided against herself, a being who sees herself as victim and whose victimization determines her being-in-the-world as resistance, wariness, and suspicion" (21). In this sense, a woman's feminist "birth" involves an act of negation and transcendence, an acknowledgement that she has been diminished in her being and mutilated to some extent, and a willingness to wage war against those parts of society and her self that have been undermining her attempts at freedom. In second wave feminist texts, "woman" becomes the subject/object of a variety of interrogations that examine how she is constructed and defined; how her ambitions and moves are regulated and controlled; and how she has been kept in the rank of a second-class citizen. The "woman question" comes to be seen as a problem to be debated and solved, with an important distinction being made between "woman" – the myth – and "women" – the real historical beings (Beauvoir 26; Lauretis 5).[6] Monique Wittig, for example, argues that as feminists "our first task ... is to always thoroughly dissociate 'women' (the class within which we fight) and 'woman,' the myth" and thus, "we have to destroy the myth inside and outside ourselves" (313).[7]

Feminist critics suggest that the myth of "woman" has been kept alive and perpetuated in unison with another mythical construct: "the eternal feminine". Indeed, femininity has been used to seduce women into accepting their subjugated status – sugar-coating the otherwise bitter pill that is womanhood. Following the lead of Simone de Beauvoir's *The Second Sex* (1953), many early second wave writers concentrate on the cultural and social formations of gender in order to "dethrone the myth of femininity" and discard the notion of feminine essence (30). Beauvoir starts with the widely known postulation that "one is not born, but rather becomes, a woman" and she then poses the "woman question" as a "problem of feminine destiny" (295, 82). It is civilization as a whole that produces the "creature" described as feminine – strangely situated in an intermediary position "between male and eunuch" (295). Stressing throughout her work that the words "*woman* or *feminine*" refer to "no archetype, no changeless essence whatever", Beauvoir is adamant that it is not "*natural* for the female human being to make herself a *feminine* woman" (30, 428; emphasis in original). She identifies femininity as a kind of "prolonged infancy" that sets woman aside from "the ideal of the race" and enfeebles her mind (142). For Beauvoir, it is clear that this ideal is to be found in the masculine realm of "transcendence" and progress, whereas woman is doomed to a life of "immanence" and repetition (467).[8] Given the opportunity, woman could well show herself as rational, active and efficient "as a man", but at present, Beauvoir laments, she is too busily occupied seeking "the false treasures" of femininity to undergo her apprenticeship "in liberty" (539, 729, 720).[9] In Beauvoir's eyes, the emancipated "modern woman" is diametrically opposed to the "feminine woman": whereas the former accepts masculine values and "prides herself on thinking, taking action, working, creating, on the same terms as men", the latter makes herself "object and prey" and thereby renounces her claims as sovereign subject (727, 691). These two female destinies are incompatible as woman's independent activities and successes are in contradiction with her femininity (291). Moreover, by becoming feminine, woman not only betrays herself and her own kind but also reduces man to "her carnal passivity", occupying herself in catching him in her trap and enchaining him by means of the desire she arouses in him (727).[10] In so doing, woman makes herself into a "thing", condemned to play the part of the Other who is refused access to society by right of being human, what Beauvoir calls "the human *Mitsein*" (436, 109). In these circumstances, the key question for Beauvoir is not as to why women should reject the limitations imposed upon them by their sex but why they accept them so easily and apparently willingly (429).

Subsequent feminist analyses take up and further a number of points highlighted by Beauvoir: the need to de-essentialize the biological identity of woman and investigate the social construction of gender; women's right to equality on the same terms as men; and the clash between feminist and feminine impulses, the desire to assert herself as a "complete, unmutilated person" or be a "true woman" who accepts herself as the Other (539, 291). These ideas became central to ensuing feminist politics and fundamental to much social and political enquiry into issues such as the sexual division of labour and women's familial relations. Beauvoir's text also offered important insights into the workings of femininity, arguing that women are in effect complicit in the production of their own femininity and, consequently, in the gendered status quo that puts them in a position of subordination. Beauvoir talks about the "charm of passivity" and the "temptations of convenience" that convince women to yield to femininity (360, 168): "It must be admitted", she writes, "that the males find in woman more complicity than the oppressor usually finds in the oppressed" (730). She pinpoints an unmistakable class bias by identifying this "parasite" as "noble or middle-class" women who sell themselves to privileged men and thereby achieve a relatively influential and powerful social standing (141).[11] Quoting Balzac's injunction that men treat woman as slave while persuading her that she is queen, Beauvoir maintains that while these women behave with apparent freedom, their "equality in inequality" is rather doubtful as it masks both male despotism as well as female cowardice (493, 730). Succumbing to her "anxiety of liberty", woman enters a vicious circle whereby she agrees to become "what-in-men's-eyes-she-seems-to-be" in order to secure her place and not devaluate herself sexually and socially (730, 169, 692). Beauvoir is aware that a "greater moral effort" is required in choosing the road of independence but ultimately there is no other option as a woman who "remains a parasite" cannot "take part effectively in making a better world" (169, 606).

This belief was to be voiced again by other feminist writers like Germaine Greer for whom successful "feminine parasites" are among the chief enemies of "the revolutionary woman" who has overcome the "fear of freedom" (23–6). Greer's first book, *The Female Eunuch* (1970), offers an enquiry into the construction and naturalization of the feminine body, suggesting that women are conditioned to conform to society's expectations of femininity because they gain value only by being valuable to men. She seeks to raise a universal feminist consciousness based on the understanding that woman "could begin not by changing the world, but by re-assessing herself" (16). Dividing her polemic into sections on "Body", "Soul", "Love", "Hate" and "Revolution" (supposedly encompassing the feminine/feminist experience), Greer is convinced that "women must learn how to question the most basic assumptions about feminine normality in order to reopen the possibilities for development which have been successfully locked off by conditioning" (17). In many ways *The Female Eunuch* can be said to be part of a radical feminist tradition that wants to posit a fracturing of the discourse of normative femininity and feminine identity. For example, Greer argues against the liberal feminist goal of putting women in the workplace, contending that working women remain preoccupied with winning male approval. Her view of a positive revolution is equivalent to the theory of the proletariat outlined in classic Marxist thought and her solution involves women's retreat from their labour. As she reveals, "Women represent the most oppressed class of life-contracted unpaid workers, for whom slaves is not too melodramatic a description", concluding that "if women are the true proletariat, the truly oppressed majority, the revolution can only be drawn nearer by their withdrawal of support for the capitalist system" (369, 25).[12]

While this notion of women as a proletarian sisterhood might be appealing to a flourishing feminist movement, it does not necessarily capture the imagination of more mainstream feminists. In these founding feminist texts, to be described as middle-class, white and feminine can almost be considered as an acknowledgement of complicity and collusion, for these are exactly the kinds of female "parasites" that Beauvoir and Greer are concerned about. Beauvoir, for example, highlights that the myth of woman not only fulfils a purpose of "utility" but is also "a luxury" (289). While it is important for any woman who wants to avoid social devaluation to "live out her feminine situation in a feminine manner", middle-class women are offered particular, material inducements to complicity, beyond the "inauthentic longing for resignation and escape" (692, 325). Beauvoir notes that most bourgeois women have accepted "this gilded confinement", holding on to their chains because they cling to the privileges of their class (142). Freed from her male provider, the middle-class woman would have to work for a living and, as a result, she has "felt no solidarity with working-women". It is for this reason that "in the ruling classes" women remain parasites subjected to "masculine laws" and eager "accomplices of their masters" (160, 638). While such drastic views and entrenched class boundaries are no longer current or even relevant in today's society, these depictions nevertheless draw attention to the historical, social, class and racial "baggage" of femininity and the construction of the feminine woman as an exploitative hanger-on, a co-conspirator of patriarchy who helps to undermine the advances of other, feminist-minded women.

Indeed, it is these susceptible and privileged beings that Betty Friedan chose to address in her best-selling *The Feminine Mystique* (1963), in which, like Beauvoir, she sets out to examine the effects of nurture (in the guise of advertising, popular psychoanalysis, education and economics) upon women in forming the state of femininity. Friedan's white, middle-class perspective (and bias, some would argue) is revealed by the book's subject and target audience: the post-war phenomenon of the educated American housewife who is experiencing a crisis of identity whereby she "no longer know[s] who [she is]" (64). The book is based on the results of a questionnaire that Friedan circulated among her former college classmates, 15 years after they graduated, and it exposes an apparently unnameable dissatisfaction felt by these socially advantaged women who embarked on their life journey thinking they would be "New Women" but ending up as "Happy Housewives" (60). From the start, Friedan rejects the assumption that these women's difficulties are minimized or diminished by the fact that they "have luxuries that women in other times and lands never dreamed of"; on the contrary, she writes, "the strange newness of the problem" is that it cannot be understood in material terms as poverty or sickness (23–4). The situation is more perplexing and less tangible as, despite increased opportunities for higher education and professional careers, these women are fleeing into marriage and turning back to the hearth. *The Feminine Mystique* exposes the internal and psychological dilemmas of suburban housewives who are not realizing their full potential and suffer from an internalized sense of limitation, a "false consciousness" (although Friedan shies away from this Marxist-inflected term). She presents us with an analysis of the crises, limitations and aspirations of these supposedly parasitic women, "these daughters of the American middle class" to which she herself belongs (24).

According to Friedan, the 15 years after the Second World War were characterized by a strange turn towards nostalgia that sees both men and women look for the comforting reality of home and children (160). The experience of war has played an important part in this development as it caused the "American spirit" to fall into "a strange sleep": eager to avoid the frightening uncertainty and cold immensity of the changing world, men as well as women, liberals as well as conservatives have found excuses to not face their problems and, as a result, Friedan bemoans, "the whole nation stopped growing up" (164). Women in particular have been affected adversely by this home-bound trend and they have fallen into a trap of "helpless conformity" that makes them suppress their "ability and education to discover and create" in favour of housework and rearing children (164, 59). War, however, was not the only reason for women's retreat from the public arena as there was also a major shift in popular media and women's perceptions of themselves. Looking at a range of women's magazines from the 1930s onwards, Friedan notes that there has been a change in female imagery from the adventurous pre-war career woman distinguished by her "spirit, courage, independence [and] determination" to the homebodies of the 1950s who have decided to "give up the world and go back home" (33–4). Friedan, a journalist by trade, admits that she herself has helped to create this image: "I have watched American women for fifteen years try to conform to it. But I can no longer deny my own knowledge of its terrible implications. It is not a harmless image ... what happens when women try to live according to an image that makes them deny their minds?" (59).

Friedan is concerned that post-war women have made a mistaken choice – "trading [their] individuality for security" (180) – and they have to suffer the consequences: a nagging doubt and a growing divergence between the reality of their lives as "women" and the image of "woman" which they are trying to match. In Friedan's words, this constitutes "the problem that has no name", a widespread frustration felt by educated, pseudo-emancipated women who – "insecure in their ... freedom" (89) – have backtracked on their dreams of equality and now have a vague, undefined wish for " 'something more' than washing dishes, ironing, punishing and praising the children" (54). What makes this problem so difficult to overcome is that while it places women firmly in the home it also offers a comforting, "protective shade" to those who agree to remain within its narrow bounds (208). Therein lies the power and persuasiveness of the ideology of the "feminine mystique" that convinces women that they should "desire no greater destiny than to glory in their own femininity" (13). Friedan's widely quoted description is instructive:

> The feminine mystique says that the highest value and the only commitment for women is the fulfilment of their own femininity. . . . It says femininity is so mysterious and intuitive and close to the creation and origin of life that man-made science may never be able to understand it. . . .The mistake, says the mystique, the root of women's troubles in the past is that women envied men, women tried to be like men, instead of accepting their own nature, which can find fulfilment only in sexual passivity, male domination, and nurturing maternal love.
>
> (38)

The mystique builds on essentialist ideas that tightly link femininity with female biology, sexuality, motherhood and victimization. At the same time, the feminine mystique is also deceptively modern as it makes use of growing consumerism – with its associated forms of advertising and shopping – and fashionable psychoanalysis to bring about "the sexual sell" (181). Friedan's discussion of the housewife illustrates this point: 1950s advertising, for example, embraced the "cult of the housewife" by construing domestic labour in capitalist terms and constructing the homemaker as a competent businesswoman surrounded by labour-saving devices.[13] In this way the feminine mystique updates and exalts the "Occupation: Housewife", manipulating the unwitting homemaker into thinking that she can achieve a sense of identity and purpose by "the buying of things" (16, 182).

However, Friedan urges her readers not to fall for this recycled fantasy: "women once again are living in the old image of glorified femininity. And it is the same old image, despite its shiny new clothes, that trapped women for centuries and made the feminists rebel" (90). Friedan is resolute that women cannot allow themselves and/or others to confine them to this "genteel prison" as in the end this self-incarceration can only result in a "slow death of mind and spirit" (83). Friedan echoes Beauvoir in her delineation of femininity as a case of arrested development whereby women who choose the path of feminine adjustment simply refuse "to grow up, to face the question of their own identity" (67). At times, Friedan's emotive language features potentially insulting and even misogynist metaphors, such as her description of housewives as prisoners, "walking corpses", inhabiting a "comfortable concentration camp": "In a sense that is not as far-fetched as it sounds", she writes, "the women who 'adjust' as housewives, who grow up wanting to be 'just a housewife', are in as much danger as the millions who walked to their own death in the concentration camps" (265). Other images include brain-injured soldiers, schizophrenics and mentally retarded people (272, 270, 224). Moreover, Friedan suggests that women who adopt this passive non-identity are not only infantile, dependent and victimized but also progressively dehumanized, "stunted at a lower level of living, blocked from the realization of her higher human needs" (274). She maintains that the feminine mystique implies a choice between "being a woman" and "risking the pains of human growth" and hence, once again, femininity finds itself opposed to humanity (275).[14] Woman's energies then must be directed towards her human progress and maturity and "she must learn to compete...not as a woman, but as a human being" (328).

For both Friedan and Beauvoir, the way out of the feminine trap is economic freedom, education and "gainful employment": "education is and must be the matrix of human evolution", and once educated, women can draw on "work" as "the giver of self and...the creator of human identity" (Beauvoir 689; Friedan 322, 290).[15] Once the curse that is upon "woman as vassal" is broken and she ceases to be a parasite, "the system based on her dependence crumbles" and she can be active and productive in her own right (Beauvoir 689). The solution to "the problem that has no name" is deemed to be relatively straightforward: stop conforming to the feminine mystique and make a commitment to the more masculine (and presumably "human") world of work.[16] There is a notable difference between Friedan's and Beauvoir's proposed "life plans" for women in the sense that Beauvoir's account is aligned more closely with a feminist rhetoric and collective activism: "there is no other way out for woman than to work for her liberation", Beauvoir asserts, "[t]his liberation must be collective, and it requires first of all that the economic evolution of woman's condition be accomplished" (639). In addition, she is convinced that "sooner or later [women] will arrive at complete economic and social equality, which will bring about an inner metamorphosis" (738). Beauvoir's strategy for liberation thus works from the macro- to the micro-level, whereas Friedan focuses more on individual self-transformation as the way forward. Both writers, however, believe that women have a personal responsibility for producing this change and sometimes only have themselves to blame for their subjugated position.[17]

This is an inherent feature of most liberal feminist writings that concentrate on individual autonomy and self-determination; Friedan's analysis seems to imply that if women's revolution was to fail, this would largely be their own fault. Even though she appears to criticize the patriarchal social structure that insists that women put their efforts into housewifery and childcare, Friedan largely omits men's responsibilities and roles from her examination.[18] At no point does she propose that women relinquish their marital/maternal duties; on the contrary, she is keen to point out that women need not sacrifice marriage and motherhood: "It is not a question of women having their cake and eating it ... [W]ith the vision to make a new life plan of her own, she can fulfil a commitment to profession and politics, and to marriage and motherhood with equal seriousness" (329). However, while the needed social changes are hinted at, there is no definite challenge to existing work/family patterns.[19] In fact, there is an assumption that women would somehow manage to juggle their domestic and public commitments. As Rosemarie Tong observes,

> *The Feminine Mystique* failed to consider just how difficult it would be for even privileged women to combine marriage and motherhood with a career unless major structural changes were made within, as well as outside the family.... Friedan sent women out into the public realm without summoning men into the private domain.
>
> (24)

Friedan's work has been submitted to rigorous criticism, not least because of her own social positioning and the constituency she addressed in her book: white, married with children and comfortably middle-class. Having grown up in the American heartland of Peoria, Illinois, and describing herself in the preface as "a wife and mother of three small children" (9), Friedan was convinced that feminism must appeal to a suburban audience, a crowd she vaguely referred to as "the mainstream" and "Middle America".[20] If Friedan's objective for women's equality within the public sphere is not always expressed or analysed in the most sustained and comprehensive manner (and at times, even smacks of political hopefulness and naivety), this might be to do with her insistence on the importance of the middle class as key to the feminist movement's success. When, on the back of the extraordinary success of *The Feminine Mystique*, Friedan helped to set up the National Organization for Women (NOW) in the United States in 1966, her message was unequivocal: "Participation in the Mainstream is the Real

Revolution" ("An Open Letter" 384). As NOW's founding slogan con-
veyed, revolution had nothing to do with overthrowing the basic fabric
of society and the relationships between men and women, as many
radical feminists were suggesting (Friedan later termed this "orgasm
politics"). As Deborah Siegel reveals, Friedan's brand of feminism was
more informed by the liberal optimism of the Kennedy era and can be
seen as "a natural extension of American democratic values": "feminism
was not a countercultural program of dismantling and overthrow but
a realization of one's rights as a citizen" (*Sisterhood, Interrupted* 79). For
Friedan, "politics" therefore meant legislation, elections and civil service
but not the intrusion into women's private spaces, like their bedroom.
NOW's statement of purpose accentuates that women are supposed
to fully participate in the mainstream of American society, "exercis-
ing all the privileges and responsibilities...in truly equal partnership
with men" (quoted in Siegel 82). Friedan wanted heterosexual women
to be able to identify as feminists, without having to question their
intimate connections with men – seemingly heralding later postfeminist and popular feminist engagements with heterosexual, mainstream
femininity.

Certainly, one of the most astounding inconsistencies and potential
ideological U-turns that Friedan presents us with is her ambivalent relation to femininity. While in 1963, Friedan was unwavering in her belief
that reigning definitions of femininity were antagonistic to human
growth, she was also worried about the implications of a complete rejection of femininity. When in 1968 a group of radical feminists stormed
a conference in Boston to perform a ritual act of haircutting on one
of their blonde, long-haired members, Friedan's reaction was one of
intense criticism: calling it a "hysterical episode", she was appalled by
the message that these campaigners were trying to convey, that is, that
"to be a liberated women [sic] you had to make yourself ugly".[21] As I
will discuss in the following chapters, this incident highlights not only a
stylistic difference but a deeper philosophical and ideological split that is
symptomatic of liberal feminists' difficult relationship with their radical
sisters, for whom the cultivation of a stereotypically feminine appearance – such as long hair – has political ramifications. In 1971, Friedan
performed an even more astonishing turnabout when she began writing
a regular column for *McCall's*, a women's magazine. In "Betty Friedan's
Notebook", she continued her struggle to "feminize" feminism, fully
aware of the irony that the author of *The Feminine Mystique* was now
writing for a magazine once considered a cause of "the problem with no
name". Now she assured her readers that "femininity is being a woman

and feeling good about it, so the better you feel about yourself as a person, the better you feel about being a woman. And", she added, "it seems to me, the better you are able to love men" (quoted in Siegel 91). As I will elaborate in Chapter 3, Friedan's "feminine turn" is indicative of a larger shift towards pro-family conservatism that some feminist strands underwent subsequent to the heyday of the second wave. First, however, I want to look at how the triangulation of feminism, femininity and victimization was depicted in radical feminist discourse that rose up alongside liberal feminism, but diverges from its emphasis on public empowerment and middle-class heterosexuality, and its proposed strategy of joining rather than undoing "the system."

2
Burning the Bra: Second Wave Enemies of Glamour

As I have discussed in the previous chapter, liberal feminism is characterized by a belief in the equality and "sameness" of men and women;
indeed, Simone de Beauvoir had no qualms ending her pathfinding *The
Second Sex* on the word "brotherhood" (741). Beauvoir was adamant
that "woman...cannot be transformed unless society has first made
her really the equal of man" (737–8). It was fraternity between men
and women that was meant to bring about this "utopian fancy" and
press for changes in the status quo. While many liberal feminists continued in this direction in the late 1960s and early 1970s, those feminists
who saw their politics as more radical began to deviate from this
egalitarian perspective by focussing more on the differences between
men and women and on the need for a political "sisterhood".[1] They
argued that the liberal feminist stance was only pushing society into
accepting women in the same positions as men, without otherwise
altering the social order. One of the popular slogans of the period
claimed that "Women who strive to be equal to men lack ambition"[2] –
which was reinforced by contemporary activists like Ti-Grace Atkinson,
who proclaimed that liberal feminism is "worse than useless" and the
only successful way forward is confrontation through a "declaration
of war" against men and society (quoted in Nicholson ed. 3; Gamble
ed. 302). While liberal feminists like Betty Friedan shied away from
a "bedroom politics" and concentrated on working within American
democratic society, radical feminists wanted to explore the depths of
women's oppression, from their intimate relations with men to their
own internalized victimization.

It is here that consciousness-raising became vitally important as it got
to the core of women's subjugated state, in society as well as their own
home and bodies. Female revolution in consciousness was deemed to be

the crucial first step to a wider social revolution, facilitating an awakening of previously brainwashed women and an acknowledgement that all aspects of their lives were tainted by patriarchal influences. Robin Morgan's ardent introduction to the anthology *Sisterhood is Powerful* (1970) illustrates this:

> Everything, from the verbal assault on the street, to a "well-meant" sexist joke your husband tells, to the lower pay you get at work (for doing the same job a man would be paid more for), to television commercials, to rock-song lyrics, to the pink or blue blanket they put on your infant in the hospital nursery... everything seems to barrage your aching brain... You begin to see how all-pervasive a thing is sexism – the definition of and discrimination against half the human species by the other half. Once started, the realization is impossible to stop... To deny that you are oppressed is to collaborate in your oppression. To collaborate in your oppression is a way of denying that you're oppressed.
>
> (1)

Morgan's emphasis on the ubiquity of sexism underscores the demand for an all-encompassing enlightenment, including areas of engagement that had been considered too private for a feminist inspection. Radical feminists recognized the full potential of CR strategies that not only looked outwards to fight women's discrimination but also targeted their interiorized subjugation and "nature". As Morgan's veiled threat to her more sceptical readers implies, denial of victimization is not an option; nor is there the possibility to conceive of oppression in different, perhaps less drastic, terms – quite the opposite, anything less than a complete transformation of self and a "radically" raised consciousness is seen to involve collaboration and collusion with a hostile patriarchy.[3]

Many theoretical texts that emerged from the radical feminist movement focused on the notion of "patriarchy" and broadened its meaning (beyond the original definition as the rule of an elder male in a kinship structure) to include the institutionalized oppression of all women by all men. In *Sexual Politics* (1970), for example, Kate Millett argues that patriarchy is a political organization and the primary form of human oppression, underpinning all other social relations: "If one takes patriarchal government to be the institution whereby that half of the populace which is female is controlled by that half which is male, the principles of patriarchy appear to be two fold: male shall dominate female, elder male shall dominate younger" (25). Millett popularized the phrase "sexual politics" to describe "the 'socialization' of both sexes to basic patriarchal polities with regard to temperament, role and status", including stereotyped lines of sex category ("masculinity" and "femininity") (26). Patriarchal power is maintained predominantly through ideological control, "a most ingenious form of 'interior colonization'" (25): "[O]ne is forced to conclude", Millett writes, "that sexual politics...is, like racism...primarily an ideology, a way of life, with influence over every other psychological and emotional facet of existence. It has created, therefore, a psychic structure, deeply embedded in our past" that "as yet, no people have succeeded in eliminating" (168). Women have been targeted by this "psychological weapon" and they have internalized patriarchal ideologies of womanhood and femininity and, with them, their own inferior status (58). Hailed as "the Bible of Women's Liberation", Millett's book identified patriarchy as a socially conditioned belief system that achieves universality and longevity by passing itself off as "nature"; demonstrating in detail how its attitudes and systems penetrate literature, philosophy, psychology, politics and life (quoted in Siegel, *Sisterhood, Interrupted* 42; Millett 58). Her analysis of patriarchy as entrenched in social reality and even knowledge – living in the "mind and heart" to effect the conditioning of its subjects (177) – proved to be very influential and was crucial in the development of feminist thinking.[4] For Millett, women are the victims of a false patriarchal ideology that is politically deployed against them and deprives them of any but "the most trivial sources of dignity or self-respect" (54). Indeed, she notes that "like all persons in their situation (slaves are the classic example here)", women are obliged to "seek survival or advancement through the approval of males as those who hold power" (38, 54). Social change thus comes to be seen as "a matter of altered consciousness" that involves both transforming one's own "personality" and forming a coalition with like-minded "alienated elements" – "blacks", students, youths and the poor (362–3). Millett's goal is a "cultural revolution" that goes beyond political and economic reorganization by eliminating conformity to sexual stereotypes and sexual-social categories as a whole.

In radical feminist writings, there is an unmistakable partition between two states of mind and being – raised or non-raised – and a definite need to distinguish enlightened "new feminists" from "token women" who are in league with their (male) oppressors and "delight in docility" (Millett 362; Daly 334). Separatism thus became a defining characteristic of much radical feminist politics – in relationship to men as well as other women, particularly Beauvoir's female/feminine "parasites".[5] In this chapter, I want to focus on a number of radical feminist texts that concretized the dichotomy between feminism and femininity and established the figure of "the feminine anti-heroine" set up in opposition to "the feminist heroine" (Hollows, *Feminism, Femininity and Popular Culture* 17). In conjunction but somewhat antithetically, this radical feminist critique of femininity (manifested by a rejection of fashion and beauty practices) also gave rise to the stereotype of the desexed "bra-burner", propagated by an unsympathetic mass media. These mixed messages not only highlight the women's movement's unhappy relationship with the media, but also point towards contradictory constructions of femininity that are more likely to divide rather than unify women/feminists. Radical feminists contend that victimization is inherent in the minutiae of everyday existence and every aspect of life previously accepted as normal, given and standard. Radicalizing one's feminist consciousness requires a meticulous scrutiny and overhaul of day-to-day patterns, routines and behaviours: "It means changing how you relate to your wife, your husband, your parents, and your co-workers" (Beal 395). These interactions are seen to go straight to the heart of patriarchy and women's most private and supposedly "natural" relations, with others as well as their own selves and bodies. Shulamith Firestone, for example, brings home this point in her famous statement that "a revolutionary in every bedroom cannot fail to shake up the status quo" (36). Some radical feminist texts, like Firestone's *The Dialectic of Sex* (1970) and Millett's *Sexual Politics*, go beyond cultural gender norms and discuss biology as a defence for the ideological oppression of women. Here, it is not just femininity that is seen as a chief reason for women's subordination, but the female body itself and its function as a vessel for human reproduction. In radical feminist writings, the relationships between the "f-words" (feminism, femininity, femaleness) are stirred up, with proposals ranging from a call for an androgynous culture (Millett), a "cybernetic communism" where machines perform all kinds of labour (Firestone), to a "Hag-ocracy" peopled by "A-mazing Amazons" (Daly).

If separatism was one important feature of radical feminism, then activism was certainly another. Having found their cause, feminists were keen to have their voices heard through public acts intended to draw people's and the media's attention to social injustices against women. One of the earliest and most iconic events that brought second wave feminist activism to public awareness – and inadvertently also inflicted upon feminists the mythical label of the "bra-burner" that has been almost impossible to shake off ever since – was the demonstration that feminists staged at the Miss America Beauty Pageant in Atlantic City in 1968. The protest symbolically enacted the rejection of oppressive ideals of femininity through tactics which included picket lines, theatre, lobbying visits to the contestants urging them to drop out of the contest and a huge "freedom trash can" into which they threw "instruments of female torture": bras, curlers, false eyelashes, wigs, issues of *Cosmopolitan*. As the "No More Miss America!" manifesto (1968) announced,

> The pageant exercises Thought Control, attempts to sear the Image onto our minds, to further make women oppressed and men oppressors; to enslave us all the more in high-heeled, low-status roles; to inculcate false values in young girls; women as beasts of buying; to seduce us to ourselves before our own oppression.
>
> (quoted in Unger and Unger 215)

The demonstration served a double purpose: it was an attack on male-defined femininity and on the notion that women were objects to be consumed. Members of the New York Radical Women, who spearheaded the action, wanted to deride "the degrading mindless-boob-girlie symbol" and bring to light that "women in our society are forced daily to compete for male approval, enslaved by ludicrous beauty standards that we ourselves are conditioned to take seriously and to accept" (quoted in Siegel, *Sisterhood, Interrupted* 48; Brownmiller 9).[6] To put across their view that women were treated like cattle at beauty contests – judged and rewarded purely on the basis of their looks – the demonstrators paraded a sheep on the boardwalk and crowned it Miss America.[7] The protest was a direct challenge to the beauty industry as a whole that fostered such events and thereby contributed to the objectification of women. It was also a carefully planned publicity stunt and an attempt at collective CR: it was hoped that the media would act as a mouthpiece for the feminist movement and disseminate its messages of female emancipation to a wider audience.

However, media reports of the event were less than favourable: much of the national press coverage depicted the protest in ways that made the emerging movement seem ludicrous. Imaginary flames were added by the TV stations in an attempt to ridicule the demonstrators while the *Times* salaciously referred to the "bra-burnings" (though, in reality, no bras had been burnt in accordance with Atlantic City police's request not to endanger the wooden walkway). As Coote and Campbell comment, "The media loved it. Sexy and absurd, it neatly disposed of a phenomenon which would otherwise have proved rather awkward to explain" (3). This incident reveals the uneasy relationship with the media that was going to characterize much of second wave feminism. While feminists were sure of their own motives for the demonstration, it was quickly interpreted by the press as a jealous attack on the contestants in the beauty pageant. Press coverage of the early 1970s reflects this media tendency to depict "the women's libber" as an unfeminine, ugly woman with no make-up who seeks to "stir up ferment amongst her more attractive and contented sisters" (Hinds and Stacey 161).[8] Feminists were evidently frustrated at the media's ability to twist any event to create a favourable or unfavourable reading; there was also reluctance on the part of feminists to court the media in order to get their message across: the media liked to deal with spokespeople (preferably someone attractive and eloquent) and feminists were opposed to the development of a "star system" within their ranks and demanded a rota for media appearances (Whelehan, *Feminist Bestseller* 46–7). This did not fulfil the media's desires, nor did it enable the feminist groups to present themselves (and their message) in the most favourable manner.

The media stereotype took root in the popular imagination – undermining to a large extent feminists' efforts to target the public consciousness and implant their own ideas – and, even until today, such assumptions persist.[9] The figure of the bra-burning, mannish and fanatic feminist has dominated popular representations of feminism "so long as to have become one of the most familiar symbols in the contemporary political landscape and cultural imagination" (Hinds and Stacey 153). This negative label has been propagated as a metonym for the Women's Liberation Movement with the result that "we all know what feminists are" (Douglas 7). As Susan Douglas summarizes, "they are shrill, overly aggressive, man-hating, ball-busting, selfish, hairy, extremist, deliberately unattractive women with absolutely no sense of humor who see sexism at every turn" (7). This mythologizing or demonizing of feminism performs an apparently definitive rupture between feminism and femininity in its construction of two polarized and irreconcilable categories. The iconic figure of the humourless and drab bra-burner acquires meaning in opposition to cultural stereotypes of femininity and its rejection of feminine trappings. Feminists are characterized as "enemies of the stiletto heel and the beauty parlor – in a word, as enemies of glamour" (Bartky 41). As Hinds and Stacey argue, "there is no doubt that the persistent media characterisation of the feminist, from the bra-burner onwards, condenses a range of characteristics antithetical to conventional definitions of desirable femininity" (161). The media's argument against feminism insistently proclaims that women who collectively adopt a feminist outlook and engage in activist feminist politics will effectively be defeminized and desexed as this display of public action and assertiveness is incompatible with their feminine selves. Feminism is depicted as the preserve of "only the unstable, mannish, unattractive woman who has a naturally difficult relationship to her own femininity" (Whelehan, *Overloaded* 18). This media trend reached its peak in the 1980s with the representation of "macho feminists" who apparently stop at nothing (not even boiling an innocent pet) to achieve their goals (see Chapter 3).

Contrastingly, femininity is played off against the negative image of feminism and "appears not only as more rewarding but also as a lot more fun" (Budgeon, "Fashion Magazine Advertising" 60). The feminist movement is seen to threaten women with desexualization and social annihilation, undermining their sense of identity and blocking an important source of gratification and self-esteem. Sandra Lee Bartky notes that "[t]o have a body felt to be 'feminine'... is in most cases crucial to a woman's sense of herself as female... [and] a sexually desiring and desirable subject"; hence, "the radical feminist critique of femininity... may pose a threat not only to a woman's sense of her own identity and desirability but to the very structure of her social universe" (77, 78). As I will discuss in Chapter 4, advocates of femininity insist that it is not the terrain of female submission and containment but an empowering and active position that allows the female/feminine subject to express her self in confident and autonomous ways. Femininity is depicted in individualistic terms as a conscious *choice*, a personal right rather than a patriarchal law that is imposed authoritatively. This conjunction of conventional modes of femininity with notions of power and agency is an important feature of postfeminist/Girl Power rhetoric that no longer understands the relationship between feminism and femininity as necessarily antagonistic.

First, however, I want to refine the binary opposition between these f-words and distinguish the media propaganda on feminist "masculinization" and asexuality from the ideas and goals expressed in radical feminist treatises. As we have seen, from its earliest beginnings (exemplified, for instance, by Wollstonecraft's *Vindication*), much feminist writing has constituted femininity as a (named or unnamed) "problem" and a major cause of women's oppression. Radical feminist writings share this sense of incongruity between feminism and femininity but they draw a clear line between, what they consider, "man-made" femininity and "real" femaleness and sexuality. For example, Kate Millett's 1970 best-seller *Sexual Politics* may have condemned sex as "a status

category with political implications" and taken male writers and ana-
lysts to task for their sexism, but she also called for a "fully realized sexual revolution ... [to] end traditional sexual inhibitions and taboos ... [as
well as] the negative aura with which sexual activity has generally been
surrounded" (24, 62). She continues, "[t]he goal of revolution would be
a permissive single standard of sexual freedom, and one uncorrupted by
the crass and exploitative economic bases of traditional sexual alliances"
(62). That same year, Shulamith Firestone's *The Dialectic of Sex* asserted
that "in our new [feminist] society, humanity could finally revert to
its natural polymorphous sexuality – all forms of sexuality would be
allowed and indulged" (187). On a more literary level, this sexualized
feminist ideal is also manifest and is perhaps best represented by Erica
Jong's heroine Isadora Wing, who, in her search for the "zipless fuck",
sought pleasure for its own sake and on her own terms:

> The zipless fuck was more than a fuck. It was a platonic ideal. Zip-
> less because when you came together zippers fell away like rose
> petals ... Tongues intertwined and turned liquid. Your whole soul
> flowed out through your tongue and into the mouth of your lover.
> For the true, ultimate zipless A-1 fuck, it is necessary that you never
> get to know the man very well .... it was passion that I wanted.
>
> (11–12)

Jong offered her readers a new kind of heroine – "a thinking woman
who also had a sexual life" – and her creation proved extremely popular,
selling 6 million copies in the United States alone (Allyn 267).[10]

Conflating sexual freedom and feminist emancipation, these critical
and fictional examples can be seen to reflect another large cultural trend
of the 1960s and early 1970s that also had an enormous impact on
the reshaping of Western womanhood: the sexual revolution. In several
ways, women's liberation and the sexual revolution overlapped, with
many of the same people involved in both causes and sharing their
key struggles. Jane Gallop, for example, remembers her own "double
transformation" during this period: "The disaffected, romantic, passive
young woman I had been gained access simultaneously to real learning and to an active sexuality. One achievement cannot be separated
from the other .... Feminism made me feel sexy and smart; feminism felt
smart and sexy" (5–6).[11] Announcing a new libertarian era of openness
and uninhibitedness, the sexual revolution bared freedoms for feminists to not only critique but also enjoy their sexual lives.[12] Curiously,
one (unlikely) early supporter of the women's movement was *Playboy*

founder Hugh Hefner, a self-pronounced hero of the sexual revolution. Hefner is quoted as saying that he was fighting "our ferocious antisexuality, our dark antieroticism" and publishing *Playboy* felt "like waving a flag of freedom, like screaming 'rebellion' under a dictatorship" (Levy 55). The Playboy Foundation even gave money to NOW to support their legal defence and education fund and Hefner himself hosted a fundraiser at the Playboy mansion, declaring that "I was a feminist before there was such a thing as feminism" (56).

However, as might be expected, such an alliance was not going to be everlasting, and feminism's struggle with *Playboy* in particular has been well documented ever since Gloria Steinem put on a satin bunny outfit when she went undercover as a waitress in the New York Playboy Club in 1963.[13] Shulamith Firestone expressed her scepticism already in the early 1970s, commenting that "women have been persuaded to shed their armour" "under the guise of a 'sexual revolution'" (127). The sexual revolution – "if it brought no improvements for women" – proved to have "great value" for men: by convincing women that "the usual female games and demands were despicable, unfair...and self-destructive, a new reservoir of available females was created to expand the tight supply of goods available for traditional sexual exploitation" (127–8). Women dare not make the "old demands", Firestone continued, because they are keen to be "groovy chick[s]" and, as a result, have been disarmed of the little protection they had to fight sexual harassment (128). As Imelda Whelehan explains, while the sexual revolution proclaimed a sea change in social attitudes, it did not automatically alter "women's sexual identity or their power relationships with men"; sexual revolution thus came to be seen as a "chimera where women were being sold the idea of sex as liberation but often it cast them in just as strong a thrall to men, with new pressures to perform sexually at every occasion" (*Feminist Bestseller* 109).

Moreover, though the goals and agenda of radical feminism were undoubtedly sexual, they were not necessarily *hetero*sexual. Jong hints at this when her heroine's quest for sexual enlightenment is repeatedly thwarted by her lover's (the appropriately named Adrian Goodlove) inability to live up to the promise of this surname and achieve an erection ("it was no good.... He was only at half-mast and he thrashed around wildly inside me hoping I wouldn't notice" [134]). Isadora even relinquishes her fantasy of the "zipless fuck" when she foregoes the opportunity to have sex with a stranger on a train, feeling disgust rather than desire. "Perhaps", she muses, "there was no longer anything romantic about men at all?" (332). In effect, sex proved to be a "thorny issue at the heart of radical feminist politics", not only causing a split with advocates of the sexual revolution but also being divisive within the movement itself (Whelehan, *Feminist Bestseller* 53). Gradually, calls would emerge to unseat normative heterosexuality, either through "political lesbianism", celibacy and anti-pornography legislation.[14] These sex-critical stances reached their most radical height in the late 1970s and early 1980s with the "pornography wars" that saw two distinct oppositional factions develop: on one side, the anti-pornography and pro-censorship camp influenced by the writings and political activism of Andrea Dworkin and feminist law professor Catherine Mackinnon, who contend that "[t]he oppression of women occurs through sexual subordination" ("Against the Male Flood" 30);[15] diametrically opposed were "sex-positive" feminists who maintained that "women have the right to determine, for themselves, how they will use their bodies, whether the issue is prostitution, abortion/reproductive rights, lesbian rights, or the right to be celibate and/or asexual" (Alexander 17). Contemporary postfeminist positions (like "do-me feminism") bear obvious resemblances to this sex-positive agenda that argues for sexual empowerment and subjecthood (see Chapter 4).

Radical feminist texts are thus intent on differentiating "false", male-identified versions of femininity (and sexuality) from "real", feminist-inspired femaleness (and sexuality). Mary Daly expresses this thought clearly in *Gyn/Ecology* (1978) when she states that "femininity is a man-made construct, having essentially nothing to do with femaleness" (68). Femininity is quintessentially "a male attribute" that blinds women and lures them into forgetting its "falseness" (69). By contrast, femaleness is the realm of the "Positively Revolting Hag" (also described as Crone, Spinster, Harpy, Fury) who journeys to the "Otherworld" of the Race of Women (xxii). In Daly's universe, patriarchy has colonized women's (and even feminists') heads to such an extent that it "prepossesses" them and inspires them with "false selves" (322). She condemns these "moronized" women as "man-made", "painted birds" who have been incorporated into the "Mystical Body of Maledom" and succumbed to the patriarchal invitation "to become 'living' dead women" (5, 334, 67). In effect, this is "the common condition of women under patriarchy" who are "masked" by not only one but two or three coats of the patriarchal "paint disease" (334, 336).[16] To combat this internalized colonization ("the pig in the head"), the doubly or triply "painted bird" has no other option than to "unpaint" her self and "come to consciousness" (that is, wake up from "the patriarchal state of sleeping death") (342, xvii). Daly urges her readers to free "the Hag within" and become "wild women"; this implies undergoing a radical process of exorcism and defeminization, an undoing of their conditioning in femininity and an "unravelling of the hood of patriarchal woman-hood" (343, 15, 409). As Daly writes, "spinsters must... constantly unweave the ghostly false images of ourselves which have been deeply embedded in our imaginations" (409). Yet, she also issues a warning to those brave enough to follow "the call of the wild" that they will be persecuted not only by men but also by feminine "token women": the wild woman who "sheds the paint and manifests her Original Moving Self... is attacked by the mutants of her own kind, the man-made women" (343, 334).

Daly's analysis is more wide-ranging than that of other radical feminists (like Millett) in the sense that she attempts to attack sexism at its roots, in the very language used to articulate one's oppression. Arguing that reality is constructed through male-imposed, androcentric language (or "semantic semen" [324]), she advocates its deconstruction and its replacement with "gynocentric writing". As she explains, "[s]ince the language and style of patriarchal writing simply cannot contain or carry the energy of women's exorcism and ecstasy, in this book I invent, discover, re-member" (24). Using idiosyncratic neologisms and linguistic puns to expropriate negative gendered words, Daly engages in what she calls "a daring Piratic enterprise" that plunders material from the "patriarchal thieves", unmasks hidden reversals and invites her audience to listen to words in a different way (xxvi). For example, Daly reminds us that the word "glamour" originally meant "a magic spell" and used to refer to witches or "castrating bitches"; this is in marked contrast to modern definitions that characterize "glamorous" women as "made up and done in", while feminists are decidedly "unglamorous" (188). Daly's attempt to create a new language that is "Furiously and Finally Female" illustrates radical feminism's separatist agenda that envisages a woman-identified environment and a different "Hagocentric psychic space" (29, 341).

In *The Dialectic of Sex*, Shulamith Firestone focuses more on sexuality in her vision of a feminist utopia that allows women to escape female biology and the processes (and handicaps) associated with it. Firestone moves beyond heteronormative conventions, representing monogamous, "aim-inhibited" relationships as a purely temporary, transitional necessity before the ideal state of "natural polymorphous sexuality" can be achieved (205). For her, this involves "trans-sexual group marriages", a dismantlement of traditional family structures and their replacement with the transient social form of the "household", and, most controversially, sexual freedom for children (205, 207, 215).[17] In her view, women have more in common with children than their fellow men: whereas men and women are seen to live in "different halves of reality", women and children share a bond of oppression, being stuck in the "same lousy boat" (148, 65, 81). In her quest for freedom, a feminist – being an "ex-child and still oppressed child-woman" (93) – has to integrate the liberation of children as the myths of femininity and childhood are interrelated (82). Like other feminists before her, Firestone's critical trajectory involves a now familiar condemnation of femininity, reiterating previous accounts that women live "under a system of patronage" that perpetuates the illusion of free choice (124). Women only love "in exchange for security" and hence "romantic love" is defined as "love corrupted by its power context" (125, 131). In line with earlier analyses, Firestone calls for a rejection of feminine appearance and behaviour, declaring that "our final step must be the elimination of the very conditions of femininity" in order to "clear the way for a fully human condition" (94).[18]

Firestone radicalizes these lines of enquiry, both by going beyond cultural norms of gender and by delving further into women's private lives, behaviour and consciousness. For example, one proposed anti-feminine action includes a "smile boycott" and an abandonment of the desire to please: as she explains, "[t]he smile is the child/woman equivalent of the shuffle; it indicates acquiescence of the victim to her own oppression" (81). According to Firestone, the "tapeworm of exploitation" has burrowed deep into women's lives, pervading "all culture, history, economics, nature itself" (12, 3). Patriarchy has taken advantage of women's biology, in particular their reproductive capacity, to handicap them and hinder their advancement. "In all stages and types of culture, women have been oppressed due to their biological functions", Firestone writes, and – reproduction being a chief reason for female subordination – the only solution for her is the removal of this fundamental impediment from the social order (67). This biological revolution is meant to come about through technological developments in artificial reproduction that will liberate women from the experience of pregnancy – a process she describes, with brutal conciseness, as "barbaric", "the temporary deformation of the body of the individual for the sake of the species" (180–1).[19] She believes that "women have no special reproductive *obligation* to the species" and – "Humanity" having begun to "transcend Nature" – future advances in technology will provide the means to overthrow oppressive natural conditions (209, 10; emphasis in original).

For Firestone, this implies a seizure of not only control of reproduction but also other social relationships, like work. Indeed, she is convinced that cybernetics will create the technological possibilities for a "full takeover by machines of increasingly complex functions, altering man's age-old relation to work and wages" (176). Machines will act as "the perfect equalizer" obliterating patriarchal systems based on the exploitation of both labour and sex (183). Overall, Firestone's alternative structure – a "cybernetic communism" – is based on four key demands: control of the functions of childbearing/child-rearing through artificial reproduction and the socializing of childcare; economic independence and the obsolescence of the labour force through cybernation; integration of women and children into the larger society ("Down with school!"); the sexual freedom of all women and children (185–7).[20] Undoubtedly, this dream of a feminist utopia – inspired by a Marxist model – is revolutionary and uncompromising in its view of patriarchal history. Firestone's objective goes beyond a consideration of social structures (and women's unequal position within them) and targets the sex distinction itself (11). Once the tyranny of sexual/biological division is removed through an embrace of technology, the social and cultural formations that lend it ideological support – the family, cultural myths of femininity, romance, love, marriage and motherhood – will also collapse. Firestone's radical feminism "bursts through" traditional categories of thought – biological, sexual, cultural, social and economic (3): "feminism, when it truly achieves its goals, will crack through the most basic structures of our society . . . [and] question the basic relations between the sexes and between parents and children" (36, 37). Firestone is resolute that the goals of feminism cannot be achieved "through evolution, but only through revolution" (30).

What strikes one as a twenty-first-century reader about these radical feminist treatises is the distinctively angry tone of such criticism and the undeniable sense of optimism and confidence that change was not only necessary but also viable and realizable in a relatively short span of time: Millett, for example, is positive that there is no need for a "lengthy evolutionary process" as "the deliberate speed fostered by modern communication" makes it possible for "groups . . . [to] become organized . . . in a matter of some two years" (363). In retrospect, some of the policies and demands are extremely visionary as to appear naive, such as Firestone's ardent belief in the potential of technology and her suggestion that "no one will be 'working' " in a "new culture based on a radical redefinition of human relationships and leisure for the masses" (183). Her dream of a cybernetic communism that "resolve[s] all the basic dilemmas that now arise . . . to obstruct human happiness" reads somewhat like utopian science fiction to a contemporary audience whose lives heavily depend upon and are governed to some extent by technology (213). Far from easing the workload and creating the possibility for "humane living", technological advancements – many would argue – have enslaved us further and turned us into "techno-junkies" addicted to email and mobile phones (184). To be fair, Firestone's feminist revolution is accompanied by a caveat that acknowledges the limitations of her plans (laid out, as she says, by "a solitary individual") that are not meant to provide "final answers" and inevitably are "sketchy": "the reader could probably draw up another plan" that would satisfy his/her requirements "as well or better" (203).

This highly individualistic attitude points towards some of the problems that were going to trouble radical feminists after their political prime in the early 1970s, revolving around questions about how these proposals could be translated into social reality and who was really addressed by their radical agenda. As a number of critics have highlighted, Daly's feminism, for example, seems to have given up on most women and instead concentrates on a "chosen few" – in Morris's words, Daly is a "political elitist" who differentiates between "the elect-in-a-state-of-grace" and "those beyond the pale" (quoted in Hollows, *Feminism, Femininity and Popular Culture* 15). Her distinction between "real women" and feminine dupes is bound to alienate those who conceive of their femininity (and feminism) in different, more diverse, terms and who do not agree with this polarity. In years to come, new (post)feminist voices would emerge to support a resignification of femininity that wants to loosen and even sever its links with female victimization. "Difference" and "diversity" would become the buzzwords of the following decades and questions would be asked about whether feminism could ever unite women (beyond the markers of class, race and sexual orientation). This is not to say that radical feminism was uniform and invariable; quite the contrary, the ideas and theories put forward by these thinkers were radically utopian and distinct – for example, there is no conformity or agreement as to what is meant by femininity and femaleness (a deep, mystical quality for Daly; a biological trap for Firestone). Yet, these internal disparities were overlooked in favour of an overriding concept of "sisterhood", allied in a struggle against a common set of oppressions and oppressors. As Whelehan notes, "the problems that united women coming out of a male-dominated political framework seemed larger and more urgent than those which spoke to other aspects of a woman's identity" (*Feminist Bestseller* 161). By the 1980s, however, there was a gradual shift away from radicalism, and feminists had to face a harsh reality: "women's liberation was everywhere and yet it was nowhere. An era had passed" (159–60). As I will discuss in the next chapter, the 1980s marked a difficult period of uncertainty for feminism – subsequent to the political excitement of the second wave – when it had to confront and re-address its estranged relationship with the media, its oppositional critique of femininity and an increasingly contentious sisterhood.

3
Boiling the Bunny: The Backlash and Macho Feminism

Ever since *Fatal Attraction* was first released in 1987, the film has become synonymous with one particular scene – the boiling rabbit. Cinema audiences were shocked and scared as they witnessed the motherly and caring Beth (Anne Archer) discovering her daughter's dead pet simmering in a pot upon the stove. The child screams in fear, unable to find the animal, and her husband Dan (Michael Douglas) jumps up, already certain of who is to blame for this gruesome crime – his mad, pregnant mistress Alex Forrest (Glenn Close). Principally as a result of this heinous attack on the happy American family, moviegoers cheered during the final scene that saw Alex being both drowned and shot.[1] This raving madwoman seemed so incredibly deranged and turned increasingly dangerous in her actions that contemporary audiences came to feel an overwhelming sense of hatred for her, as well as sympathy for her intended victims. Alex became the embodiment of evil in the film and, following her vicious murder of an innocent animal, she also gave rise to a new cultural stereotype and description of neurotic and menacing womanhood: the bunny-boiler.[2] Susan Faludi explains that as soon as the film came out it mesmerized the media that reported on "Real Life Fatal Attractions", advising the unsuspecting public that "[i]t's not just a movie: All too often, 'casual' affairs end in rage, revenge, and shattered lives" (145). Depicting the descent of a titillating flirt into a deadly nightmare, the film was said to encourage a monogamy trend and slow the adultery rate. It was seen as a warning to unfaithful husbands who were tempted to stray from their safe, domestic havens; but predominantly, it was also meant as a cautionary tale for/against unmarried women. While the husband was clearly in the wrong betraying his wife and endangering the family unit (and, implicitly, the whole of society whose moral health and stability depend upon it), his greatest mistake

65

was his failure to recognize the new danger that faced 1980s America: emancipated, single women.

Here was a novel kind of woman that Hollywood and the media in general were keen to classify and typecast: career-focused and financially independent; sexually confident and unabashed; demanding equality and respect from men, the 1980s single woman was clearly the beneficiary of feminist advancements in the public and private spheres.[3] Yet, inhabiting a previously inconceivable social position, she was also unhinged, deranged and potentially threatening – as far as filmmakers and press writers were concerned, she was a time bomb, ready to explode at any moment and destroy the American family in its entirety. The 1980s bunny-boiler was perceived to be infinitely more dangerous than the bra-burner; whereas the latter confined herself to a rejection of feminine accoutrements, the bunny-boiler – bolstered by the successes of the women's movement – did not hesitate to assert her rights and use violent means to achieve her goals. Moreover, she also harboured more risks for men to get involved with her because, unlike the unfeminine bra-burner, she appeared to be more seductive, appealing and heterosexual. In *Fatal Attraction*, Alex Forrest's frizzy blonde hair and flirtatiousness lure Michael Douglas's character away from his domestic life and his hearth angel wife. As I will discuss in Part II, the two women enact a modernized version of a well-known polarization between, what the screenwriter James Dearden calls, "the Dark Woman and the Light Woman", or in this case, the raving Singleton and the dutiful wife, the sexualized temptress and the good mother (quoted in Faludi 149).[4] This 1980s siren and the freedoms she exhibits hold some attraction for a family father who wants to "spice up" his normal routine by participating in her wild, unregulated life and aggressive sexuality. While undeniably exciting, Alex's heterosexuality also breaks away from patriarchal conventions and calls for a changing definition of femininity and a more equal relationship between partners. Rather than exploring the potential of a progressive, late-twentieth-century version of femininity and sexuality, *Fatal Attraction* endorses a conservative, pro-family agenda that identifies the single woman as a sadistic, sexual predator – one tabloid even dubbed Glenn Close's character the "MOST HATED WOMAN IN AMERICA" (Faludi 145). The film's final message and brutal dismissal of Alex Forrest leave no room for doubt as to what is the only possible outcome for this type of woman.

As the sad case of the bunny-boiler exemplifies, popular representations of feminists (or emancipated women) were becoming more drastic and antagonistic in the 1980s. In the media's eyes, ridicule was no longer a sufficient response to the perceived threat of feminist liberation and enfranchisement; nothing but a bloody double-kill would do to rid society of the evil of single career women who had taken on board feminist lessons and insisted on their implementation in their daily lives and interactions with men. The bunny-boiler appeared to be an abject by-product of an altered social reality that saw women's increased access to and involvement in a buoyant post-war economy and workforce. Feminism had undoubtedly played an important role in emboldening women to challenge gender discrimination and transform the dynamics of the workplace. This was meant to be the age of the "Superwoman" who could "have it all" and juggle home, children and job (see Part II). However, where the bunny-boiler went off course was in her insistence on transposing her professional ambition and competitiveness to the private realm and thereby enforcing a new structuring of domesticity and heterosexuality. As far as the media was concerned, this was one step too far: working women were now an economic fact and necessity that could no longer be denied and had to be tolerated as long as they were still willing to perform their traditional motherly/wifely roles in addition to their new work responsibilities. As soon as singleness and sexuality were added to this mix, what resulted was a power-crazed lunatic that was seriously threatening the sanctity of the home.

The horror-inspiring image of the bunny-boiler was at the extreme end of a range of new female representations that emerged as a result of second wave influences on social and cultural formations. Her forceful expulsion gave a clear indication as to how far women's public successes and demands for equality could be taken and introduced into the domestic heart of society. There were obvious boundaries between private and public womanhood, and the family – the traditional motor and microcosm of Western society – was clearly off limits. The example of the bunny-boiler not only underlined the media's scepticism and hostility towards feminism – at best, a half-hearted nod to women's professional advancements – but also raised questions regarding feminists' treatment of domesticity and femininity. While feminists had worked hard to get women out of the house and into the office by exorcizing the "feminine mystique", they did not necessarily provide the answers that would help women to combine their "half-lives". Looking back on 20 years of feminist activity, second wave veteran Betty Friedan comes to the conclusion that "[t]he women's movement did not fail in the battle for equality" but "[o]ur failure was our blind spot about the family" (*The Second Stage* 203). In her aptly entitled *The Second Stage* (1981), Friedan laments that in her search for public achievement, the career woman often adopts an approach based on "female machismo" that sees her ape male power and strength in an attempt to "mask her vulnerability, her economic independence, her denigration by society and denigration of herself" (56). In playing out the "superwoman game", women are locked in "excessive reaction against female powerlessness – *or* female machismo – deny[ing] themselves certain real strengths as women and becom[ing] doubly passive" (58; emphasis in original). In an apparent reversal of her previous critical stance that urged women to move out of "the protective shade of the feminine mystique", Friedan now asked them to "go back to their feminine roots" and principles – "the sensitive, tender, intuitive, life-cherishing values that have always been associated with women" (*Feminine Mystique* 208; *Second Stage* 275, 164).

Friedan's feminine turn is seemingly at odds with her earlier convictions and it has been criticized as a "great leap backwards" and "an attack on the radical core of feminist thought and practice" (Stacey 232). In this chapter, I want to examine the 1980s as a period of external and internal backlash that changed the women's movement significantly in structure, strategy and collective identity. The 1980s are generally seen as a difficult decade for feminism, both in terms of popular representations as well as in terms of inner divisions that – although present from the beginning of the second wave – were causing rifts within the women's movement and fracturing the communal ideal of sisterhood. Nancy Whittier describes "the Eighties" as a "grim symbol of antifeminism" and "a tough period of retrenchment": "the 1980s contained massive opposition and setbacks for feminism that drove longtime activists out of social movement organizations and into more individual forms of agitation. 'Feminism' became a dirty word in many circles" (191, 194). Yet, she also explains that "the 1980s women's movement was not 'in abeyance' in the same sense as the post-World War II women's movement"; new recruits continued to enter and in some ways the movement can even be said to have grown "more visible and accepted" during this time (194, 195).

In effect, feminism lost much of its core position and identity as it was pulled in two directions by internal and external forces: on the one hand, feminists were confronted with a wider range of issues, which meant that more attention had to be paid to diversity and differences among women, particularly in terms of racism, classism and heterosexism.[5] While much of second wave feminism's agenda and outlook relied on the notion of collectivity to foster political change, now other determinants, like race, class and sexual preference, gained importance and could no longer be subsumed under the umbrella term of "sisterhood".[6] As Whittier summarizes, "in short, feminist collective identity, or how participants understood what it meant to be a feminist, changed in the 1980s", with the result that, when it emerged at the end of the decade, "'[f]eminist' came to mean something quite different by 1990 than it had meant in the 1970s" (196, 191). On the other hand, feminism also became less tangible and distinct in the ways that it was perceived from without. Feminism lost much of its outsider status as many feminist activists entered more institutionalized professions in the 1980s and feminist ideas of emancipation and empowerment were appropriated and adopted by popular culture (204–11). Feminist critics at large have denounced this development as a commodification of feminism and a hijacking by the media that sends up and undermines its central tenets. Debates surrounding the issue of "feminism and/in popular culture" have focused on the ideas of co-option and incorporation to explore the interconnections between the two sites and the viability of the term "popular feminism".[7] As I noted in Introduction, this has become an increasingly complex and equivocal area of discussion, with twenty-first-century feminism indisputably being a part of the cultural field and common sense. As Rosalind Gill puts it, "most feminism in the West now happens in the media" (*Gender and the Media* 40).

I want to examine the mainstreaming and diversification of feminism in the context of 1980s backlash culture that saw profound changes in the social, political, economic and cultural climates of Britain and the United States. The backlash is often linked to the rise of the New Right and a shift in a more conservative direction that not only can be felt in politics but is also evident throughout popular culture.[8] Critics contend that the media work hand in hand with a right-wing political ideology to launch an attack on the core beliefs and politics of the women's movement and to re-articulate conventional versions of femininity and domesticity. As Ann Braithwaite writes, evidence of the backlash can be found in the "renewed emphasis on images of women that replay and celebrate more traditional definitions of femininity, definitions that were the locus of earlier feminist thinking, commentary and action" (20). The media backlash – located, for instance, in advertising, the fashion industry, popular news media, film and television – is seen to be preoccupied with presenting "an image of woman in which she [is] engrossed either with her appearance and being attractive... or with motherhood, children and a desire to retreat from the workplace in favour of the 'mommy track' – in short, with being 'a woman again'" (20). The re-embrace of femininity is understood as a "demand that the cultural gears shift into reverse" and women be confined again between the twin poles of domesticity and beauty – pressing them to "conform to comfortably nostalgic norms" and "shrinking them in the cultural imagination to a manageable size" (Faludi 92). This, it is argued, is a "false feminine vision" that hides women's reality and promotes restrictive stereotypes of femininity and femaleness that second wave feminism worked to challenge and change (78). In this case, the backlash becomes synonymous with anything considered "anti-feminist", that is anything that appears to retract and invalidate the gains and social transformations brought on by or through the feminist movement. This conceptualization of the backlash keeps intact the historically entrenched division between feminism and femininity, and it also adopts a view of backlash femininity as forever static and backward-looking: in Susan Faludi's words, "the 'feminine' woman . . . is like the ballerina in an old-fashioned music box, her unchanging features tiny and girlish, her voice tinkly, her body stuck on a pin, rotating in a spiral that will never grow" (92).

In my eyes, the above outline of the backlash as "anti-feminism" points to a facile attitude towards feminism, femininity and popular culture that glosses over some of the complexities, contradictions and overlaps that mark these fields of enquiry. The backlash is not just a retrogressive, anti-feminist position that simply replicates long-standing patterns of femininity – Imelda Whelehan, for example, portrays it as an "over-simplifying" rhetoric that repeatedly makes the "banal point that feminists are just a nasty bunch of spoilsports" and endorses a "retro-sexist" nostalgia for the "old order of babes, breasts and uncomplicated relationships" (*Overloaded* 32, 178).[9] This interpretation of the backlash offers a delimited understanding of feminism, femininity and popular culture that overlooks their diverse relationships and engagements with one another. As Ann Braithwaite comments, "the politics of backlash thus become a politics of rejection" and "a kind of shorthand for a distinction between a more 'authentic' feminism on the one hand, and a suspect, tainted, and usually commercialized rendition of feminism on the other" (26). Rather than focusing on how the backlash (re)acts against feminism, Braithwaite suggests that one might alternatively take into account "how much something about feminism has instead saturated pop culture, becoming part of the accepted, 'naturalized,' social formation" (19). Without doubt, the descriptions of womanhood that appear in the 1980s highlight the incorporation and denigration of feminist ideas in their transition to cultural representation – from all-achieving "Superwoman", over-achieving "macho feminist" and bunny-boiling murderess. Yet, they can also be seen as comments on and responses to a late-twentieth-century context that has been influenced and altered by the second wave. In this sense, these depictions do not simply endeavour to roll back the gains made for women's social and political equality and send them back to the "genteel prison" of the feminine mystique (Friedan, *The Feminine Mystique* 83). The 1980s return to femininity does not have to be conceptualized merely as a diminishment of the accomplishments of women/feminists; instead, it also draws attention to the fact that femininity is not a one-dimensional, retrograde construction bound to a number of graven images. This point of view is especially interesting and rewarding when we consider the feminine turn in feminist thinking (exemplified by Friedan's call for "second-stage" feminism) and the possibility of "feminist femininities" in 1990s expressions of Girl Power (Chapter 4).

The term "backlash" certainly achieved its current reputation and infamy with the publication of Susan Faludi's best-selling book of that title in 1992. According to Faludi, since the early 1980s there has been a sustained attempt by the media to undo the ground gained by the second wave and take women back to the subordinate roles of a bygone era. As Faludi explains, "the last decade has seen a powerful counter-assault on women's rights, a backlash, an attempt to retract the handful of small and hard-won victories that the feminist movement did manage to win for women" (12). This "pop-culture version of the Big Lie" stands "the truth boldly on its head" and "proclaims that the very steps that have elevated women's position have actually led to their downfall". The backlash targets the growing social category of working women and announces that, in their search for professional success on male terms, they are bound to end up single, unloved and fraught with neuroses. Faludi outlines the backlash tenets that have been propagated in a range of media texts in the 1980s and early 1990s and that are based on the assumption that female identity is troubled and tormented:

> professional women are suffering 'burnout' and succumbing to an 'infertility epidemic.' Single women are grieving from a 'man shortage.' ... Childless women are 'depressed and confused' and their ranks are swelling.... Unwed women are 'hysterical' and crumbling under a 'profound crisis of confidence.' ... High powered career women are stricken with unprecedented outbreaks of 'stress-induced disorders.' ... Independent women's loneliness represents 'a major mental health problem today.'

(1–2)

As Faludi explains, these female predicaments have been laid at the door of the feminist movement that has supposedly "gone too far", providing women with more independence and choice than they can handle and thereby wrecking their relationships with men (xiii). The backlash claims that "women are unhappy precisely *because* they are free. Women are enslaved by their own liberation", grabbing "the gold ring of independence, only to miss the one ring that really matters" (2; emphasis in original). Feminism is said to be responsible for "the sad plight of millions of unhappy and unsatisfied women" who, thinking they could combine career and family, have jeopardized an essential part of their femaleness (Walters 119). Suzanna Danuta Walters sums up the backlash argument whereby feminism "promised more than it put out", "we thought we wanted equality, but realize instead that we cannot have it all" (121). Attempting to live up to an ambitious "Superwoman" image, working women have been positioned in a no-win situation as either they are condemned to a "double-day/second-shift" existence or they recognize that their professional success has come at the cost of relationships and marriage (122). Backlash propaganda aims to dichotomize and create a dissonance between women's private and public, feminine and feminist aspirations, splitting their lives into "half-lives" (Faludi 491). Moreover, the backlash not only warns women that they cannot have it both ways and must choose between home and career, but also makes the choice for them by promoting wedded life and domesticity as a full and fulfilled existence. In other words, women are told that "if they gave up the unnatural struggle for self-determination, they could regain their natural femininity" (490).

Faludi is adamant that the backlash can be attributed to an entirely hostile media that acts as an anti-feminist force to sabotage and undermine the women's movement and slander it as "women's own worst enemy" (2). She insists that the "so-called female crises have had their origins not in the actual conditions of women's lives but in a closed system that starts and ends in the media, popular culture and advertising – an endless feedback loop that perpetuates and exaggerates its own false images of womanhood" (9). In particular, professional single women are castigated by the popular press and pilloried for their unmarried state and the error of their independent ways. Working Singletons are cautioned that, unless they hurry and change their overly liberated lives, they are going to end up loveless and manless as "single women are 'more likely to be killed by a terrorist' than marry" (124). In fact, "to be unwed and female" comes to be seen as an "illness with only one known cure: marriage" (122). Unattached career women are

pathologized and defined as abject and deficient, selfish and emotionally stunted, and ultimately regretful about neglecting their essential
roles as wives and mothers. The backlash seeks to segregate single working women and represent them as "defective units", "alone and isolated
only by their own aberrant behaviour" (376). Singleness is described as
a woman's personal psychosis, self-inflicted and curable only through
extensive "feminist-taming therapy" and self-transformation (372) – of
course, in *Fatal Attraction* Alex Forrest proved to be beyond such reme-
dies, having jeopardized not only her "natural" (that is, caring and
domestic) femininity but also her sanity. As Faludi notes, single women
are taught to see that "what they think is a problem with the man is
really something inside them", and therefore, it can be dealt with only
through individual, rather than collective, responsibility (376). Specifically, the Singleton's feminist convictions have become a trap as the
focus on career has engendered a negligent and/or misguided attitude
towards her heterosexual commitments and femininity – again, the
example of the bunny-boiler is instructive here as it reveals just how
mistaken and dangerous single women can be in their (mis)conception
of heterosexual relations and the gender roles associated with them. This
personalizing and individualistic trend results in the fragmentation of
any sense of commonality among women and the depoliticization of
their anxieties that are portrayed as purely personal ills, unrelated to
patriarchal pressures and confining social structures.

The backlash thus endeavours to convince women of their need to
scale back their feminism/professionalism and rekindle their interest
in romance and marriage. The disparagement of single womanhood
is accompanied reversely by an enhancement and resignification of
domesticity that repackages women's retreat to home and husband in
activist terms and rhetoric. As Elspeth Probyn reveals, this marks a
"new traditionalist" agenda that articulates and naturalizes a "vision
of the home to which women have 'freely' chosen to return" (149).
New traditionalism centralizes and idealizes women's apparently fully
knowledgeable choice to abstain from paid work in favour of family life
and values. By contrast, the women's movement is represented as "the
enemy of the New Traditionalist", having unleashed "a drab, macho
feminism of hard-faced women" who are determined "to carve their
place in the world, no matter whose bodies they have to climb over to do
it" (277–8). "Macho feminism" has deceived women into believing that
they can be happy only if they are treated (and treat themselves) like
men (278). However, new traditionalists emphasize that female fulfilment really lies in the pleasures and "freedoms" afforded by femininity

and domesticity.[10] The domestic sphere is re-branded as a domain of female autonomy and independence, far removed from its previous connotations of drudgery and confinement – as I will discuss in Part II, this resignifying approach is particularly relevant for twenty-first-century housewives who try to make sense of domestic life in postfeminist terms.

As far as Faludi is concerned, the "back-to-the-home movement" is nothing more than the creation of the advertising industry and, in turn, "a recycled version of the Victorian fantasy that a new 'cult of domesticity' was bringing droves of women home" (77). Couched in the language of women's liberation, the return to the domestic realm veils and conceals the political assault on women's rights, their re-imprisonment in the home and regression to a stance of feminine passivity. This "linguistic strategy" is seen as an inherent part of the backlash's conservative programme that seeks to re-label the terms of the feminist debate, control the definition of "equality" and ultimately "switch the lines of power through a sort of semantic reversal" (269). The backlash thus employs resignifying techniques to work against the feminist movement, individualize women's problems and splinter their collective struggle for emancipation while promoting its own stereotypical values and reasserting the primacy of traditional gender roles.

While Faludi acknowledges a more nuanced understanding of the backlash in her introduction – whereby it contains a series of mixed messages about feminism that take into account the struggle for women's rights and the social changes wrought by the feminist movement[11] – her overall appraisal is damning. As she summarizes, the backlash decade has produced "one long, painful and unremitting campaign to thwart women's progress" (492). Interestingly, Faludi employs a similar rhetoric of relapse in her description of postfeminism that, in her eyes, is simply interchangeable with the backlash. She maintains that "post-feminism is the backlash", "meaning not that women have arrived at equal justice and moved beyond it, but simply that they themselves are beyond even pretending to care" (15, 95). This indifference, Faludi is convinced, "may, finally, deal the most devastating blow to women's rights" (95). Her concluding words and solution are surprisingly hopeful – considering the depths and lengths she goes to in her discussion of the backlash as cultural regression and anti-feminism – and recall previous second wave strategies and thinking: "productively, women can act" and revive the feminist movement for "no one can ever take from women the justness of their cause" (498).

Faludi's extensive analysis of the backlash has been instrumental in the unveiling of a conservative, right-wing ideology and agenda that was prevalent in 1980s Western culture and society. Since the publication of *Backlash: The Undeclared War against Women* the notion has become a standard feature of many feminist investigations, to the extent that it is now used "to critique the perceived political implications of almost any issue having to do with women, and especially to denounce a range of current representations of women throughout popular culture" (Braithwaite 18). However, Faludi's mobilization of the term "backlash" (and postfeminism) to describe a reaction against the women's movement also runs the risk of dismissing the nuances and complexities inherent in both contemporary feminist theories and popular culture overall. The ways in which critics like Faludi employ these terms suggest that there is a necessary conflict between "genuine" 1970s feminism and femininity/popular culture. To subscribe to such determinate definitions means that one can only ever read the backlash (and postfeminism) as a retrograde stance that harks back to a pre-feminist world. Contrastingly, as Charlotte Brunsdon has observed in her evaluation of postfeminism, another useful interpretation could highlight "a changed context of debate on feminist issues" which is marked by a shift "in popularly available understandings of femininity and a woman's place" (*Screen Tastes* 101–2). This line of enquiry might allow us to break loose from the definitional constraints that a conception of the backlash (and postfeminism) as "anti" necessarily entails, as well as move beyond the stifling dichotomy between feminism and femininity that ultimately rigidifies each identity.

This is precisely what Betty Friedan tries to achieve in *The Second Stage* (1981), in which she argues against "polarizing rhetoric" that has been employed and manipulated by differently minded political extremists, including radical feminists. According to Friedan, the appearance of incompatibility is a false impression, created and put forward in the "first stage" of the women's movement that was "defined by that old structure of unequal, polarized male and female sex roles" (40). However, after almost 20 years of feminist activity, she is convinced that "it's over, that first stage" and "what's needed now is to transcend those terms, transform the structure itself" (27, 40). The goal of "second-stage" liberation is thus to rise above "the polarity between women and women and between women and men, to achieve the new human wholeness that is the promise of feminism" (41). Friedan's sights are set on a particular duality that she herself had helped to formulate in her ground-breaking earlier work: "There is a reconciling of seeming opposites that has to take place now, a dialectical progression from thesis-antithesis (feminine mystique-feminism) to synthesis" (81). This "new turn in the cycle" brings women back to "a familiar place" – their femininity/domesticity – but this time, Friedan stresses, they return to it "from a different vantage point". In effect, the second-stage path takes women/feminists "full circle back", but "it's no longer ... a Doll's House" that they enter.

As the title of Friedan's book indicates, she is engaged in a kind of retrospective, revisionist exercise that questions some of her earlier assumptions and "take[s] [her] way beyond [her] previous concerns, opening strange doors" (15). She acknowledges that something is "going wrong" within the women's movement to the extent that an "unarticulated malaise", "nervousness" and "weariness of battle" now have replaced the preceding exhilaration and "great momentum" that characterized the first stage (15, 20, 26, 18). Though Friedan does not explicitly refer to temporal referents, her usage of the term "first stage" is meant to designate the Women's Liberation Movement of the 1960s and 1970s that intricately linked the feminist goal of equality with collective sexual politics. There is some disillusionment apparent in Friedan's recollection of how "simple and straightforward" "our agenda then seemed" and how "easily" "our early battles were won", coupled with a newly gained awareness that "the radiant, inviolate, idealized feminist dream" has led women/feminists to a "dead end" (24, 254, 27). While she appreciates that "the women's movement has changed all our lives and surpassed our dreams in its magnitude", she also concedes that "it's not so easy to *live* ... solely on the basis of that first feminist agenda" (26–7; emphasis in original). In fact, "[t]he equality we fought for isn't livable, isn't workable, isn't comfortable in the terms that structured our battle" (40).

In Friedan's eyes, the first-stage political programme concentrated on breaking through "the barriers that had kept women from moving as equal persons in the mainstream of society" and this often created a mistaken view of the movement as a sexual war of women against men (170). Somewhat paradoxically, the first stage also supplied women with a "masculine" model of success – what she calls "Alpha-style leadership" – that was employed by "all previous liberal and radical movements of 'outs' wanting to get 'in'" (244).[12] This resulted in a kind of "female machismo" that "locked women in violent reaction against their own identity" and made them exchange their feminine/domestic powerlessness for masculine careerism and a male "warrior model" (56, 45, 194). She is resolute that "[t]he women's movement is over, in terms of the dominant Alpha, masculine mode that polarized women against men in the sexual politics of the first stage, and also polarized women against women" (248). This kind of hierarchical, authoritarian and task-oriented leadership now has to be replaced with the "Beta" mode, which emphasizes flexibility, sensitivity and relational power, all of which are supposedly "feminine" in origin.

Friedan's demand for feminist progression can clearly be understood within the context of her anti-radicalism and anti-extremism, already evident in *The Feminine Mystique*. As I observed in Chapter 1, Friedan's liberal feminist approach hinges on her belief in the necessary connection with the American, middle-class heartland and, as such, she is opposed to the sexual politics of radical (lesbian) feminists. In *The Second Stage*, this ideological division is again brought to the fore: "our roots [are] in the middle American mainstream", she vows, and "equality and the personhood of women never meant destruction of the family, repudiation of marriage and motherhood, or implacable sexual war against men" (47).[13] She dismisses and denounces sexual politics as "a serious ideological mistake", "a red herring" and "a pseudo-radical cop-out from the real and difficult political and economic battle for equality for women in society" (47, 313, 51). Countering "radical lesbian 'separatists' " – Friedan explicitly mentions both Daly and Millett, who encouraged women to not "shave [their] legs" and view men as "vampires" feeding on female bodies and minds (48) – she is adamant that sexual politics and "personal bedroom wars" are "an irrelevant, self-defeating acting out of rage" (318, 257).

Her particular point of contention is that the sex-role distinction fostered by first-stage sexual politics often engendered an antagonism between feminism and the family, a "polarization between the feminist who wants equality and 'choice,' and the woman for whom 'the family' is security" (203). The sexual politics of the first stage thus not only pitted women against men but also women/feminists against themselves, denying "the reality of woman's own sexuality, her childbearing, her roots and life connection in the family" (51). Reinforcing her non-dualistic worldview, Friedan maintains that "[t]here are *not* two kinds of women in America" (228). Nor are the needs of men and women irreconcilable; in effect, she envisages a second-stage coalition with men and – rephrasing a famous anti-rape slogan ("Take Back the Night!") – she encourages "women, with men" "to take back the *day* – take a stand on regaining human control over what was once called women's sphere (family, children, home) and join men in jobs, unions, companies, professions asserting new human control over work" (257; emphasis in original). Admittedly, Friedan's second-stage solution and her call for a new order are only vaguely defined and she provides no sustained analysis of how the restructuring of home and workplace is to be accomplished. This is in line with her main objective and focus, which is not on providing answers but helping to "ask new questions" and "put the right name to...new problems" (34). Importantly, these problems and difficulties no longer solely reside outside the feminist movement but they are caused by its increasing diversification and internal rifts.

Friedan singles out feminism's "anti-family" perspective as an area of feminist dispute and she refuses to discount it as pure backlash and "enemy propaganda": "It is not just a conspiracy of reactionary forces", she writes, "though such forces surely play up and manipulate those fears" and she demands that women/feminists look inward and "begin to openly discuss feminist denial of the importance of family, of women's own needs to give and get love and nurture, tender loving care" (22). In an apparent critical turnaround, she asks her readers (and feminist sisters) to revisit "unfinished true battles of feminism" and not turn their backs on "the life-serving core of feminine identity" (32). The radical feminist pendulum has swung too far in its reaction against femininity – as Friedan says, "we blush even to use that word now" (41) – insofar as women are denying "certain painful feelings, certain yearnings, certain simple needs" for fear of being trapped again in "the weakness, the helplessness, the terrible dependence that was women's lot before" (38). The limitations of and predicaments caused by the feminine mystique are no longer Friedan's primary concern as she shifts her critical eye and attention to the feminist movement itself: feminism is now seen to be in danger of breeding its own "problem that has no name", a "*feminist* mystique" that threatens to "harden into a similarly confining, defensive mystique" than its feminine counterpart (31). According to Friedan, shattering the debilitating hold of the mystique of feminine fulfilment was an important ideological project of earlier phases of feminist thinking – "[i]t was, is awesome", "that quantum jump in consciousness" (31) – but "saying no to the feminine mystique and organizing to confront sex discrimination was only the first stage" (40). In fact, "if the movement is to fulfil its own revolutionary function in modern society", the challenge ahead is to discover a "new mode of thought" that allows us to re-introduce and confront femininity (and domesticity/family) on different terms (84, 239).

Friedan implicitly acknowledges that there is room for disapproval and a possible irony in her re-embrace of femininity and domesticity: "There was a time when such an idea would have made me cringe", she admits, but immediately rebuffs criticisms of this kind, asserting that "there is a truth here. Not a new feminine mystique" (195). What reappears in the 1980s is not "the old feminine necessity" but a "new human politics" that "will enable us to take back the day *and* the night" (31, 343; emphasis in original). In this sense, even though an "either/or approach might seem simpler", the solutions that Friedan now seeks to uncover "are inherent in the paradoxes, which imply 'both/and' thinking" (234, 240). As she declares, "the picture that emerges is something quite different from either feminine or feminist mystique, integrating, in new forms, elements recognizable from both. The reality is richer, the problems and the pleasures more complex, interesting, reassuring, surprising" (55–6).[14] In order to "turn this new corner" and get to the second stage, there is no option in her eyes but to break out of feminist rhetoric, go beyond the assumptions of the first stage of the women's movement and "test life again" (40).

Friedan's vague depiction and almost philosophical belief in "human liberation" and possibility "as women and men" has been criticized as a neo-Victorian, essentialist espousal of the "women's sphere" and an example of "the new feminist conservatism" that "discards the most significant contributions of feminist theory", providing in their place "a feminism that turns quite readily into its opposite" (Faludi 357; Stacey 235). In Judith Stacey's estimation, Friedan can be seen as a "disenchanted" liberal/feminist who responds to both "the failure of liberalism" and "the setbacks of feminism" (227, 224). Susan Faludi is even more scathing in her description of *The Second Stage*: the "book is punctuated with the tantrums of a fallen leader who is clearly distressed and angry that she wasn't allowed to be the Alpha wolf as long as she would have liked" (356). For Faludi, Friedan's feminine veer amounts to nothing less than treason and political disloyalty: by "accepting the New Right language, Friedan has walked right into the New Right's 'pro-family' semantics trap" (358). She puts forward the question "Why [is] Friedan stomping on a movement that she did so much to create and lead?" and her answer is quick to follow and unequivocal: this is once again an example of a regressive backlash that makes even established feminists "turn and bite [their] tail" (355). Stacey concurs by saying that "the new conservative attempt to fortify the family … exempts it from analysis and returns it to its prefeminist status as an ahistorical essence", concluding that "the logical terminus proves to be classical patriarchy" (233–4, 236).

Friedan is by no means the only second wave feminist who critically revisits some of her earlier assertions and beliefs. As Faludi observes, "[b]y the mid-1980s, the voices of feminist recantation became a din, as the media picked up the words of a few symbolically important feminists and broadcast them nationwide" (352). She cites Susan Brownmiller, author of the 1975 landmark work on rape, *Against Our Will*, and Germaine Greer, whose book *Sex and Destiny: The Politics of Human Fertility* (1984) champions chastity and arranged marriages and, in her own words, represents an "attack upon the ideology of sexual freedom" (quoted in Faludi 352). Greer's case also exemplifies a move away from feminist collectivity in favour of a celebration of difference and heterogeneity of female experience.[15] Like Faludi, Judith Stacey also reads these public feminists' return to femininity, privacy and the family as part of a wider conservative trend that seeks to "avoid all forms of direct struggle against male domination" (221). Yet, she also admits that the problem cannot be located solely outside the feminist camp as "one more alien antagonist" (237). Feminists, like Friedan and Greer, are responding to "genuine" social difficulties and a second wave theoretical tendency to focus purely on "the negative social and psychological effects of the housewife/mother role" (237–8). Stacey argues that the emergence of pro-family/feminine feminism also has "powerful personal roots in the collective biographical experiences of a particular generation of feminists" (238). In the late 1960s and early 1970s, many feminists, who were then in their twenties and early thirties, were intent on avoiding the traps of motherhood and marriage and they were keen to experiment with sexuality and collective households (Firestone's notions of "cybernetic communism" and "polymorphous sexuality" are obvious examples). Stacey notes that this has resulted in "three sorts of personal traumas": " 'involuntary' singlehood, involuntary childnessness, and single parenthood" (239). As I will discuss in Part II, these are exactly the kinds of problems that trouble postfeminist generations of women and give rise to female categories and figures like the "Singleton". However, Stacey's solution to these new, feminist-related concerns looks remarkably worn and equally as sketchy as Friedan's: "I believe that 'old' unreconstructed feminists must forge a political theory and programme that comes to grips with the difficult issues that the new conservative feminism helps to identify" (242).

What both these anti-backlash and pro-family critics ultimately highlight is the lack of confidence and certainty about the future, both of feminism and of femininity. In her book, Friedan distinctly addresses a generation of "daughters" who need help to "break through the mystique I myself helped to create" (34). "[T]his part is over", she writes, and "it is very important indeed that [the daughters] start thinking about the movement in new terms" (340).[16] While she admits that there are certain predicaments ahead – there are "new, uncomfortable realities...that are hard to put into words because they do not fit either the new or old images of women" (34) – her tone is still confident and encouraging, revealing her liberal optimism: "by the year 2000, I doubt there will be any need for the likes of... Gloria Steinem or Betty Friedan. The arguments about equal rights for women will be nostalgic history" (236). As time has proven, Friedan's positive assertion that "the daughters no longer have to play games" has been confounded by the increasing complexity of their lives and the "games" they now enter into (341). These postfeminist daughters not only insist on bringing back femininity into the feminist framework but they also suggest that to be feminine can be interpreted as a feminist statement. However, simultaneously, it has also been shown that to shatter the "old" does not necessarily set the scene for the "new". Instead, the daughters of the second wave cannot get away from the complications and paradoxes inherent in a postfeminine subject position that is caught between the aspirations brought on by (feminist) change and the awareness of a culture that is still degrading women.

4
Going Pink: Postfeminism and Girl Power

If, as we have seen, the 1980s can be discussed as a rather muted period of disillusionment, revisionism and political reprisals against second wave feminism, the following decade came to represent a more upbeat, rejuvenated and "popular" version of feminism, both in terms of its increasingly mediated existence as part of the cultural field as well as in terms of its capacity to act as a commodity, selling empowerment and agency to female consumers. It was during this time that "postfeminism" became more recognizable and concretized as a cultural phenomenon and journalistic buzzword; while there had been some mention of postfeminism early in the 1980s (predominantly, interpreting it as symptomatic of a backlash against feminism [for example, Bolotin]), the 1990s witnessed a veritable explosion of the term in popular culture and its diversification into a number of sub-categories: "do-me" feminism, power feminism, DIY feminism, "bimbo" feminism, raunch feminism and, perhaps most famously, Girl Power (Neustatter; Shalit; Wolf; Albury; Levy; Kim; Siegel, *Sisterhood, Interrupted*). Although varying in terms of content and focus (in particular, the degree of sexualization and the age groupings of the women/girls addressed), these differently named classifications are part of a prevalent, late-twentieth-century postfeminist discourse that blends a more mainstream – or commoditized (depending on your view/critique of popular culture) – and individualized version of feminism with a range of feminine and/or sexual markers. In an attempt at renovation and innovation, feminism is reconstructed (and its language refurbished) by prefixing it with another ("feminine") classifier; indeed, this results sometimes in oxymoronic formulations like "bimbo feminism" that attracts more attention as a media catchphrase rather than an actual description or characterization that women can identify with (Siegel 10).

Other postfeminist manifestations – like "power feminism", "do-me" feminism and Girl Power – are more clearly connected to female pleasure and (sexualized) agency, intermingling feminist-inspired notions of free-dom, liberation and empowerment with (hetero)sexuality, embodiment and fashion that have traditionally been associated with femininity.[1]

Taken as a whole, these 1990s expressions of postfeminism argue not just for an overhaul and modernization of feminism – or, less posi-tively, "a ritualistic denunciation" that renders feminism "out of date" (McRobbie, "Post-Feminism and Popular Culture" 258) – but also for a reinterpretation of femininity that disrupts its previous signifying link with female victimization. Postfeminism interrupts the cycle of, what queer theorist Emily Apter has called, "gynophobia", the femi-nist reaction against femininity that equates the latter with "weakness", "castration" and "passivity". It constructs a suture between feminism and femininity that can be articulated in different ways, depending on various levels of relationality and overlap; while in some cases (such as "do-me" feminism and, to some extent, Girl Power) there appears to be an unproblematic correspondence whereby femininity/sexuality is understood as a feminist statement, I am more interested in the com-plex interactions and paradoxes that emerge in the spaces between these f-words. I believe that it is here – in this blurring of the binary – that a postfeminist femininity (or "postfemininity") surfaces that transcends and reconfigures existing victim/power dualities. At the same time, how-ever, we need to take care not to rest on our interpretative laurels and halt our critical interrogations at an uncontested assertion of postfem-inism's contradictoriness, its "both/and structure" (Projansky 69). As Rosalind Gill and Elena Herdieckerhoff have recently observed in their discussion of romance in chick lit, "it is not enough merely to point to [the] coexistence [of contradictory discourses]; what is important is the work they are doing" (500). Equally significant, I would add, is that we fully comprehend and investigate the spectrum and potentialities that postfeminism/postfemininity open up, both for a consideration of the complex discursive and contextual interactions that characterize the twenty-first century as well as for a re-conceptualization of contempo-rary forms of critique and agency, subjectivity and objectivation. In this sense, our discussion of how the prefix "post" affects and modifies both feminism and femininity will also necessarily involve a much wider examination of how we conduct critique, use definitional strategies and analytical structures to (re)present the self and/in society.[2]

Significantly, I do not understand postfemininity as a simple rever-sal of logic that equates femininity/sexuality with freedom; on the contrary, in my eyes, the postfeminist connection between feminism and femininity is highly controversial and polysemic and, as such, it is indicative of a number of social, cultural, economic, theoretical and political developments that characterize a late-twentieth- and early-twenty-first-century Western context. On the one hand, the appearance of a postfeminine subject position in the 1990s can be linked to a widely theorized "gender quake" brought on by – very broadly defined – a post-modern questioning of gender norms in conjunction with the "coming out" of queer theory around this time. Taking cues from theorists like Judith Butler, I propose that the insight that gender is a cultural product, a "kind of doing", can be employed productively within a heterosexual frame to analyse the changeability and unsettledness of feminine signifiers that destabilize and resignify conventional meanings ascribed to gender difference (Butler, *Undoing Gender* 1).[3] Some critics might object to the use and appropriation of a theoretical model that has developed within a non-heterosexual critical milieu, very much *in reaction to* heteroreality and normativity.[4] However, as Kath Albury notes, such paradoxes inevitably come to light when we start to interrogate and experiment with forms of heterosexuality: there is an assumption that "like breathing, heterosexuality is something you 'just do'" and she admits that "[her] personal stance on her heterosexuality could be called queer precisely because heterosexuals are not supposed to be aware of [their] heterosexuality" (vi, 39).

In Butler's theories, heterosexuality is assigned a hegemonic status and normative quality – whereby "gender norms operate by requiring the embodiment of certain ideals of femininity and masculinity, ones that are almost always related to the idealization of the heterosexual bond" (*Bodies* 231–2). Yet, she also allows for a denaturalization of heterosexuality by revealing that "'imitation' is at the heart of the *heterosexual* project and its gender binarisms": "hegemonic heterosexuality is itself a constant and repeated effort to imitate its own idealizations", and as a result, it can lay no claim to "naturalness and originality" (125; emphasis in original). As Butler insists, terms of gender designation (such as "masculine" and "feminine") are "notoriously changeable" and "never settled once and for all but [they] are constantly in the process of being remade" (*Undoing Gender* 10). Femininity can thus be "done", and by extension "undone", in the sense that it no longer refers to a stable gender monolith but it has become available for another set of significations and a different "scripting".[5]

However, as I pointed out in Introduction, this act of resignification should not be understood as an annihilation of the feminine signifier and a "clean" break that erases pre-existing associations; rather, any reinterpretation or modification of femininity builds upon social and cultural patterns of that term, creating layers of feminine meanings that overlap in significant ways and give rise to contradiction and ambiguity.[6] The potential for "newness" and a possible challenge to, what Beauvoir named 50 years earlier, "the eternal feminine" can be discovered in the contemporary signifying link that has been established with feminism and notions of self-determination and power. What postfemininity thus achieves – drawing on Beauvoir's imagery again – is a depolarization of "the 'feminine' woman" (who makes herself into "a thing") and "the emancipated woman" (who "refuses the passivity man means to impose on her") (727).[7] By contrast, the postfeminine woman actively demands her sovereignty – not as an object and prey – but as a feminine subject who has taken on the difficult task "to do as she pleases in shaping the concept of femininity" (692).[8]

Other (perhaps less theoretical and more historically distinctive) factors that inform the emergence of postfeminism/postfemininity are connected to the increasing importance of media visibility and consumer culture. Certainly, the types of femininity and feminism that come to the fore in the 1990s are constructed (to varying degrees) in mediated forms and through consumption. Angela McRobbie, for example, uses the term "commercial femininities" to refer to the feminine subjectivities that are produced by/in popular culture, particularly in women's magazines ("More!"). This embrace of consumer culture represents a marked point of differentiation from second wave feminism that, as we have seen, has been critical of the media's misogyny and believed in the power of separatism over, what Imelda Whelehan terms, "the spin game" (*Feminist Bestseller* 138).[9] Here it is important to realize that empowerment and agency – goals that both second wave feminists and postfeminists claim – are envisaged differently, whereby second wave notions of collective, activist struggle are replaced with more individualistic assertions of (consumer) choice and self-rule. As Sarah Banet-Weiser has observed, within this contemporary context, "empowerment cannot be theorized as separate from market strategies but is rather a *constitutive* element in these strategies" (216; emphasis in original). Indeed, the notion of freedom is often directly tied to consumer culture and the ability to purchase, with women's agentive powers premised upon and enabled by the consumption of products and services, frequently associated with femininity/sexuality. This is especially relevant for 1990s expressions of Girl Power that – in its most commercialized form – combines an emphasis on feminine fun and female friendship with a celebration of (mostly pink-coloured) commodities and the creation of a market demographic of "Girlies" and "chicks".[10]

In this rapidly changing cultural landscape, feminism's role and situation in a media/consumer society have been the subject of many discussions; doubts have emerged whether it can still exist as a discrete politics once it has been incorporated into popular culture; and its fight for female emancipation and equal opportunities has been normalized (even though the material reality has not yet been attained). The main issues revolve around individualism and popularization/mainstreaming – two closely related points that have also been raised and debated vigorously in critiques of postfeminism and its politics of representation and (controversially) emancipation.[11] In effect, consumer culture has become a site for tension (and contention) around the concept of the individual within (post)feminism and the kind of political action it makes possible. The move towards individual, consumer-oriented empowerment has propelled the consideration of several complex questions: Can feminism be political and popular at the same time? Once feminism has become a commodity, does it still have the power to enforce social change? What happens to female agency once it has undergone a process of individualization and commoditization? What kind of politics can appear in a "representation nation" where media display is paramount (Klein)? Many critics are sceptical of and even hostile towards this "free market feminism" that, it is argued, works "through capitalism" and is purely centred on the self and "based on competitive choices in spite of social conditions being stacked against women as a whole" (Whelehan, *Feminist Bestseller* 155).[12] This view has been disputed by a number of (mostly younger) feminists who encourage non-collectivism and an awareness of one's consumer status as part of their political agenda. The so-called "DIY feminism", for example, favours individuality as a positive articulation of political motivation and appropriates cultural images of women to effect a distanciation from previously intended meanings.[13]

In the remainder of this chapter, I want to focus on Girl Power as a particularly popular and influential postfeminine/postfeminist stance that illustrates some of the problems and debates around commercialization and individualization within feminism that I have mentioned.[14] I suggest that Girl Power encapsulates the spectrum and paradoxes inherent in postfeminist femininity, encompassing a sexualized politics, an emphasis on style and youth as the site of emancipation, a hip marketing strategy and consumer slogan, all based around a playful/ironic reconfiguration and consumption of feminine signifiers. Countering criticisms by (predominantly) second wave feminists who decry the appearance of 1990s Girl culture as a "depressingly durable" and insidious kind of media indoctrination, I propose to examine it through a multi-layered postfeminine lens that reveals a range of significations and gives rise to a contradictory form of feminine/sexual identity that confounds existing power/victim, subject/object dualities (Greer, *The Whole Woman* 28). As Stacy Gillis and Rebecca Munford have observed in relation to the postmodern, consumerist feminism of the pop icon Madonna, "[t]he politics of subjectivity need to incorporate an understanding of the agency within self-representation as well as the appropriation of that agency" – "in short, the 'power' and the 'girl' in girl power need to be interrogated rather than dismissed outright" (173). Indeed, it is in the connection between these two concepts – "girl" and "power" – that we witness the possibilities for an altered understanding and reformulation of femininity that takes into account its relation to – rather than disconnection from – feminism and discourses of female empowerment and assertiveness.

The term "Girl Power" has become naturalized in popular culture, where it usually refers to a media-friendly way of articulating a playful, sexualized subjectivity and agency that resist more passive, compliant versions of femininity. David Gauntlett, for example, defines Girl Power as "a celebration of self-belief, independence and female friendship" and he draws a direct link with music culture, and in particular the arrival of the Spice Girls on the pop stage in 1996: "Mixing conventional glamour with feisty, ultra-confident, 'in your face' approach, the Spices – driven by Geri Halliwell – really did push the 'girl power' agenda for a while" (217–18).[15] Neatly packaged into five different facets of 1990s British femaleness – Sporty, Scary, Posh, Ginger and Baby – the Spice Girls (with their "Girl Power" battle cry) declared their intention to shake up the music scene (and society with it). In an interview, Ginger Spice (aka Geri Halliwell) describes the powerful community made up by the Spice Girls and their fans: "When you speak to them, they've got such balls! It's like we've collected a whole group of our people together" (quoted in Gauntlett 217). The girls' message that was to be repeated in innumerable interviews and song lyrics (such as their debut single "Wannabe") is about "fulfilling your dreams, going against expectations and creating your own opportunities for success" – in tandem with the "freedom" to flaunt their femininity/sexuality through a display of hot pants, platform shoes and Wonderbras (218). As their self-penned manifesto *Girl Power!* (1997) emphasizes, the Spice Girls position themselves as late-twentieth-century modernizers offering an updated, "feminized" version of feminist empowerment: "Feminism has become a dirty word.

Girl Power is just a nineties way of saying it. We can give feminism a kick
up the arse. Women can be so powerful when they show solidarity" (48).

The suggestion that feminism deserves a good shake-up (a "kick up the
arse") has been denounced by a number of commentators as illustrative
of an anti-feminist backlash in popular culture that turns feminism into
a "dirty" word and presents it as obsolete and old-fashioned. Imelda
Whelehan, for example, argues that the band's comment – though a
seemingly genuine gesture of pro-female camaraderie – shows "how girl
power as a rhetorical device is all too prone to appropriation for essentially patriarchal ends. It inevitably promotes the widespread view that
feminism is nothing but a tangle of infighting factions who never gave
serious consideration to the idea of female solidarity" (*Overloaded* 45).
At their height, Whelehan writes, the Spice Girls "offered a vision of
success, youth and vitality to the young in a world where youthful,
childless, sexually attractive women are the most visible fetishised image
of femininity" (46). If Girl Power can at all be called a version of feminism, it is a purely individualistic one that "bears no relation to the
'bigger' issues" as the Spice Girls "seem to have forgotten, or remain
blissfully unaware of, the social and political critiques offered by second-
wave feminism" (47). For critics such as this, the crux of the matter
seems to revolve around both the personalized address of the Girl Power
slogan as well as the historicizing logic that creates a competitive generational model between second wave feminist mothers and postfeminist
daughters, politically informed women and culturally astute girls.[16]

Another, associated, point of contention relates to the notions of
commercialization and mainstreaming that are viewed by many as a
"selling out" of feminist principles and their co-option as a marketing
device. As numerous feminists (and others) have hastened to emphasize,
the Spice Girls are a "manufactured" band, hand-picked by the British
pop mogul Simon Fuller and 19 Management, and as such, their motivations and commitment to female emancipation and empowerment
have been called into question – whereby "empowerment" is seen to be
defined merely in terms of their own financial gain. In her discussion
of *Girl Power!*, Whelehan suggests that, in the absence of "clear directions" and anything "resembling a political programme", the audience,
comprised of young girl readers, nonetheless is aware of "what to do
next: when you turn to the final page the 'secret' of girl power is ultimately revealed – merchandising" (48). Whelehan insists that, despite
the Spice Girls' salute to female independence and self-confidence,
the (mostly adolescent) fans who emulate the band's celebrated styles
do so through "costly mimicry rather than doing it for themselves".

Middle-of-the-road, consumerist Girl Power is implicitly differentiated from a more "authentic", unadulterated kind of feminism that does not follow the dictates of the marketplace and insists on a noticeable, and politically usable, level of independence from mainstream media.

This is a viewpoint taken not only, as we have seen, by second wave feminists – who take a "hard line", anti-media approach – but also by the so-called "third wave feminists", who – while still being critical of the media – try to bridge the gap between consumption and critique.[17] The very invocation of "third wave feminism" and the mobilization of the adjective "third" indicate a desire to establish a link with previous feminist waves and ensure a continuation of feminist principles and ideas. As the self-declared third wavers Leslie Heywood and Jennifer Drake make explicit, "to us the second and third waves of feminism are neither incompatible nor opposed" (3). Mimicking the nomenclature of its predecessors, third wave feminism acknowledges that it stands on the shoulders of other, earlier, feminist movements. Yet, at the same time, its agenda does not mirror the preceding waves straightforwardly. Rather, it "makes things 'messier'" by embracing second wave critique as a central definitional thread while emphasizing ways that "desires and pleasures subject to critique can be used to rethink and enliven activist work" (7). In particular, unlike its second wave predecessor, the third wave situates itself within popular culture and understands a critical engagement with the latter as the key to political struggle.[18] As Heywood and Drake put it, "we're pop-culture babies; we want some pleasure with our critical analysis" (51). Feminism's third wave thus faces the paradox of "an often unconscious knowledge of the ways in which we are compelled and constructed by the very things that undermine us" (11). The reclamation/recuperation of all things feminine is seen as an inherent part of this method of critique. Rather than rejecting femininity, third wavers are eager to create new feminine models based on contradiction and conflict: "we want not to get rid of the trappings of traditional femininity or sexuality so much as to pair them with demonstrations of strength or power" (Klein, "Duality" 223).[19]

How to walk the tightrope between critique and participation is made explicit in the case of Girl culture that many third wave feminists embrace as emblematic of their political stance and critical practice. However, it is not the marketable "girl" that third wave feminists have adopted as their heroine but the non-conformist "grrrl", who emerged in the 1990s from the US underground punk scene and the Riot Grrrl movement.[20] Described as "an infusion of punk and feminism", the Riot Grrrls (epitomized by bands such as Bikini Kill and Bratmobile) staged a rebellion against dominant representations of girlhood and the patriarchal structures they encountered in the music scene (Feigenbaum 132). One of the most prominent and public faces of the grrrl movement who has been held up as a third wave feminist icon is Courtney Love, lead singer of the punk rock band Hole and wife of the late Kurt Cobain. To Heywood and Drake, Love personifies the third wave and its politics of ambiguity: she is "[g]lamorous and grunge, girl and boy, mothering and selfish, put together and taken apart, beautiful and ugly, strong and weak, responsible and rebellious" – "bridg[ing] the irreconcilability of individuality and femininity", she combines traits that defy a narrowly defined second wave identity and delineate third wave flexibility (5). At the same time, there is an insistence on continuity that links the third wave inextricably to the second. Addressing issues such as sexual abuse and eating disorders in song lyrics, weekly meetings and zines, the Riot Grrrls are said to have forged "a unique feminist space for young women" that, it has been suggested, is not "that structurally dissimilar to that sustained by the second wave consciousness-raising groups and support networks" (Gillis and Munford, "Genealogies and Generations" 170).

While the third wave's connection with its predecessor can be described in terms of both permanence and change, its relation to – or rather disconnection from – postfeminism is often deemed to be less equivocal and ambiguous. The distinction between "third wave grrrls" and (postfeminist) "girls" is a case in point: as Rebecca Munford has noted, the grrrl movement – with its emphasis on style and femininity – can be understood as part of a "politics of *identification* that is vital to both individual and collective empowerment" (147; emphasis in original). "Spice Girls-style girl power" on the other hand is often no more than a "fashion statement", "a ready site for postfeminist colonisation" (148–9). Munford seeks to rescue "Girl Power" from postfeminism's trivializing grip by pointing out that the phrase – although popularized by the Spice Girls in the mid-1990s – was actually coined some years earlier by members of the Riot Grrrls. Hijacked by the popular media, the term was then hollowed out and "deprived of its radical and activist history" (Gillis and Munford, "Genealogies and Generations" 170). This differentiation between "grrrl" and "girl" illustrates a common perception of a much wider divide between the (sub-cultural and activist) third wave and (mainstream and depoliticized) postfeminism. From its initiation, the third wave has resolutely defined itself against postfeminism; in fact, third wave pioneers Rebecca Walker and Shannon Liss were keen to establish an ideological and political split between the two, pronouncing "[w]e are not postfeminist feminists. We are the third wave!" (quoted in Siegel, *Sisterhood, Interrupted* 128). Heywood and Drake also emphasize that, within the context of the third wave, "'postfeminist' characterizes a group of young, conservative feminists who explicitly define themselves against and criticize feminists of the second wave" (1).[21] Despite their generational differences, second and third waves of feminism are thus united in their condemnation of an exceedingly popular and retrograde postfeminism that is in line with the economic, political and cultural forces governing the market and mainstream media.

In my eyes, this rhetoric of antagonism reflects a conceptual inadequacy and critical short-sightedness that provides a limited reading of postfeminism (as anti-feminist backlash) and fails to take into account its multiplicity and complexity. I have argued throughout for a more nuanced and productive interpretation of the prefix "post" and its relations to feminism, whereby the compound "postfeminism" is understood as a junction between a number of often competing discourses and interests. In Patricia Mann's words, postfeminism can be described as a "fertile site of risk" that reaches "beyond the boundaries of a feminist audience" (207, 118). This expanded understanding of postfeminism allows us to address the paradoxes of a late-twentieth- and twenty-first-century context in which feminist concerns have entered the mainstream and are articulated in politically contradictory ways. As I have written elsewhere, the distinction between postfeminism and the third wave is misleading in the sense that it rests on an overly simplistic view of postfeminism as defeatism that, as one third wave critic notes, "shuts down ongoing efforts to work toward change on the level of both theory and practice" (Genz, "Third Way/ve"; Sanders, "Feminists Love a Utopia" 52).

Of course, there are undeniable and important differences between both movements, significantly at the level of foundation and political alignment; yet, there are also a range of similarities as the third wave and postfeminism both posit a challenge to second wave feminism's anti-popular and anti-feminine agenda and engage in a reformulation and resignification of femininity. As Sarah Banet-Weiser has suggested, postfeminism is "a different political dynamic than third wave feminism", with the latter positioning itself more overtly as a kind of feminist politics that extends the historical trajectory of previous feminist waves to critique contemporary consumer culture (206). Postfeminism, on the other hand, does not exist as a budding political movement and its origins are much more impure, emerging from within mainstream culture, rather than underground sub-culture.[22] Unlike the third wave, postfeminism is not motivated by a desire for continuity and a need to prove its feminist credentials; what Baumgardner and Richards term a "scrambling to be better feminists and frantically letting these women [second wave feminists] know how much we look up to them" (85). However, this unwillingness or rather indifference to situate itself in the generational wave narrative need not imply that postfeminism is apolitical and merely concerned with lifestyle and commodities. On the contrary, in another context, I have analysed the notions of a postfeminist politics and/or a political postfeminism that – while not identical to other, particularly feminist strategies of resistance – adopt a more flexible and open-ended model of agency that is doubly coded in political terms and entwines backlash and innovation, complicity and critique (see "Third Way/ve").[23] With this in mind, I maintain that there is an overlap between third wave feminism and postfeminism, and, unlike other critics, I do not interpret this as a "dangerous and deceptive slippage" but rather an unavoidable consequence of the contradiction-prone social, political and cultural environment in the contemporary West (Munford 150).

This decidedly complex configuration of postfeminism also informs my understanding of twenty-first-century femininity that women can take up as self-conscious social actors rather than passive objects of the male gaze. In my eyes, femininity has to undergo a similar process of complication and diversification that highlights the spectrum of feminine meanings and explores the middle ground between victimization and power, subject and object. This implies that one has to take into consideration femininity's potential for change, creation and agency, which a number of critics have sought to do. For example, in his discussion of the discourse of Girl Power – which he admits is "a commercial tool" (220) – David Gauntlett contends that the commoditization of female strength and success should not detract from the positive impact these notions have on young girls/women: "Whilst it was easy for cynics to criticise the 'girl power' idea as a bunch of banal statements about 'believing in yourself' and 'doing whatever you want to do,' it was still an encouraging confidence boost to young women and should not be dismissed too readily" (219).[24] Moreover, Girl Power's relation to and treatment of feminism need not be judged too pessimistically: Kathy Acker – one notable exception to the generalized feeling (within the feminist movement) of distrust and rejection of Girl Power – highlights the band's appeal to women, beyond class and educational boundaries. In an interview she conducted with the Spice Girls for the British newspaper the *Guardian*, she discusses their ability to represent "the voices, not really the voice, of young women and, just as important, of women not from the educated classes" (19). In this sense, Girl Power underscores an intellectual, middle-class elitism and anti-sexual bias within feminism: "it isn't only the lads sitting behind babe culture...who think that babes or beautiful lower and lower-middle class girls are dumb. It's also educated women who look down on girls like the Spice Girls, who think that because...[they] take their clothes off, there can't be anything 'up there' [in their brains]." Sheila Whiteley puts forward a similar argument in her description of the Spice Girls as an antidote to the "heavy" media image of feminism: "The impact of the Spice Girls...was to provide a new twist to the feminist discourse of power and subjectivity. By telling their fans that feminism is necessary and fun...they sold the 1990s as a 'girl's world' and presented the 'future as female'" (216–17).

Beyond the music scene, the idea of "Girl Power" (or rather "power femininity") was also adopted and embraced by the so-called "Girlie feminists" who celebrate feminine paraphernalia and place it at the centre of their feminist philosophy.[25] As Jennifer Baumgardner and Amy Richards explain, the term "Girlie" depicts the "intersection of culture and feminism" and it "encompasses the tabooed symbols of women's feminine enculturation – Barbie dolls, make-up, fashion magazines" (136). Girlies see themselves as reacting to (and against) "an anti-feminine, antijoy emphasis" that they perceive as the legacy of "Second Wave seriousness" (80). "Girlie" feminism performs a glamorous makeover of the drab and unfashionable women's liberationists of the past and it effects a "shift from the *monstrous outsiders* of the 1960s and 1970s to the *incorporated Ms* of the 1990s" (Hinds and Stacey 155; emphasis in original). The feminine Girlie is both a response to the bra-burner epithet that has haunted media representations of feminists as well as "a subversion of the pin-up image" (Whelehan, *Overloaded* 37). Girlies are adamant that they can compete successfully alongside their male counterparts and attain equality without sacrificing all forms of "pink-packaged femininity" (137). In fact, their empowerment and assertiveness are directly linked to their feminine identities and their ability to resignify feminine signifiers and language. Girlies insist that they are not trapped by their femininity but they can gain control by acknowledging and using their insider position within consumer culture. Girlie feminism thus combines cultural confidence with feminist awareness and it emphasizes that the traditional/patriarchal connotations of girlishness can be interrupted by alternative modes of production/consumption:

> Using makeup isn't a sign of our sway to the marketplace and the male gaze; it can be sexy, campy, ironic, or simply decorating ourselves without the loaded issues.... What we loved as girls was good and, because of feminism, we know how to make girl stuff work for us.[26]

(136)

The myths of femininity that have historically been imprinted on the female body as signs of docility and subordination are revitalized in Girlie rhetoric that establishes a distance between image and identity and, in this new signifying gap, redefines feminine modes and subjectivities. The central tenet of Girl Power is that femininity is powerful and empowering, endowing the female subject with the agency to create her self and negotiate the possibilities of her gender role. Women can use their femininity to compliment and even further the qualities of subjecthood and independence endorsed by the feminist movement. Girlie feminism thus offers a way out of the one-sided attention to the restrictions of feminine conventions that has obscured women's/feminists' engagement in the constructions of femininity. The claim of a new meaning for old symbols establishes a space for the inventive and potentially subversive use of cultural signs and a refashioning of feminine identities. Rather than focusing on the dehumanizing aspects of gender socializations, Girlies expose and exploit their constructed nature in order to reveal the creativity and fluidity of feminine traditions and subjectivities. As Baungardner and Richards write, "believing that feminine things are weak means that we're believing our own bad press.... it is a feminist statement to proudly claim things that are feminine, and the alternative can mean to deny what we are" (134–5).

Taken to its logical conclusion, the Girlie feminist stance makes a case for femininity politics or "femmenism" that forges its political theory from the re-appropriation of feminist discourses into the readings of femininity. Jeannine Delombard describes this feminine politics by alluding to Audre Lorde's famous precept: "femmenism is using the master's tools to dismantle the master's house" (22).[27] Femmenism implies using the signs and accoutrements of femininity to challenge and resignify the notions of gender formations. Gender is understood as an analytical category, to be questioned and reworked from within its own conventions. Femmenism relies on feminist theory's deconstructive strain to conceptualize femininity as a construct and artifice and, instead of dismissing the feminine *tout court*, it argues for its reconstruction and resignification. As Ang notes, gender identity is both "multiple and partial, ambiguous and incoherent, permanently in process of being articulated, disarticulated and rearticulated" (125). While I welcome this diversification and undoing of femininity that unfastens its heteronormative connections and associations with female victimization, I am also aware of the historical stronghold of these norms and the prevailing cultural stereotypes of womanhood. In this chapter, I have argued that the redefinition and resignification of femininity always entails contradictions as it continually threatens to re-inscribe and reinforce phallocentricity. As I have suggested, the resignificatory process is positioned ambiguously as an appropriation and deconstruction from within, vacillating between complicity and critique, agency and confinement. Accordingly, the Girlies' assertion of dynamic self-fulfilment and feminine self-expression is not unanimously liberating but can also appear as a trap of conformity and disempowerment. Speaking from this side of the debate, numerous critics have disputed the notion of freely choosing feminine/sexual subjects. For example, Ariel Levy, author of *Female Chauvinist Pigs* (2006), contends that what some are calling "the new feminism" is really "the old objectification", disguised in stilettos (81). She blames a phenomenon she dubs "raunch culture" – the "glossy, overheated thumping of sexuality in our culture" exemplified by programmes such as *Girls Gone Wild* and *Sex and the City* (31) – for co-opting the ideals of sex radicalism and feminism by equating sexually provocative behaviour with freedom. As Levy writes, "[r]aunch culture isn't about opening our minds to the possibilities and mysteries of sexuality. It's about endlessly reiterating one particular – and particularly commercial – shorthand for sexiness" (30). The women who adopt this kind of raunchy "trash culture" are dismissed unceremoniously as "FCPs" – "Female Chauvinist Pigs" or "women who make sex objects of other women and of themselves" (44, 4). Rosalind Gill is equally pessimistic in her examination of the move in popular media "from sex object to (desiring) sexual subject", maintaining that "sexual subjecthood" represents "a new 'higher' form of exploitation" that shifts "an external judging male gaze to a self-policing narcissistic gaze" (*Gender and the Media* 89–91). Women are offered the promise of autonomy and endowed with the status of active agents by voluntarily objectifying themselves and actively *choosing* to employ their capacities in the pursuit of a feminine appearance and a sexualized image. One of the most disturbing aspects of this shift, Gill notes, is that it makes critique "much more difficult" because "objectification is no longer seen as imposed from outside, but rather is self-chosen" (90).

I do not wish to deny the relevance and accuracy of these critiques; on the contrary, it is important that we keep reminding ourselves that, in the midst of the promise of innovation, there lurks a spectre of conformity and commoditization that has to be taken into account in any examination of contemporary forms of femininity (and feminism). My aim here is to draw attention to a more nuanced and varied understanding of femininity that not just focuses on its limitations but also allows for its potentialities. This means that we have to open ourselves up to new modes of critique, subjectivity and agency that might not fit our pre-exiting models and frameworks. Perhaps, one useful way of looking at the postfeminine subject is provided by the Foucauldian concept of *assujetissement* (or "subjectivation"), which explains the process of subject formation as involving "both the becoming of the subject and the process of subjection" (Butler, *The Psychic Life of Power* 83).[28] In this oxymoronic formulation, the subject is instituted through constraint and s/he inhabits a contradictory site that is constraining and liberating, productive and oppressive. This doubled process may help us to comprehend and explore the paradoxes of a postfeminist femininity that can work in empowering and subordinating ways and that establishes links with feminist discourses of female emancipation without fully relinquishing its heteronormative, patriarchal connections. As regards Girl culture, I have sought to show that – in spite of some homogenized representations – it encompasses an eclectic range of movements – including punk feminist Riot Grrrls, lip-glossed Girlie feminists and Girl Power – that are influenced by mainstream media, consumer culture, neo-liberal politics, gender theory and, significantly, feminism. How and in what configuration postfeminism and postfemininity emerge from this mix and what effect this has on our conceptions of critique and subjectivity remain areas of debate that necessitate a continuous critical engagement and questioning.[29] We face the challenge of emancipating femininity from its monolithic existence in both feminine and feminist mystiques to become part of a more complexly articulated female identity and autonomy. This will allow us to go beyond narrow and unitary descriptions of femininity (and postfeminism) and discover feminine subjectivities *in between* the poles of feminist agency and patriarchal objectification. As we will see in Part II, it is in this newly developing and relatively unexplored "grey area" that we witness a spectrum of postfeminine identities emerging that transcend previous depictions of feminism and femininity.

Part II
Postfemininities

5
The (Un)happy Housewife Heroine*

> Woman is shut up in a kitchen or in a boudoir, and astonishment is expressed that her horizon is limited. Her wings are clipped, and it is found deplorable that she cannot fly. Let but the future be opened to her, and she will no longer be compelled to linger in the present.
>
> – Simone de Beauvoir, *The Second Sex*

When *Cosmopolitan* magazine announced in its June 2000 issue that young twenty-something women had become the new "housewife wannabes", the relationship between domesticity and female/feminist emancipation seemed to have been turned on its head (Dutton). While for the last century women had fought to expose the oppression and subjugation inherent in their domestic subject positions and bring about a "click" moment,[1] now it appeared that they were eager to re-embrace the title of "housewife" and rediscover the joys and crafts of a "new femininity". Suddenly, "domesticity" became the buzzword of the new millennium, and housewives, fictional and real, were emerging in all areas, determined to regain entry into their doll's house that, not 40 years ago, they seemed to have left for good.[2] From Nigella Lawson whipping up tasty treats on TV (and simultaneously managing to look infinitely glamorous) to Brenda Barnes famously giving up her job as president of Pepsi-Cola North America (and, with this, her $2 million annual salary) to spend more time with her three children,[3] there was no denying that domesticity was experiencing a comeback, a twenty-first-century renaissance. Critics from all arenas were keen to comment on this cultural trend: while "new traditionalist" politicians and journalists were welcoming this reaffirmation of family values, feminist critics largely denounced this retro-boom as a backlash that returns women to the subordinate roles of a bygone, pre-feminist era (see Chapter 3).

In this chapter, I employ an alternative, postfeminist/postfeminine frame to interpret the revival of domesticity and the figure of the housewife. I contend that postfeminism offers a new mode of conceptualizing the domestic as a contested space of female subjectivity where women/feminists actively grapple with opposing cultural constructions of the housewife. In particular, a postfeminist/postfeminine lens allows us to transcend a critical impasse (trapped by a dualistic logic) and re-imagine the homemaker as a polysemic character caught in a struggle between tradition and modernity, past and present. The twenty-first-century housewife is no longer easily categorized as an emblem of female oppression but she re-negotiates her domestic/feminine stance, deliberately choosing to "go home". Postfeminism thus undermines static constructions of the housewife by reclaiming domestic femininity as a site of undecidability, of meaning in question. In this sense, we need to focus our critical efforts on the contingent and shifting relationships between women and the home – a venture that is made all the more difficult by the complexity of our current historical and cultural moment in which domestic femininities have been bent into new configurations that intertwine positive and empowering elements with destructive, misogynist ones. The contemporary figure of the housewife is inscribed with multifarious significations, vacillating between patriarchal scripts of enforced domesticity, feminist critiques thereof and postfeminist re-appropriations that acknowledge agency and self-determination. As I have maintained throughout, my intention is not to argue the case of postfeminist housewifery/femininity as either a new utopia or the trap of nostalgia.[4] It is less a choice between retro- and neo-femininity/domesticity than an endeavour to examine the ambiguities inherent in a "post" position. It is in this in-between space that the potentialities and intricacies of the postfeminist housewife are revealed.

To begin, I want to revisit some second wave feminist accounts of the housewife that have shaped and contributed to twenty-first-century understandings of domesticity. The relationship between second wave feminism and domesticity has often been described as troubled and fraught with problems and difficulties (Gillis and Hollows). Without doubt, one of the most influential second-wave texts that brought the housewife to universal attention and elevated her to a political figure was Betty Friedan's *The Feminine Mystique* (1963). Friedan was instrumental in the exposure of the "happy housewife myth" that traps women as helpless prisoners in a "comfortable concentration camp" (or the 1950s family) that uses "the pretty lie of the feminine mystique" to enact a denigration into "genteel nothingness" (245, 180, 89). The housewife was singled out by Friedan as the epitome of female non-identity and passivity, a perfect illustration of patriarchal constructions of Woman as an apathetic, dependent and purposeless being. Her utter and complete rejection of the housewife leaves no room for interpretation: "A woman's work – housework – cannot give her status; it has the lowliest status of almost any work in society" (236); hence Friedan's crushing verdict that " 'Occupation: housewife' is not an adequate substitute for truly challenging work, important enough to society to be paid for in its coin" (218).[5] Friedan was adamant that the very condition of being a housewife has a progressively dehumanizing effect which makes it impossible for a woman "of adult intelligence" to retain a sense of identity and self (264). Enlightening these brain-damaged "schizophrenics" comes to be seen as a political duty for their feminist sisters, with CR sessions acting as a lifeline to pull these domesticated dupes from their "housewife trap" (270, 314).[6] "[C]onvinced [that] there is something about the housewife state itself that is dangerous", Friedan advises women to "say 'no' to the housewife image" and realize their full abilities by pursuing a career outside the home and performing a meaningful role in the public sphere (264–5, 297).

The Feminine Mystique sparked a cultural revolution by foregrounding a domestic dystopia that denies women their potential and even humanity. Friedan cemented into feminism the idea of housewifery as pathology, depicting the political position of the housewife as a catalyst for feminist agency and activism: "the real cause both of feminism and of women's frustration was the emptiness of the housewife's role" (212). Here, the housewife is clearly defined as a tragic non-self, an unvarying "Other" against whom the notions of modern emancipated womanhood and feminism are constructed. Following Friedan, many second wave feminists believed that "the only solution was for women to reject their investment in domesticity and understand that it would never really bring them any real fulfilment" (Gillis and Hollows 6). The underlying assumption is that feminism and domesticity are mutually exclusive and irreconcilable, leaving the housewife with no other position to assume (and role to fulfil) than that of a docile and self-alienated instrument of patriarchy. Friedan was by no means the only feminist critic who dismissed domesticity as a primary site of female subjugation and imprisonment. Ten years earlier, Simone de Beauvoir had already lambasted the career of the "wife-servant" as "tiresome, empty [and] monotonous" (472). Mirroring the fate of Sisyphus, the housewife is caught in a cycle of "endless repetition" and – as her "battle against dust and dirt is never won" – she ends up "mak[ing] nothing, simply perpetuat[ing] the present" (470). Woman is yet again confined in "immanence", as her "work within the home gives her no autonomy; it is not directly useful to society, it does not open out on the future" (475). Beauvoir is sceptical of any positive characteristics and rewards that might be associated with the housewife state, asserting that "[h]owever respected she may be, she is subordinate, secondary, parasitic".[7] Even more disturbingly, in her never-ending "war against dust, stains [and] mud", the housekeeper "submits to it in a kind of madness" that may even have life-threatening consequences: "She becomes bitter and disagreeable and hostile to all that lives; the end is sometimes murder" (471).

Similar arguments emerged throughout the late 1960s and 1970s, politicizing the perceived relationship of women with the home whereby the latter is denounced as a prison and the homemaker as a victim (or worse, an enemy of feminism). For Germaine Greer, the housewife is no more than a "permanent employee" whose life is "not real": it is "anachronistic", "thwarting" and plainly pointless as it "has no results", "it simply has to be done again" (*The Female Eunuch* 272, 312). Greer condemns the life of the full-time housewife as one of absolute servitude, turning women into "the most oppressed class of life-contracted unpaid workers, for whom slaves is not too melodramatic a description" (369). In *Gyn/Ecology* (1979), Mary Daly adopts an even more radical stance, encouraging her readers to discard conventional femininity *tout court* and become "wild women". One of the largest-scale investigations of housewives was provided by Ann Oakley's sociological research in the early 1970s, which examines the social value and material undervaluation of women's domestic labour. Oakley argued that the primacy of the housewife role in modern industrialized societies plays a major part in obstructing women's progress towards equality. "Housework", she announced, "is work directly opposed to the possibility of human self-actualization" (*The Sociology of Housework* 222).[8] Juxtaposing the identities of the feminist and the housewife, she claimed that "an affirmation of contentment with the housewife role is actually a form of antifeminism, whatever the gender of the person who displays it. Declared contentment with a subordinate status – which the housewife role undoubtedly is – is a rationalization of inferior status" (233).

This summarizes the second wave's opposition to the figure of the housewife and its restricted definition of domesticity/femininity as based around hearth and home. As Judy Giles has observed, in many second wave narratives, "'leaving home'...is a necessary condition of liberation" and domesticity is presented as "something that must be left behind if women [are] to become 'modern' emancipated subjects" (141–2). As a result, the housewife is "othered" in many second wave articulations and it operates as an object of feminist critique, necessarily antagonistic to the notions of emancipation and subjectivity. This not only creates a dichotomy between private and public spheres, between the downtrodden housewife and the feminist revolutionary but also offers little room (or hope) to re-evaluate the meaning of home (and the housewife) within feminism. Domesticity is thus denied a place in the feminist discourse of female liberation as well as the changing land-scape of modernity and progress. As Justine Lloyd and Lesley Johnson note in their discussion of post-war melodrama, the figure of the home-maker is cast "as a case of arrested or incomplete development within the terms of modernity" (10). The housewife statically remains in her old-fashioned, homely prison, unable to take part in the gender devel-opments and transformations of a rapidly changing world. In this sense, a woman's domestic place and housewife status can evolve only in one possible way or direction, in that they are to be left for good. Once her consciousness has been raised by a feminist awakening, she should be immune to the feminine mystique and resist its deceptively "protective shade" (Friedan, *The Feminine Mystique* 208). In Greer's words, "women have been exposed to too many other kinds of life to revert to four walls and people two foot high without strain" (312).

These ideas were taken up by a number of writers and filmmakers in the 1960s and 1970s who describe the physical and mental dan-gers inherent in the housewife role: From Sue Kaufman's *Diary of a Mad Housewife* (1967) to the homemaking robots in Ira Levin's *The Stepford Wives* (1972), female domesticity acquired sinister and even murderous connotations, literally killing off the woman and leaving behind a fem-inine automaton, a mechanized doll of patriarchy. In Kaufman's novel, after 11 years of "functioning beautifully", New York housewife Bettina Munvies Balser is suddenly afflicted with a "new looniness", an inability to channel her "Normal Feminine Drives" into her home life as a wife and mother (6, 12, 21). She uses her diary to write herself back to sanity, and with her newly gained self-awareness, she propels herself into a set of experiences, most notably an extramarital affair. The entries provide the possibility of self-help as Bettina uses her imagination to escape the four walls of her apartment and her privileged, yet mundane, existence. Importantly, Bettina does not suffer from any physical exhaustion or material hardship as the daily drudgery has been taken over by her maid

Lottie; her illness stems from her frustration with her housewife role and her thwarted artistic ambitions. As a young woman, Bettina studied art history and engaged in an affair with a married sculptor; yet, after being abandoned by her lover, she finds herself suffering from anorexia and eczema. Pushed into therapy by her parents, Bettina's dreams of being a painter are crushed by her analyst Dr Popkin who advises her to settle for her womanly vocation and "be what you are" (25). For Bettina, "that took a lot of doing" but in time, she writes – ventriloquizing her doctor's views – "I finally learned to accept the fact that I was a bright but quite ordinary young woman, somewhat passive and shy, who was equipped with powerful Feminine Drives – which simply means I badly wanted a husband and children and a Happy Home" (25). She submits to her destiny by throwing "herself into the Feminine Role" and marrying corporate lawyer Jonathan to whom she quickly bears two children.

Problems start to appear after a while when Bettina finds herself unable to make the transition into, what she calls, the "second phase" of her "Feminine Passive Role": "Women like me, after a certain number of years of Fulfilling [sic] themselves in domestic necessities, are supposed to leave the seclusion of the lair and re-enter The Great World, where they're supposed to snap-to and get *with* it right away" (75; emphasis in original). Her "madness" is also linked to her husband's professional success and wealth, concomitant with his increasing acting out of "The Forceful Dominant Male", as Bettina puts it (41). As he moves into new social circles (becoming, for example, a patron of the arts), he insists that Bettina keeps up with him, "change[s] and grow[s]" to live up to the persona of an upper-middle-class wife (75). One again, Bettina yields to his demands: "I understood that unless I wanted to divorce Jonathan, or have Jonathan divorce me, I had to jump when he said Jump . . . . I knew I would jump. And jump and jump" (113). Apart from her diary, the only other outlet that Bettina can rely on to relieve her of her assumed role and the recurring vertigo and sweats she experiences as physical manifestations of her insanity is her sexual encounters with the playwright George Prager. In her affair – that Bettina recounts with a frankness that is reminiscent of later second wave novels like Erica Jong's *Fear of Flying* (1973) – she enters, ostensibly voluntarily, in a sadomasochistic relationship. George is "the classic Heel, the Sadistic Rake whom certain kinds of women find irresistible – and I, by virtue of my current crazy condition, have become that kind of woman. The perfect Willing Victim, moth to the flame, all that old stuff" (197). The liaison ends violently with a pregnancy scare and George ridiculing and questioning her motives ("Madame Ovary. That's you") (286). In the end, there is simply no viable alternative and Bettina settles for her "niche" and a life as a paragon-housewife, "the lady with the apron", "Tabitha-Twitchit-Danvers-Me" (283, 295).[9]

As Imelda Whelehan has suggested, "the depiction of these women's lives where 'nothing' seems to happen offers the perfect insight into examples of the seemingly invisible and constant re-enactment of male power" (*Feminist Bestseller* 80). *Diary of a Mad Housewife* is clearly inspired by feminism's uncovering of the perils of patriarchy and the exposure of "the problem that has no name" (Friedan, *The Feminine Mystique* 54). However, there is no attempt to go beyond this realization and politicize the relationship between women and the home. Whelehan dubs this feminist confessional fiction – also exemplified by Lois Gould's *Such Good Friends* (1970) and Sheila Ballantyne's *Norma Jean the Termite Queen* (1975) – "the 'mad housewife' novels": written in a confiding form, these books "anatomize domestic labour and its impact on the married woman and in so doing bring together both First and Second Wave accounts of the housewife role" (67). The central protagonists are "well educated, intellectually questing and often artistically inclined"; "much of the drama takes place in the women's heads" and the female characters are "in danger of losing their hold on rationality in face of the ways domestic duties threaten to rob them of all sense of self" (75–6, 67).

According to Whelehan, later in the mid-1970s, a more activist kind of feminist fiction emerged: "the consciousness-raising novel" exemplified by Jong's *Fear of Flying* and Marilyn French's *The Women's Room* (1977), which has been described as "the first and last international bestseller of the women's movement" (O'Faolain). For the group of young married women/mothers in *The Women's Room*, their mundane lives and domestic chores engender a sense of entrapment:

> The unspoken, unthought-about conditions that made it [housewifery] oppressive had long since been accepted by all of them: that they had not chosen but had been automatically slotted into their lives, and that they were never free to move (the children were much more effective as clogs than confinement on a prison farm would be). Having accepted the shit and string beans, they were content.
>
> (103)

The novel follows the life of Mira, from her teenage years to her marrying and becoming a mother, through to university, CR sessions and the struggles to live and love as a feminist in a male-oriented society. Mira's politicization is gradual, largely brought about by her contact with other women and her entry into higher education. Initially, like other "mad housewives", Mira is presented as a victim of patriarchy: after narrowly escaping rape, she decides to give up her hopes and "dream of choosing and living a life of her own" and she withdraws into marriage (50). As she admits her defeat, "[s]he was a woman and that alone was enough to deprive her of freedom.... She was constitutionally unfree. She could not go out alone at night...she couldn't defend herself: she had to depend on a male for that.... She would live out a half-life, like the rest of women" (48–50). Mira believes that in order to protect herself against "a savage world", "[t]here was no way out" but "a woman had to be married" (50, 176). She experiences her marriage to the (aptly named) Norm as a dulling of her mind and senses and a surrender of her liberty and independence. At home with her two boys and her husband, she is no more than an "unpaid servant, expected to do a superlative job. In return, she was permitted to call this house hers" (206). She discovers the power of female friendship and community, first in suburbia, where she finds herself to be part of "a secret sisterhood" of young mothers and housewives, and later through a CR group at university (86). After Norm leaves her for another woman ("Mrs Perfect Norm" [336]), Mira recognizes that she has been duped by, what one might call, the feminine mistake – "[s]he had done everything right, she had been perfect, and he had still come home saying, 'I want a divorce'" (336) – and she decides to go back to her studies and become a student. At Harvard, Mira undergoes a series of intellectual, feminist, political and sexual awakenings, as she learns to live "without a [feminine] face" and critically re-evaluate society and her role within it (333).

While there are moments of exhilaration and excitement about "designing the perfect world" – including a sexual revolution and "ecstasy" that Mira encounters in her relationship with fellow student Ben (454) – the novel's overall tone is dark and discouraging about the possibilities of a new feminist age (452). As Whelehan notes, looking back, *The Women's Room* is "an unremittingly gloomy book, as if French is determined to emphasize that women still have a long way to go and that the way is treacherous" (94). In its cataloguing of female oppressions, the novel does not make "a clear distinction between polemical tract and literary work" and, as such, it has been criticized for its "missionary zeal" and "nannyish hectoring" that might come across as preachy and anachronistic to contemporary readers (Gerrard quoted in Whelehan 96). This is especially evident in the case of Mira's friend Val, whose radical stance is expressed in an unwavering and frenzied voice that reinforces stereotypes of the angry feminist: after her daughter

Chris has been raped, Val leaves "the male world" and becomes a member of a militant feminist organization ("the lunatic fringe") that adopts the view of a gender war – "it was males against females, and the war was to the death... all men are rapists... all men are the enemy" (622–34). Mira's sisterhood of friends falls apart when Val is tragically killed by the FBI following one of her radical feminist operations; nor is there a more optimistic conclusion to Mira's heterosexual partnership with Ben as the relationship comes to an end when she refuses to fulfil his life plans and have another child. Ultimately, the best that Mira and the other women in the novel can hope for is survival. As Mira – who, as is revealed in the final pages, is the disembodied first-person narrator who has appeared throughout the (mainly third-person) narrative shifting the focus of the other characters and commenting on their actions – remarks dejectedly, "This is not the world I would have wished.... I have opened all the doors in my head. I have opened all the pores in my body. But only the tide rolls in" (686–7). For these housewives-cum-feminists, there is no resolution, no clear path to a better, feminist future and a different understanding of domesticity; as Isolde – another member of Mira's CR group – puts it, "I hate discussions of feminism that end up with who does the dishes.... But at the end, there are always the damned dishes" (83).[10]

If survival is an option for the women in French's novel, then the fate that awaits the housewives of Stepford, Connecticut, is infinitely more frightening, as the seemingly idyllic scenery and domestic perfection hide a dark secret of murder and technology: the Stepford husbands are killing off their wives to substitute them with domestic sex-machines whose interests do not go beyond housekeeping and pleasuring men. *The Stepford Wives* dramatizes anxieties regarding the changing roles of women in 1970s society and the home, literalizing Betty Friedan's notion of housewifery as a progressive "dehumanization" that turns woman away "from individual identity to become an anonymous biological robot in a docile mass" (267). While Friedan's metaphor was meant to illustrate the plight of the post-war American housewife who is incarcerated in suburbia, Ira Levin's 1972 novel (and the film adaptations that followed) transformed the passive and submissive homemakers into uncanny living dolls that have long replaced their more demanding human counterparts.[11] The novel as well as Bryan Forbes' 1975 film version open with the main protagonist Joanna Eberhart and her family leaving the city behind in order to move to affluent and comfortably middle-class Stepford. Initially ambivalent about the decision – that, it is soon clear, was fuelled by her husband Walter – Joanna begins to settle into, what is described as, "a nice town with nice people" (1). Yet, she soon notices that most of her new neighbours are unnaturally attached to their roles as housewives and mothers, with the notable exception of cynical Bobbie Markowe, herself a newcomer and equally bewildered by the Stepford wives' domestic perfectionism. Joanna and Bobbie strike up a close friendship and together they reach the conclusion that "[s]omething fishy is going on here! We're in the town that time forgot." After unsuccessfully trying to organize CR sessions for the other wives, Joanna – watching one of her neighbours fold her laundry in colour-coded piles – realizes how artificial these women's lives are:

> That's what she was, Joanna felt suddenly. That's what they all were, all the Stepford Wives: actresses in commercials, pleased with detergents and floor wax, with cleansers, shampoo and deodorants. Pretty actresses, big in bosom but small in talent, playing suburban housewives unconvincingly, too nicey-nice to be real.[12]

(40)

Of course, what Joanna does not understand at this stage is that the Stepford wives are not real, flesh-and-blood women but robots acting out patriarchal – and in particular their husbands' – scripts of femininity and domesticity. The evil mastermind behind the plot is Dale "Diz" Coba, the president of the Men's Association – the nickname "Diz" is in fact an allusion to his former employment as an electronics expert at Disneyland and, as such, the town of Stepford resembles a simulated suburban landscape, peopled by "disneyish", cartoon characters who perform idealized and nostalgic versions of womanhood. The novel suggests that it was the growing autonomy and "raised" feminist consciousness of the Stepford women that precipitated the murderous actions of the Men's Association: notably, Carol Van Sant, one of the most formidable examples of Stepfordian domesticity, was actually the leader of the local women's group that, we are informed, once hosted Betty Friedan. Ultimately, neither Joanna nor Bobbie can escape the technological might and patriarchal control of the Men's Association. The novel comes to a climax when Joanna is betrayed by her husband, who uses their children to keep her in Stepford – children are thus effective as "clogs", as Marilyn French puts it in *The Women's Room* (103). Desperate to find them, Joanna returns to Bobbie's house that – a sure symptom that something is amiss – now is in pristine order, resembling "a commercial". There Joanna is killed by the robotic double of her best friend, reinforcing Friedan's claim that the housewife trap makes it impossible for women to "retain a sense of human identity, the firm core of self or 'I' " (264).

The 1975 film version provides an even more chilling ending, as here it is Joanna who kills the Bobbie-replicant by stabbing her with a kitchen knife and causing a horrifyingly comic malfunction, whereby the robot goes into domestic overdrive, stumbling around her kitchen and repeatedly offering coffee to Joanna. Still on the lookout for her children, the latter then arrives at the Men's Association – fittingly, a dark, Gothic manor house – where she is finally murdered, not as one might expect, by her husband or the other men, but by her mechanized, man-made Other. Unbeknown to Joanna, she has in effect provided the Men's Association with all the personal details – allowing, for example, her voice to be recorded and her portrait to be sketched – they need to build her automated doppelgänger, identical to her in look, apart from an enlarged bust and black eyes. This simulacrum continues to perform her motherly and wifely duties to the satisfaction of her husband/children and she is finally assimilated into the domestic and consumerist fantasy world of the Stepford wives: the concluding scene shows the "new" Joanna gliding in a long dress through a bright supermarket, filling her trolley with goods and exchanging meaningless pleasantries with the other shopping wives. *The Stepford Wives* is unequivocal in its assessment of victims and culprits: this is men against women (or rather feminists), men who brutally reinforce their desire for a Victorian "Angel in the House", murdering any independent female thought and progress. The doomed women of Stepford are clearly punished for their (feminist) desires to transcend their domestic selves and enforce an egalitarian relationship with their husbands. The novel and film also convey another implicit message that underlines the antagonism of feminism and housewifery and contains a warning to the burgeoning feminist: the housewife role has to be discarded, or else it will kill you. This denies the possibility for a potential re-interpretation and emancipation of domesticity/femininity, denouncing it not only as rigid and restricted but also as anti-feminist and dangerous. All that survives in Stepford is a fully automated *femme*, not a woman, much less a feminist.[13]

Slaves, prisoners, schizophrenics and, even more dehumanizing, robots – these labels have been branded on the housewife by second wave feminist critics, writers and filmmakers to the extent that now, it seems, the home has become an almost "guilty" pleasure for some women. Without doubt, the anti-domestic stance was an important and necessary phase in Western feminist history and politics as it uncovered the widespread subjugation and entrapment suffered by the vast majority of women. The housewife emerged from these critiques as an instantly identifiable figure that epitomizes everything that is wrong with patriarchy. At the same time, this positioning of the housewife as a patriarchal object and victim meant that she became exempt from any feminist approval or appreciation as she was seen simplistically and one-sidedly as a non-feminist. While there is no denying that the housewife was and remains a pillar of patriarchal control, I also maintain that her relationship with feminism has to be reassessed in order to open up the realm of possibility that has been withheld from her. My point is not to provide housewifery with a radically new meaning that wipes out its previous significations of drudgery and confinement; in a sense, invent a neo-femininity that constructs a new domestic dream of female self-actualization. These subordinating elements relentlessly continue to haunt and restrict the female homemaker, reflecting her lack of power and social status. What I argue for is a re-interpretation of the housewife as a flexible feminist subject that is liable to change and eligible for innovation and progress.[14] The "unhappy housewife myth" now has to be demythologized in order to keep women from objectifying and pathologizing their domestic personas. In an uncanny echoing of feminist fears of denial and backlash, the contemporary homemaker is loath to admit her existence: "I'm not a housewife, but . . . ."[15] Countering fears of housewifely stultification and brainwashing, I want to underline the fact that domestic femininity encompasses a diverse spectrum of ways of being and living that need to be re-examined in (post)feminist terms.[16]

To place domestic femininity and the housewife in such a postfeminist frame has a number of advantages: it both keeps intact feminism's critique of domesticity without foreclosing other significations and possibilities of renewal and loosens women's historic connections with *Kinder, Küche, Kirche* without breaking those ties completely, instead exposing the tensions between domesticity and feminism, home and work, tradition and modernity. In contemporary society, the housewife is caught up in an array of relationships and tensions within both domestic and public arenas and she has to re-negotiate her place in this changed social context. The challenges and paradoxes of a postfeminist femininity/domesticity can no longer be conceptualized along a sharp split between feminism and housewifery, agency and victimization, work and family life. This is to acknowledge that femininity/domesticity is changeable and can operate in a variety of ways, acquiring a range of different meanings that have come to the fore in the postfeminist present.

Postfemininity remains difficult to pin down and critics have often given in to the analytical temptation to retreat to a safe binary order that differentiates housewives from feminists, mothers from career women, domesticity from paid work.[17] Detractors often detect a veiled attack on feminism that hides behind the deceptively stylish façade of professional TV homemakers and domestic goddesses (most recently incarnated by the impossibly groomed but nonetheless "desperate" housewives of Wisteria Lane). As I have previously discussed, Susan Faludi, for example, dismisses the renewed interest in the housewife as a conservative backlash that packages domesticity in feminist activist rhetoric. This is concomitant with "new traditionalist" discourse that articulates a vision of the home to which women have freely chosen to return (Chapter 3). In *The Meaning of Wife* (2004), Anne Kingston also comments on this romanticization of domesticity that lures the housewife into a dream of "mystique chic":

> Increasingly, housework – an endeavour reviled for decades as drudgery, as the source of women's psychiatric problems, as the very root of female oppression – was presented as both fashionable and, even more perversely, a surefire route to female satisfaction. Call it mystique chic. Call it the ultimate backlash to *The Feminine Mystique*.
> (65)

Kingston explores how in a chiastic reversal of the home/work dichotomy domesticity has been mythicized into an edenic space of fulfilment and freedom from the shackles of working life. Whereas work outside the home is now an inevitable economic requirement for most women, "homework" has become the sanctuary of a few privileged, financially secure housewives. This refuge from the workplace is at best a nostalgic illusion and at worst a ruse to return women to "the same kind of idealized domesticity that, ironically, had given rise to the twentieth-century feminist movement in the first place" (102).

These doubts and critiques are often justified and reinforced by contemporary writers and filmmakers who struggle to depict a post-feminine/postfeminist stance. Sophie Kinsella's *The Undomestic Goddess* (2005) depicts the domestication of a high-powered lawyer who flees her city job (interestingly portrayed as an abusive partner, "a bad relationship" [112]) for the "freedom" of being a housekeeper in the Cotswolds. Initially uneducated in the arts of cooking and cleaning, she is soon initiated into this secret world by "a cooking witch", the mother of Samantha's love interest Nathaniel. Samantha experiences this domestic realm as a revelation that transforms her "old conventional, monochrome" persona into a more colourful (that is, blonder) and feminine self, "a new me. A me with possibilities" (162, 163). The novel does not engage in the home/work debate and is careful to avoid any standpoint that could be politicized: "What about feminism?", a journalist asks after Samantha's double life (a housekeeper with a degree from Cambridge and an IQ of 158!) has sparked a public tabloid discussion on "The Price of Success". "I'm not telling women anything", she replies, "I'm just leading my own life…I don't want to be a role model" (318, 326); tellingly the only openly and undeniably feminist figure in the novel is Samantha's mother, a successful lawyer who disapproves of housewives and unapologetically puts her career before her family. The solution sits well with a neo-liberal individualism that gives primacy to "choice" ahead of all other political dictums. Samantha's final farewell to her city friend Guy is a case in point: "Don't define me! I'm not a lawyer! I'm a *person*" (361; emphasis in original). Yet, her desire for "a simpler life" (334), like "the Waltons" (329), cannot escape a smack of nostalgia that puts into question this conversion to domesticity.

Here the domestic is being held up as a rural fantasy that Samantha has unjustly and unnaturally been kept away from by her academic education and feminist enlightenment. As the media furore caused by the exposure of Samantha's double life demonstrates, in today's society "being *only* a housewife" is frowned upon, and for a highly trained, successful professional it is an unthinkable forbidden pleasure. Samantha's voluntary domesticity is not only an anachronism but also an affront to her own mother and, sequently, decades of feminist struggles. In this sense, her domestication can clearly be read in terms of a generational conflict that pits the domineering feminist mother against her rebellious postfeminist daughter. A model of a 1980s Superwoman, Samantha's mother is depicted stereotypically as a career-focused workaholic and strident feminist who is thoroughly anti-domestic ("She disapproves of women taking the name of their husband. She also disapproves of women staying at home, cooking, cleaning, or learning to type, and thinks all women should earn more than their husbands because they're naturally brighter" [32]). She has no qualms missing her daughter's birthday and her only maternal advice consists of a capitalist battle cry: "You have to be better than the others" (34). Samantha repudiates the values handed down from the feminist motherhood in favour of a long-repressed domestic dream, a nostalgic site ruled by individual fantasy rather than collective reality. *The Undomestic Goddess* endorses the idea (backed by "new traditionalist", backlash rhetoric) that "something's gotta give" in women's public/private predicament, and in case of doubt, female ambition should be directed towards hearth and heart.

There have also been – variably successful – attempts in popular culture to combine women's roles at home and at work and we have been presented with a number of different interpretations of the modern working housewife. During the 1980s, *Scarecrow and Mrs King* (1983– 1987) depicted the adventures of a recently divorced housewife and mother – the eponymous Mrs Amanda King – who inadvertently gets caught up in the dangerous world of espionage when she is asked to protect a package handed to her by a secret agent. Amanda (Kate Jackson) soon gets involved in the whole assignment and she ends up working for "The Agency" (a government branch dealing with intelligence and defence), unbeknown to her two sons and her mother. Her partner Lee Stetson (Bruce Boxleitner) – code named "Scarecrow" – is initially reluctant to work with her; she is not necessarily spy material but a stereotypical "Middle American homemaker" ("Filming Raul"). Many of the series' comic moments derive from the different world views that the work partners have: when flying down enemy agents in a helicopter, Amanda is asked, "Have you ever flown a whirlybird before?" "No", she replies, "but it's a lot like my dishwasher. You give it a good kick and it goes". As Lee/Scarecrow discovers during their missions – that, befitting for the decade, rely on a Cold War premise and mostly involve Soviet spies – Amanda's domestic abilities can be an asset and, gradually, he is converted to her normality:

AMANDA: You know. That's your whole problem. You're out of touch.
LEE: Out of touch with what?
AMANDA: The way normal people do things.
LEE: I'm normal.
AMANDA: Oh sure. You think sunbathing in Borneo is normal. You know most people just want to get through a day with healthy kids, friends they can count on, a regular job, and a roof over their heads.
LEE: Fine. That normal I'm not. ("There Goes the Neighbourhood")

At the end of the fourth season, Lee has exchanged his womanizing ways for a relationship with Amanda and they even have a secret marriage. Throughout her adventures, Amanda's family has been kept in the dark about her dealings as a spy – they have been told that she works for a production company – and so finally, Lee is introduced to her sons only as a boyfriend, not her husband.

While *Scarecrow and Mrs King* clearly updates the figure of the housewife, endowing her with "agency" – in more than one way – it still keeps intact (for most of the series) the division between private and professional spheres, between Amanda's life as a homemaker/mother and her job as a government agent. While there might be reasons in the narrative for this – her status as a housewife acts as a cover identity that protects her family – the series nonetheless makes a concerted effort to hold on to a conservative idea of domesticity that puts limits on Amanda's agency. As such, it makes a clear distinction between Amanda and her colleague Francine Desmond (Martha Smith), another top-level agent who corresponds more closely to the image of a power-suited, tough and independent working woman. From the start, Francine is dismissive of Amanda's suburban domesticity and she has learnt to fight her way through a male-dominated society. In one episode ("Fearless Dotty"), both Francine and Amanda recount their different reactions to being mugged on the street:

> FRANCINE: What happened to you?
> AMANDA: I was mugged.
> LEE: You were what?
> AMANDA: I was mugged. In the middle of the street in broad daylight.
> LEE: Well that's terrible.
> FRANCINE: That's funny. The same thing happened to me just last week. I was outside the airport making a surveillance pass and all of a sudden I felt this big arm lock around my neck from behind.
> AMANDA: What did you do?
> FRANCINE: I spiked his instep with my heel, thumbed his eye sockets, pressed my forearm against his larynx and then brought up my knee in a lifting motion.
> AMANDA: I just screamed.
> FRANCINE: Hmm . . . so did he.

Here, we are not meant to applaud Francine for her survival skills and fighting bravado and disapprove of Amanda's passive behaviour, exemplary of a feminine victim; rather, Francine's violent actions are indicative of her overly masculinized persona and her lack of femininity/domesticity. In another episode ("Life of the Party"), Francine tries to justify her indifference to domestic issues but she is again shown up for being deficient:

> FRANCINE: Amanda, I am an expert at hand to hand combat, small arms weaponry, wealthy men between 30 and 40 but definitely not a kitchen person.
> AMANDA: Look. Francine. You gotta do it, okay? Now you know how to cook, don't you?
> FRANCINE: I know how to hire a cook.

By contrast, Amanda is not only happy to keep her agency secret but she also minimizes the importance of her job. When complimented on being a "mother, housewife and agent", she self-effacingly replies, "Well, I'm not really a real agent. I mean I don't even own a trench coat" ("Welcome to America, Mr. Brand"). Ultimately, the series repeatedly makes the point that, while a woman can be a housewife *and* a spy, being a spy without being a housewife is a less attractive option as the woman-spy might be in danger of losing her most endearing feminine traits.

Renny Harlin's 1996 film *The Long Kiss Goodnight* addresses a similar subject matter but from a different angle: here, the housewife identity is a cover-up, an illusion that hides the self of the female agent. The main protagonist Samantha Caine (Geena Davis) is a suburban mother and schoolteacher who has been suffering from amnesia for a number of years and she has no memory of her past – including who is the father of her daughter Caitlin (Yvonne Zima). Samantha's former life only resurfaces as a series of flashbacks and unexplained impulses that do not add up to her current life situation and experience: for example, when Caitlin injures herself while skating on the ice, Samantha tells her in an uncharacteristically harsh and uncaring manner, "Stop being a little baby.... Life is pain. Get used to it." When she is attacked in her home by an escaped convict, she dispatches him with lethal self-defence skills she did not know she possessed. To protect herself and her child from more harm, she enlists the help of private investigator Mitch Henessey (Samuel L. Jackson) to look into her past. The truth is revealed by mysterious Dr Nathan Waldman (Brian Cox) and it turns out to be scarier than Samantha ever anticipated – her knife-throwing expertise while chopping vegetables for dinner does not point towards, as she first guessed, her being a chef but she is in fact an assassin trained by the US government. As Waldman informs her, "the schoolteacher business was your cover.... You bought your own cover. It was a fantasy. Samantha never existed." The "real", pre-amnesiac self, Charly

Baltimore, is woken up from her dormant state when she is captured and tortured by her old enemies. The transformation scene in which Samantha is disavowed and Charly comes to the surface is characterized both by her fierce, unstoppable violence and by her increased sexualization. As Samantha is left behind with all the trappings of conventional feminine beauty (long hair, polite speech, flowery dresses), Charly emerges as a muscled killing machine who adopts a more transgressive, sexualized femininity (short, ultra-blonde hair, black eye make-up, cigarette smoking). Shortly afterwards, she tries to seduce Henessey, in an attempt to renounce her suburban life (including her fiancé and child) and "kill the schoolteacher". As she tells him, "I didn't ask for the kid. Samantha had the kid, not me. Nobody asked me." It is only after Caitlin has been kidnapped that she is forced to come to terms with the domestic side of her personality and she rescues herself and her daughter while also thwarting a fake terrorist attack.

Admittedly, the ending that sees Samantha/Charly reunited with her daughter and fiancé (who has been absent from the entire "Charly" plot) enjoying a bucolic picnic could be read as a nod towards a "new traditionalist", pro-family agenda that disallows a more progressive understanding of domesticity and excludes the possibility of an interracial romance – there is undoubtedly a sexual tension between Charly and Henessey that is never resolved. What *The Long Kiss Goodnight* achieves though is a kind of reconciliation of the protagonist's double identity – tough assassin *versus* well-mannered housewife/mother. By choosing not to detach herself from all domestic engagements – most importantly her maternal role – Samantha/Charly affirms a new kind of postfeminine agency that transforms submissive domesticity into a tougher, more sexy and powerful version of it. This more aggressive domestic strain is revealed at the picnic when she expertly throws a knife at an annoying cricket or when she drives her convertible car with a suitcase of money and a gun right next to her. Moreover, Samantha/Charly has also successfully taught her daughter to be an agent rather than a victim: it is, in effect, Caitlin who saves her mother at the final standoff with her pursuers, as she leans over Charly's seemingly lifeless body, whispering "[s]top being a little baby. You're not dead…. You get up now" – in an obvious echo of her mother's earlier instructions.

This postfeminine housewife has adopted a different kind of domestic femininity that is no longer tied to notions of female victimization, subjugation and madness. While Samantha, as a consummate housewife, was undoubtedly troubled by her disconnection from her past – lacking what Friedan called a "firm core of self" (264) – her new personality brings together elements of both identities in a chaotic, contradictory wholeness that attests to the heterogeneity of contemporary women and their diverse roles in society and the family. The figure of the housewife is currently undergoing a process of re-interpretation and re-negotiation that allows us to read it within the terms of a feminist discourse of emancipation. While there are a range of fictional housewives who have appeared on screen and in print (and continue to do so), postfeminine domesticity has now become an everyday reality for most women combining feminist aspirations and feminine desires, career and family life. As Jean Railla emphasizes in her "Crafty Manifesto" on her "feminist home economics" website (www.getcrafty.com), "Being crafty means living consciously and refusing to be defined by narrow labels and categories. It's about embracing life as complicated and complex, and out of this chaos constructing identities, which are feminist and domestic, masculine and feminine, strong and weak" (par. 23). The route to this new domesticity cannot be uncovered by approaching the housewife as a problem that demands an *either/or* answer and forces us to take sides.[18] The task then is to rethink domestic femininity itself and analyse its various significations without resorting to predetermined definitions and demarcations. To see the housewife through a multifaceted postfeminist lens is thus a challenge facing critics, writers as well as homemakers in the twenty-first century.

6
Having It All: The Superwoman

Life is too short to stuff a mushroom.

– Shirley Conran, *Superwoman* (1975)

If, as we have seen, much of second wave feminist writing, fiction and activism was designed to lead women out of the kitchen, then the logical question that followed necessarily had to consider where they should go next. For Betty Friedan, there was no doubt that the first step in a woman's "new life plan" had to involve a rejection of the housewife image in order to prepare her to make "a serious professional commitment" (*Feminine Mystique* 316). Friedan's goal was to start a sex-role revolution and to accomplish this she advocated that housewives and mothers should enter the public sphere and take up paid employment. "Even if a woman does not have to work to eat", Friedan writes, "she can find identity only in work that is of real value to society" – by which she meant, "work for which, usually, our society pays" (301). She makes reference to women's "psychological need to be economically productive" and optimistically describes the "numerous opportunities for the able, intelligent woman": "In Westchester, on Long Island, in the Philadelphia suburbs, women have started mental health clinics, art centres, day camps. In big cities and small towns, women all the way from New England to California have pioneered new movements in politics and education" (300–1). "Over and over", she continues, "women have told me that the crucial step for them was simply to take the first trip to the alumnae employment agency, or to send for the application for teacher certification" (303). Although Friedan acknowledges that there might be "a number of practical problems", these – she argues – can be overcome easily enough if a woman is truly committed: "those problems only seem insurmountable when a woman is still half-submerged in the false dilemmas and guilts of the feminine mystique – or when her desire for 'something more' is only a fantasy, and she is unwilling to make the necessary effort.... It is amazing how many obstacles and rationalizations the feminine mystique can throw up to keep a woman from making that trip or writing that letter" (303).

Friedan employed a dualistic breadwinner/housewife model that puts emphasis on remunerated work that is intended for "serious use in society", concomitant with a devaluation of economically and socially unrecognized housework or community-based "busywork" (316, 300).[1] For her, social status and personal fulfilment were inextricably determined by work roles and, as such, access to market work was deemed to be of primary importance in women's fight for equality and emancipation. Rather than re-evaluating the housewife role and demanding a systematic overhaul of the public sphere to include female workers, the onus was on the individual woman to adapt herself to the job market and "sustain the discipline and effort that any professional commitment requires" (304). As a result, the blame for failing to gain, what Friedan called, a "no-nonsense nine-to-five job, with a clear division between professional work and housework" could be laid at the door of the female job seeker who was considered to be too scared/lazy – in Friedan's terms, not "committed" enough – or she had to have a vested interest in her domestic role and the "Occupation: housewife" (304). In retrospect, these assertions do not only seem overly confident and naive – betraying Friedan's middle-class bias and liberal optimism – but also rely on misogynist stereotyping that belittles the housewife and her work within the home. As Joan Williams has noted, Friedan helped to establish the "traditional feminist strategy for women's equality", that is, for "women to work full time with child care delegated to the market" (40). This "full-commodification model" denigrates and erases the housewife role (and the labour associated with it) while glorifying market employment that is credited by Western capitalist/patriarchal societies in general and men in particular. Women are thus encouraged to adopt a male model of work and little thought is given to how they are supposed to negotiate their private and public commitments. According to Williams, Friedan "strategically downplayed the changes necessary to incorporate mothers into the workforce" and "minimized the question of who would take care of the children" (44). Friedan's evasion of these difficult issues was strategic, for "she knew full well what was required for a wife and mother to go back to work": when she herself returned to work in 1955, she hired "a really good mother-substitute – a housekeeper-nurse" (44). *The Feminine Mystique* carefully avoids the question of how to integrate domestic and professional engagements, but, as Williams puts it, "it soon returned to haunt women" (44).

In the early days of the second wave, the potential drawbacks of the full-commodification model were outweighed by an eagerness and anticipation about the prospect of going out to work. Articles in the early to mid-1970s are characteristically upbeat about the excitement of market employment and the challenges of merging this new role with existing wifely/maternal duties: "I don't think you have to make a choice", one contributor to the women's magazine *McCall's* wrote in 1974, "I never felt I had to compromise my femininity to continue to work. . . . It makes perfect sense to me to move from one area to another (that is, home to office). In one day, I pick up a fabric for a chair, arrange a party, sign a business deal, pay bills and give rich attention to my husband and children" (quoted in Williams 45). Another contemporary observer is slightly less enthusiastic but still optimistic: "There is a whole generation of liberated young women who are quietly putting the ideals of revolution into practice, combining marriage, motherhood, and a master's degree, cooking and career. . . . Combining the two is far from an easy task. It is not an impossible dream but it takes hard work. The trick is in learning how; the art is in doing it well" (46).[2] Yet, many women were finding it increasingly difficult to pull off this "trick" and master "the art" of successfully synthesizing home and market work. By the mid-1970s, the initial hopefulness had waned and in its place there was fatigue and, to some extent, frustration. One woman recalled how "being a mother, wife, homemaker and career woman had . . . exhausted her physically and mentally", while another highlighted the heterosexual status quo: "My husband doesn't mind my working, but he won't help me. He says when I can't do my own work then I'll have to quit. So naturally I don't ask him to do anything for me" (46).

These tensions came to a climax in the 1980s when the "juggling" of work and family became the subject of a range of critical/popular investigations and feminism itself came into the firing line as its promise of "Having It All" became translated into an imperative of "Doing It All". This cultural shift was embodied by the figure of the over-achieving "Superwoman" who replaced the much touted 1970s career mother in the popular imagination and perception of working womanhood. Rather than artfully bringing together home and office, working women were now presented as being "doubly burdened" and "forced to be superwomen" (Friedan, *The Second Stage* 282). One feminist commentator who was intent on foregrounding the potential dangers inherent in the uncompromising perfectionism of the 1980s Superwoman was – somewhat paradoxically – Betty Friedan. While in *The Feminine Mystique* Friedan had evaded the work/family problematic – focusing instead on women's public recognition as full-time employees – she picked up the theme 20 years later, performing an often derided critical turn that emphasized women's commitment to home and family (see Chapter 3). In *The Second Stage* (1981), she describes the plight of the Superwoman and the dilemmas of the numerous women who fail to personify this image:

> The superwomen [are] trying to have it all, looking for security, status, power and fulfilment in full-time jobs and careers in the competitive rat race, like men, and trying to hold on to that old security, status, power and fulfilment women once had to find solely in home and children. Or [women are] giving up, in midstream or in advance – because who can live as that kind of superwoman? – and "choosing" to go back again and stay home, despite the economic and nervous strain. Or [women are] "choosing" not to marry or have children, and therefore seeking all identity, status, power and fulfilment in job or career – embracing, more single-mindedly than most men now, that obsessive careerism that has made so many men die prematurely of stress-induced heart attacks and strokes.
>
> (79)

Mirroring the fate of 1950s housewives that Friedan had previously exposed, (aspiring) Superwomen are caught in a "trap", "trying to be Perfect Mothers... and also perfect on the job" (113). For Friedan, this exemplifies a kind of "female machismo" that hides "the same inadmissible self-hate, weakness, sense of powerlessness as machismo hides in men". The Superwoman is thus "an easy victim of the double burden", placing unrealistic demands on herself in her work, and "getting locked into power battles with her husband over insatiable standards of housework". In opposition to her earlier belittlement of housewifery that is not "valued in dollar terms", Friedan now asserts that "it is real work" and puts forward these questions: "What would life be like if no one did that work? What if, in reaction [to feminism's focus on paid employment], [a woman] strips her life clean of all these unmeasured, unvalued feminine tasks and frills – stops baking cookies altogether, cuts her hair like a monk, decides not to have children, installs a computer console in her bedroom" (114).[3] In order to save women from an inevitable "crisis of confidence", Friedan advises them to *"transcend reaction"* and cease playing out the "superwoman game in home and/or office" (114, 58; emphasis in original). Otherwise, she predicts, women, feminists and "their younger sisters" – discovering that they cannot make it as Superwomen – will "retreat in dismay from equality itself".[4]

The proposition that women can decide on their priorities and adjust an excessively ambitious image of working womanhood is at the heart of the construction of the Superwoman. The term "Superwoman" implicitly puts the responsibility (and blame) on women themselves and hence deflects attention away from the fact that women are forced to "do it all" – become "super" versions of themselves – because of the lack of support, both from their husbands as well as from their employers (Williams 46). Trying to live up to an unattainable ideal, women are pressurizing themselves to conform simultaneously to a single standard of wife- and motherhood and a male-career pattern.[5] As Geneva Overholser noted at the time, this results in an impossible, unlivable situation: "no women, even 'superwomen', can indefinitely do all that they have been doing at home plus all that men have been doing at work. Since women *are* at work, something has to give" – and the suggested response put forward in many forms of popular culture is that "women should give" (30; emphasis in original). In a similar manner, Suzanna Danuta Walters describes the "Superwoman syndrome" as a watchword of the 1980s that constructs "a female identity in crisis, a subjectivity at war with its own history, a woman bereft" (121). As Walters argues, the ideological framework of the 1980s presents "an image of troubled womanhood, of striving career women suddenly faced with the deep truth of their bottomless need for hearth and home, husband and children" (122). In popular representations, this was to be the decade of – what Imelda Whelehan has called – "the crashing of the superwoman", lending credence to the observation that "[t]here would be no straightforward way for women to gain access to the top of their professions without the perception that their success had cost them dear in personal terms" (*Feminist Bestseller* 141).

The intention of numerous 1980s texts, films and fiction was thus to focus on the work/family conflict which was portrayed as a result of women's entry into paid employment and, correlatively, their feminist beliefs and desires. In the popular imagination, feminism came to be associated with the careerist Superwoman and it was seen to be responsible for women's long working hours and their "double-day/second-shift" existence (Walters 122). As Anne Roiphe – mother of Katie, who, in the 1990s, (in)famously attacked the notion of date rape and feminism's "neo-puritan" preoccupation with women's victim status[6] – writes in *Loving Kindness* (1987), "In the early days of the [feminist] movement we thought we could do without [families]. Then we created a model of equality that left children waiting at the window for someone to come home.... We woke up to discover that our goal of equality had created a generation of gray flannel suits who played tennis to win" (quoted in Williams 47). Likewise, in *The Second Stage*, Betty Friedan cites a number of women who are suffering from "feminist fatigue" and have started to resent "the feminist label" and its "paranoid associations" (33). One, Harvard-graduate, "earlier feminist" is quoted as saying, "we were to be the first generation of superwomen.... The half-formed feminism of the early 1960s... taught us that to find fulfilment we would have to fit in – fit in to family life... fit in to career ladders... fit in to our husband's goals... fit in to the basic ideas of womanhood" (32).[7]

Suzanna Danuta Walters pointedly summarizes the assumptions underlying this critique of the feminist movement: "Feminism... promised more than it put out. We thought we wanted liberation, but we found out that we really loved too much. We thought we wanted equality, but realize instead that we cannot have it all" (121). According to Walters, this "you can't have it all" issue is expressed in popular culture by an attempt to "dichotomize mother and woman" and reduce feminist struggles and advances to personal choices that, we are told, have created "a no-win situation: we cannot have it all" (122). Instead of celebrating the "art" of combining work and home, many 1980s narratives end up severing these two life components, leaving us – in the most drastic cases – with a dualistic depiction of the idealized housewife/mother versus the demonized career woman. As I have discussed earlier, this dichotomy not only exemplifies a "new traditionalist" return to long-established, nostalgic roles and attitudes but is also symptomatic of a wider backlash culture and political shift to the right that undermines the feminist movement as a whole (Chapter 3). Relying on a backlash framework, a number of critics have highlighted that the image of the Superwoman is not, as has been suggested, the "answer to feminism" but rather "a result of the backlash against feminism's gains and principles" (Sanders, "Consuming Nigella" 153). As Lise Shapiro Sanders has recently argued, "the superwoman as a characterization (or, more likely, a stereotype) emerged in response to the failures of society to make the structural changes that would support a transformation of traditional gender roles: the superwoman was never the ideal of second wave feminism" (153). In this sense, the "monstrous creature" of the Superwoman is not so much an embodiment of the failings of feminism than a caricature thereof that is used in popular culture and politics to prove that women should never have diverged from their paths as wives and mothers (Whelehan, *Overloaded* 16).

Irrespective of our reading of the Superwoman – whether we interpret her as a side product of feminism's full-commodification premise and its underemphasis on the structural changes that are necessary for women to reach equality;[8] or, as a symptom of the backlash against feminism that works through "new traditionalist" rhetoric to call for a resurgence of "old" values and rigidly defined roles for women and men; or, most likely, a combination of both – her prevalence in 1980s popular culture (and beyond) is undisputed. Films like *Baby Boom* (1987) and *Working Girl* (1988) engage with post-second-wave career women and they provide clear indications as to how a working woman should go about fulfilling her ambitions and once this is achieved, how she should navigate the often conflicting demands of work and family life. In *Working Girl*, striving working-class secretary Tess McGill (Melanie Griffith) climbs the career ladder by using her initiative and "bending the rules", apart from the most important one which is her commitment to femininity. Unfulfilled by her typing job and armed with a night school business degree, Tess dreams of forging ahead in the big business world in New York and gladly accepts her new boss's – Katherine Parker (Sigourney Weaver) – offer to mentor her. However, when she realizes that Katherine is using her ideas and passing them off as her own, she decides to take advantage of her employer's absence to close a business deal by herself and, unknowingly, get professionally and romantically involved with Katherine's boyfriend, investment banker Jack Trainer (Harrison Ford). While Tess tries to imitate Katherine's smooth management style and upper-crust cadence, she does not make the mistake of turning herself into a power-suited, masculine career woman. Taking cues from Katherine's more classic dress sense and wardrobe, Tess tones down her over-the-top, working-class femininity – symbolized by long, big hair, plastic jewellery and mini-skirts – to emerge as a more sophisticated, refined but still undeniably feminine business woman. This is exactly what attracts Jack to her when they first meet at a merger party:

JACK: You're the first woman I've seen in one of these things that dresses like a woman, not like a woman thinks a man would dress if he was a woman.
TESS: Thank you I guess.

Dressed in one of Katherine's expensive cocktail gowns, Tess looks nothing like the other, "macho" women who, in their efforts to take on a man's world, have effectively desexed and defeminized themselves.[9] *Working Girl* is an example of, what Suzanna Danuta Walters refers to as, the "executive in a G-string theme"; or as Tess herself states, "I have a head for business and a bod for sin. Is there anything wrong with that?" Unlike her more calculating and corrupt boss, Tess has preserved a "natural" femininity/sexuality that allows her to steal Katherine's boyfriend and rewards her with a management position and her own female secretary. As Walters writes, the "bad woman here is the woman executive who has lost her 'true' womanly ways in her climb up the corporate ladder" (126). The film relies on a polarized view of modern (employed) womanhood that pits the feminine "working girl" against the professional career woman who might look the part, but acts in a decidedly unfeminine manner.[10] This duality – or slight variations thereof – is present in a wide range of 1980s popular culture that, at best, provides a compromise between career and femininity/motherhood and, at worst, positions one woman against another in a murderous showdown which only one of them can survive.

Without doubt, one of the most clear-cut, decidedly backlash films that hinges on such a deadly binary is the now classic *Fatal Attraction* (1987). As I discussed in Part I, backlash/new traditionalist texts try to convince their female readers/viewers of the impossibility and undesirability of being Superwomen as, in the attempt to juggle job and family, boardroom and babies, they jeopardize their feminine appeal and sign up for an exhausting existence filled with pain and guilt. The stigmatization of working womanhood is particularly castigatory and deprecatory in the case of single women who dare to diverge from homely femininity in search of a career. In the most one-dimensional backlash scenarios, the unattached and childless professional woman is portrayed as a figure of evil and a neurotic psychopath, designed to deter women from seeking public success and neglecting their feminine duties. She is the epitome of Otherness and insanity, directly opposed to the virtuous housewife and threatening the traditional family unit. The dichotomy of the liberated and unmarried businesswoman and her apparent antagonist, the homemaking wife, has famously been battled out in *Fatal Attraction*, which reaffirms the family through patriarchal violence and eliminates the single woman in order to restore the peace and primacy of the domestic sphere. The film's villain, Alex Forrest (Glenn Close), embodies all that counters the dominant patriarchal structure as she is an independent career woman and an autonomous free spirit, maintaining a large apartment in Manhattan's Meatpacking district and living out her sexuality and her emotions aggressively and excessively.

Alex knowingly enters into a weekend affair with married lawyer Dan Gallagher (Michael Douglas) but then refuses to obey "the rules" as she oversteps her assigned patriarchal position of the temptress/mistress and attempts to "have it all". Pregnant with Dan's child, she is resolute that she will not be "ignored" or treated "like some slut" and, as a potential mother figure, she demands "a little respect". Insisting that she is not Dan's "enemy", Alex wants her lover to "face up" to his responsibilities as a father and "play fair with [her]".

However, *Fatal Attraction* forcefully and unequivocally undercuts the single woman's social position and demands by depicting Alex's joint desires to succeed in her career and have a family – characteristic of the Superwoman – as equivalent to madness. Rather than exploring the problems her yearnings pose (that is, changing gender relations), the film trivializes Alex's anger by focusing on her increasingly psychotic behaviour and it obscures Dan's paternal duties by siding overwhelmingly with him and favouring his life inside the established family unit.[11] Dan rejects any form of liability or blame for his actions, declaring that having his baby is Alex's ill-considered and wrongful "choice" and "has nothing to do with [him]". He is determined to maintain the separation between his eccentric and self-reliant mistress and his loving and homemaking wife and thus he disputes Alex's efforts to cross the border between the two archetypes and inhabit an in-between position. As an extramarital lover, Alex has no rights and cannot claim any support as he has "a whole relationship with someone else". Her calls for fairness are presented as "irrational" and unreasonable, a symptom of her escalating psychological disintegration and loss of control.

Increasingly, the plot evolves to alienate Alex from both Dan and the audience by concentrating on her metamorphosis from a competent and attractive professional to the "Other" woman and the "working woman from hell" who pours acid onto Dan's car, kidnaps his daughter and, most disturbingly, boils the child's pet rabbit (Walters 123). Any overlap or similarity between Alex and Beth Gallagher (Anne Archer) is denied and the two female characters are polarized as the demonic Singleton versus the dutiful wife, the lonely professional woman versus the good mother.[12] Women's private and public, domestic and professional lives are seen to be incompatible and dichotomous and hence it is the wife's responsibility to be the final arbiter of familial justice and destroy her unmarried nemesis. Confirming Bromley and Hewitt's assertion that "in the 1980s the single career woman must be killed in order to preserve the sanctity of the family", Beth defeats her arch-enemy in a bloody finale, putting an end to her intrusive and violent quest to find an avenue into the family circle (23). The brutal killing is depicted as an act of self-defence and an overdue punishment for the mad seductress who unlawfully tries to enter the family unit. By eliminating her opponent, Beth also ensures that Alex's baby, a potentially perverse progeny, has no chance of survival and dies in order to safeguard the patriarchal family.

The film thus helps to re-naturalize the association between women and home, firmly relegating them to their conventional roles as wives/mothers and instructing them that their desire for a place outside the home leads to a variety of dire personal consequences and may even result in death. While the backlash's demonization of the professional single woman has had a powerful impact on subsequent generations, there also have been concerted efforts to transcend this negative image. As I will elaborate in the next chapter, the 1990s figure of the Singleton – despite still being traumatized by Alex Forrest's cautionary tale – clearly distances herself from this monstrous stereotype. Likewise in the 1980s, writers and filmmakers sought to portray a kind of reconciliation between women's private and public positions. In *Baby Boom* (1987), high-flying Manhattan career woman J. C. Wiatt (Diane Keaton) is converted to the joys of motherhood but at the end of the film she has also started a new business venture that allows her to combine home and work. The intention of narratives like this is not so much to vilify the Superwoman as to redefine (and, in most cases, downscale) her desire to "have it all". Feminism is acknowledged as a premise of modern life, and women's work aspirations are taken into account, but they are described as requiring a certain amount of readjustment. As the opening voice-over informs the audience,

> 53 percent of the American workforce is female. Three generations of women have turned a thousand years of tradition on its ear. As little girls they were told to grow up and marry doctors and lawyers. Instead, they grew up and became doctors and lawyers. They moved out of the pink ghetto and into the executive suite. Sociologists say that the new working woman is a phenomenon of our time.... Take J. C. Wiatt for example. Graduated first in her class at Yale.... She makes six figures a year.... One would take it for granted that a woman like this has it all. One must never take anything for granted.

This sets the scene for J. C.'s domestication that – in line with the film's depiction of 1980s yuppie culture and materialism – she has voluntarily postponed in her single-minded pursuit of professional success. At the beginning, J. C. – known as the "Tiger Lady" – has seemingly arrived at the pinnacle of her career when she is offered the position of partner in her firm. Responding to her boss's concerns that she might underestimate the personal sacrifices this work commitment requires, J. C. coolly responds, "I understand what it takes to make it.... I don't want it all." Her relationship with her boyfriend Steven (Harold Ramis) is reminiscent of a business transaction as they both "eat, sleep and dream [their] work" – fittingly, their sexual encounters are limited to passionless four-minute couplings. J. C.'s ordered life is thrown into turmoil when she "inherits" a toddler, Elizabeth, from a deceased relative. Her maternal instincts are aroused before long and she attempts to live up to a Superwoman image – combining her high-powered job with the high pressure world of the New York parent/child, a world in which tots attend strenuous gym classes and undergo intelligence-enhancing training. J. C.'s business career soon begins to suffer – it appears that, as her superior Fritz (Sam Wanamaker) tells her, caring for a child has made J. C. "lose her concentration" and "go soft" – culminating in her loss of lover and job. J. C.'s solution is quick to follow: she retreats to the country, where, after an initial phase of boredom, she finds a fulfilling relationship with the local vet and founds a baby-food empire. At the end of the film, when J. C. is presented with the possibility of reclaiming her identity as a savvy businesswoman – her firm is bidding to buy her new company, offering her such perks as a one-million-dollar salary – she turns down the deal and, with this, her previous way of life and objectives: "I'm not the Tiger Lady anymore.... I don't want to make ... sacrifices and the bottom line is nobody should have to."

As Joanne Hollows has recently observed, *Baby Boom* can be discussed in terms of a "downshifting narrative" that abandons urban in favour of rural femininities and promises the achievement of a "work–life balance" through geographical relocation ("Can I Go Home Yet" 108). Hollows notes that – while "it would be very easy to read the key downshifting narrative as a classic backlash tale", involving what could be interpreted as women's "failure of nerve" to fight their way to the top of the career ladder and smash the glass ceiling – downshifting can also be seen as "an opportunity to interrogate the very notion of 'having it all' ". In *Downshifting: The Bestselling Guide to Happier, Simpler Living* (2004), Ghazi and Jones pursue a similar line of reasoning: "The point is that the old feminist battles have become obsolete. The argument now is no longer about *whether* women should pursue career or motherhood or both. It is about *how* they can best combine whichever roles suit them" (quoted in Hollows 107–8; emphasis in original).[13] Although *Baby Boom* has frequently been examined as one of the "quintessential backlash texts",[14] Hollows proposes that "by now it is beginning to look like it captures an emergent structure of feeling" (105).

The notion of working womanhood (and in particular, motherhood) has continued to play an important role in popular culture that keeps thinking through the possibilities and relationships between public and personal, paid work and domesticity, feminism and femininity. In the aptly entitled *Having It All* (1991), Maeve Haran describes a wife's dilemma to reconcile the conflicting demands of public and private life, "reveal[ing] everything we won't admit about being a working woman" (cover page). Haran's main character, "high-flying executive" Liz Ward, finds herself "torn in two" and "pulled two ways" in her effort to personify "the classic nineties woman" who has "a glittering career *and* kids", a "brilliant degree", a "job in TV" and a "handsome husband" (1, 176, 70, 3, 96; emphasis in original). Having been appointed "the most powerful woman in television", the "first woman Programme Controller of any major TV company in the UK", Liz is determined "to show not simply that a woman could do it, but that a woman could do it brilliantly" (9, 31). However, in the pursuit of her professional ambition, she realizes that she has lost touch with "the things that really matter" as her "obsession with work" causes her to neglect her domestic/feminine responsibilities and duty to care for her husband and children (118, 32). While fighting "tooth and nail to be treated the same as men" and join their "club", Liz has deviated from her "natural" path as a wife and mother, denying that she "belong[s] to another species" and is essentially and fundamentally different from men (75, 6). Confronted with her husband's unfaithfulness and her own feminine failure, Liz has to reassess her priorities and admit that she cannot "have it all" but has to make a choice between "success and happiness" (80): "it was time to tell the truth. That women had been sold a pup. Having It All was a myth, a con, a dangerous lie. Of course you could have a career and a family. But there was one little detail the gurus of feminism forgot to mention: the cost to you if you did" (53).

In this novel, rather than improving and alleviating women's personal and social station, the feminist movement has placed them on double duty at home and work, saddling them with both female and male burdens. In a nostalgic search for a simpler life, Liz chooses to become a "mommy-tracker", leave her urban surroundings – "the whole melting pot of crime and dirt, greed and tension" – and settle in a "lovely, peaceful" rural idyll, "almost chocolate box in its beauty" (73, 195, 197). The novel is intent on depicting her "return home" as a quasi-feminist act: Liz "dares to be a housewife", despite her husband's assertion that he does not "want a wife at home", he "want[s] an equal…a woman who's her own person with her own life" (224, 177). After leaving her doubtful husband, the newly single Liz surrenders to "the joys of home-making…guiltily, as though she were taking a lover" (213). In this scenario, the domestic realm is redefined as an "enjoyable" environment, far removed from "the drudgery she'd gone to any lengths to avoid" (212). As a conscious and supposedly empowering lifestyle choice, this modern haven of "security and comfort" ends up seducing Liz's husband and luring him back to his wife and children (241, 240). The novel integrates feminist ideas of social enfranchisement in a domestic tale as Liz decides to re-enter the career path on a part-time basis and alongside her husband as the managing director of the employment agency "WomanPower" whose motto is particularly appropriate: "half a woman is the best man for the job" (431). The dichotomy between women's private and public desires is resolved by this part-time solution that allows Liz to have the best of both worlds and enjoy "a life in balance" (539). As Liz notes, "being at home *part* of the time gave a spice to working, and working made the time off seem all the more precious" (417).

Family and job are described as congruous and reconcilable life components that complement each other in a symbiotic alliance. Reunited with her husband, Liz optimistically proclaims that "perhaps together anything *would* be possible": she could "have it all" and fulfil her dream of "a life where I had enough work to keep my brain alive, and enough space to enjoy my children, and fun, and sex, and food, and love…and gardening" (559, 453). In this utopian vision, modern woman has achieved a compromise between her feminine and feminist personas, between professional and personal happiness. This resolution relies on a romantic egalitarian fantasy where men and women jointly abandon their excessive career ambitions in favour of an all-embracing partnership. Liz's short-lived spell as a single mother is portrayed as a necessary period of confusion during which wife and husband re-negotiate the boundaries between work and family and then re-enter their stable and newly equilibrated relationship. Although Haran advocates the extension of women's qualities from the private to the public sphere, she also naturalizes their domestic role and reifies traditional notions that women's most important work is at home. As Liz notes, she "needed to work" but "never again would she put her career before her family" (347). Haran's endorsement of a part-time settlement of the feminist/feminine, public/private dilemma understates women's economic and social pressures that might prohibit such an equilibrium. "Having it all" is qualified and downgraded to "having it part-time", allowing privileged women to avoid the conflicts between professional and private fulfilment and providing a personalized answer that might not be relevant or achievable for the vast majority of working women. A similar scenario is replayed in a number of narratives, with slight variations depending on the heroine's familial situation. In Allison Pearson's best-selling *I Don't Know How She Does It* (2003), protagonist Kate Reddy spends her time agonizing over her life as a working mother and her own failure to live up to the high, apple-pie-baking standards of the "Muffia – the powerful, stay-at-home cabal of organised mums" (50). In her own mind, Kate is constantly called before the "Court of Motherhood" that enumerates her shortcomings and chastises her for the satisfaction she gains from her job as a fund manager. In "the grey survival zone" between work and home, she is taken to almost breaking point: "When I wasn't at work, I had to be a mother; when I wasn't being a mother, I owed it to work to be at work. Time off for myself felt like stealing" (104). Kate's cynicism for "equal opportunities" legislations ("Doesn't make it better; just drives the misogyny underground" [124]), and her frustration with feminist idealism – "Back in the Seventies, when they were fighting for women's rights, what did they think equal opportunities meant: that women would be entitled to spend as little time with their kids as men do?" (273) – ultimately drive her to resign from her job and become one of "the domestic Disappeared" (176). Although the epilogue ("What Kate Did Next") points towards a potential compromise between job and motherhood (in this case, an opportunity for a global doll's house business), the underlying message is clear: trying to be a Superwoman is a futile endeavour and in the end, high-flyers will be brought down one way or another.

Imelda Whelehan has argued that "mumlit" (the grown-up version of chick lit where the Singleton settles down and has children) is characterized by a particularly "anguished" tone as the heroines encounter a set of new, more serious, problems posed by the demands of their long-term relationships and their transition to parenthood (*Feminist Bestseller* 196). While such novels are successful at highlighting the limits placed on women and their struggles between workplace and home, they also show "depressingly, that there is no solution to the work/motherhood dilemma" (195–6). Or, at least, there is no collective answer or a political engagement with the "system" as one might have come to expect from earlier second wave feminist novels. Instead of fiery calls for revolution, contemporary mumlit provides more individual, restrained attempts at resolution and a sense of open-endedness that point towards the complexity of these issues and the absence of a "quick fix". As Kate notes in the epilogue, "I think an ending may be out of the question. The wheels on the bus go round and round, all day long" (347). Her "down-shifting" move to the country is not presented as an idyllic retreat or a nostalgic panacea – as in Haran's novel – but rather a workable situation and a solution in progress. An involuntary housewife, she is "bored to the point of manslaughter" and she regrets giving up her more exciting London life – most notably, her Internet flirtations with her American business associate, suggestively named Jack Ablehammer, describing her drunken evening with him as "the best sex I never had" (350–1). While the ending of *I Don't Know How She Does It* can be read in terms of a conservative, retrograde withdrawal from the public sphere – Kate's rural business is a fitting example as it potentially works to perpetu-ate the domestic dream and confine a new generation of girls to their doll's houses – it also offers the opportunity to revisit the debates about home/career and reinterpret the notion of "having it all", whereby it is no longer determined by a number of impossible standards that set up the doomed Superwoman for an inevitable failure and feelings of guilt and unhappiness.

On screen and in print, the biggest shortcoming of the working mother seems to hinge on her inability to embody work and home roles to a Superwoman model of perfection. Towards the end of Pear-son's novel, Kate acknowledges that she does not fit into the identity categories available to women: "I am married but am not a wife, have children but am not a mother. What am I?" (291). Her assumed office persona is equally ill-fitting and inapt: while she "love[s] the work" – "the synapse-snapping satisfaction of being good at it, of being in con-trol when the rest of life seems such an awful mess" (18) – the only way to get on at her firm has been for her "to act like one of the boys" (34). Kate's method of coping has been to divide and compart-mentalize the often conflicting demands of her professional and private lives. When asked by trainee Momo how she combines children and a full-time job, she responds, "compartments, that's how. They [chil-dren] go in one compartment, work goes in another; and you have to stop them leaking into each other. It's tricky, but not impossible" (164). Kate's final decision to drop out of the rat race and work from her country home reveals her increasing struggles and strains to perform this self-division and schizophrenically separate these life components. Maybe then, the answer lies not in an attempt to fight and resolve the chaos – or, in Kate's words, "mess" – that torments so many fictional heroines but an acknowledgement of the latter as the starting point for an examination of the contradictions that women face in a postfeminist age. Of course, this is part of a much wider analysis and social development based around the deconstruction of domesticity – including the image of the self-sacrificing, pie-baking housewife – and the "ideal-worker norm" that adopts a now inaccurate, gendered model of full-time work (Williams 4).[15] The time has come to sever the Superwoman from her objective of "having it all" as contemporary women are increasingly refusing the pressures of perfectionism and pragmatically negotiating their work/home lives.[16] The postfeminine woman faces the challenge of "having it all", where "all" now refers to a complex set of private and public, feminist and feminine entanglements.

7
Making It on Her Own: The Singleton*

> All I ever wanted was to be rich and to be successful and to have three kids and a husband who was waiting home for me at night to tickle my feet...And look at me! I don't even like my hair.
>
> – *Ally McBeal*

As Janet Lee has observed in her discussion of female/feminine representations, "the term 'new woman' seems to reappear with nearly every generation"; from the " 'new woman' in the late nineteenth century, who so shocked society with her 'independence', to that of the present day, who so preoccupies the theorists of 'post-feminism' ", women have been presented with a regularly updated and evolving range of subject positions that celebrate assorted female roles and practices as improved and emancipatory versions of womanhood (168).[1] The cultural climate of the late twentieth and early twenty-first century has produced a particularly paradoxical incarnation of the "new woman" as the millennium female model is defined in terms of her relation to a highly contentious postfeminist context and times. The new "postfeminist woman" (or "PFW") has been the subject of considerable debate and she has variously been described as an anti-feminist backlasher, a sexually assertive "do-me feminist", a pro-woman pseudo-feminist and a feminine Girlie feminist (Neustatter; Shalit; Kim; Brunsdon, *Screen Tastes*). In this chapter, I suggest that these interpretative possibilities are indicative of the precariousness and equivocality inherent in postfeminist examinations of female/feminine identities. The complex interconnections between femaleness, feminism and femininity that come to the fore in a late-twentieth-century environment are embodied by the postfeminist woman who seeks to negotiate the conflicts between her feminist and feminine associations, between individual and collective achievement, between professional career and personal relationship. Like the 1980s Superwoman, the PFW wants to "have it all" but she refuses to dichotomize and choose between her public and private, feminist and feminine selves. In this sense, she takes further the Superwoman's quest by re-articulating the distinctions between feminism and femininity, professionalism and domesticity, refuting monolithic definitions of postfeminist subjectivity.

This chapter focuses on the figure of the postfeminist Singleton, the young, unattached and mostly city-dwelling woman who is caught between the enjoyment of her independent urban life and her desperate yearning to find "Mr. Right" with whom to settle down. The Singleton's predicament centres on her recognition that "having it all" implies walking a tightrope between professional and personal success/failure, between feminist and feminine empowerment. Paradoxically, the Singleton has been touted as "bold", "ambitious", "witty" and "sexy" while concomitantly being bemoaned as "shallow", "overly compulsive", "neurotic" and "insecure" (*Chick Lit USA* 1). The postfeminist Singleton moves *across* binaries, seeking to combine her career ambitions and material success with her desire for a rewarding home life, her feminist beliefs in agency and independence with the pleasures of feminine adornment and heterosexual romance. Importantly, she is unwilling to compromise on these joint aspirations and – as one famous fictional Singleton puts it – she is determined to be a "marvellous career woman/girlfriend hybrid" (Fielding, *Edge of Reason* 18).

The Singleton has been the subject of a wide range of print, broadcast and film texts that have emerged in the 1990s, depicting the experiences of single, professional women in an urban environment. Serial dramas such as *Ally McBeal* (1997–2002) and *Sex and the City* (1998–2004), based on Candace Bushnell's 1996 novel, depict the ups and downs of "sexy, hip, smart and sassy" Singletons and their "quest to find the one thing that eludes them all – a real, satisfying and lasting relationship" (*Sex and the City*, season 1). In this chapter, I pay particular attention to the Singleton par excellence, Helen Fielding's literary creation Bridget Jones whose fictional diary recounts the adventures of a British thirty-something in her attempt to navigate the tensions between heterosexual courtship and unwed freedom, between female emancipation and self-abnegation, between feminism and femininity. *Bridget Jones's Diary*, both novel (1996) and film adaptation (2001), has been credited with catching the mood of the period or summoning the *zeitgeist* and Bridget has been hailed as "no mere fictional character, she's the Spirit of the Age" (quoted in Fielding, *Edge of Reason*, inside cover). Bridget rejects the pejorative label "spinster" and its negative connotations of unattractiveness, loneliness and social ineptitude and, instead, she redefines her status by coining the term "Singleton" – a new, rebel identity with its own language and attitudes. While Bridget is striving to throw off the stigma attached to her single state and resignify it as a novel and rewarding subject position, she also remains ensnared and persecuted by her recurring fear and "existential angst" of "dying alone and being found three weeks later half-eaten by an Alsatian" (*Bridget Jones's Diary* 20). Bridget's inherent contradictoriness and deep-seated ambiguity about her lifestyle cast her as the "original Singleton" and "the patron saint of single women", "captur[ing] what … it is like to be female" (quoted in Fielding, *Edge of Reason*, inside cover). She is "a kind of 'everywoman' of the 1990s" insofar as "the current era of the single woman might as well be described as post-BJ" (Whelehan, *Helen Fielding* 12; Zeisler 2). The "Bridget Jones persona" can thus be said to have entered the cultural consciousness and become "an identifiable character in modern life" (Whelehan, *Helen Fielding* 80).

In this Bildungsroman of the single girl, Bridget struggles to make sense of her chaotic life as she "career[s] rudderless and boyfriendless through dysfunctional relationships and professional stagnation" (Fielding, *Bridget Jones's Diary* 78). Fielding identifies her character's disorientation as a symptom of a postmodern era of uncertainty, noting that "Bridget is groping through the complexities of dealing with relationships in a morass of shifting roles, and a bombardment of idealized images of modern womanhood" (quoted in Whelehan, *Helen Fielding* 17).[2] In these complicated times, women are in the process of experimenting with a new set of identities, simultaneously revolving around feminist notions of empowerment and agency as well as patriarchal ideas of feminine beauty and heterosexual coupledom. Bridget neatly expresses the tensions between the lure of feminist politics that enables her to fulfil her public ambitions and a romantic fantasy that sees her swept off her feet by a mysterious Byronic hero. These apparently conflicting impulses leave the postfeminist Singleton in a state of constant emotional turmoil and battling with the prospect that "having it all" is a demanding and complex undertaking that defies perfectionism and uniformity. In effect, 1990s representations of the Singleton respond to previous portrayals of the Superwoman by integrating "failure" as a narrative theme and embracing women who do not live up to their ideals and achieve their goals. While the Superwomen of the 1980s were driven – and ultimately overcome – by their relentless pursuit of home/work standards and their endeavour to compartmentalize their lives, Singletons confront the possibility of re-negotiating and remaking the relationships between their feminist and feminine identities. Importantly, Bridget internalizes and individualizes this postfeminist problematic as she turns her confusion inwards and interprets it as her personal, psychological dilemma. Offering an intimate engagement with and promising a closer insight into Bridget's "real" self, Fielding's novel employs the diary format and a confessional tone to provide the fiction of an "authentic" female voice bewildered by the contradictory demands and mixed messages of heterosexual romance and feminist emancipation. In this way, *Bridget Jones's Diary* exemplifies, what Daniele calls, postfeminism's "return to the I", the "implosion of personal styles and narratives" in the postfeminist "rhetoric of autobiography" (83, 81, 89). This reliance upon the subjective voice has been discussed as a postfeminist re-enactment of the CR experiences of second wave feminism. However, while fruitfully exploring the complexities of twenty-first-century femaleness, femininity and feminism, postfeminism's "personal expression nevertheless differs from the personalizing of the political effected through consciousness raising" (Siegel, "The Legacy of the Personal" 51).[3] Critics maintain that postfeminist fiction fails to move out of the protagonists' personal sphere and relate the process of confession to a wider context of female discrimination and social inequality. They argue that postfeminism's return to the personal does not provide access to feminist politics and is thus, it risks sliding into "lifestyle feminism", confined to navel-gazing introspection rather than life-changing analysis and interrogation (Dow).

Bridget Jones has been portrayed as the poster child of this self-absorbed postfeminism in her individual quest to combine her feminist ideals of egalitarianism with her supposedly "pre-feminist" concerns and overarching desire to get married.[4] Accordingly, Germaine Greer and Beryl Bainbridge famously denounced *Bridget Jones's Diary* as "an updated version of the old Mills & Boon scenario", a literary "froth sort of thing" that "just wastes time", while Erica Jong lamented that today's young women "are looking for the opposite of what their mothers looked for. Their mothers sought freedom; they seek slavery" (quoted in Whelehan, *Helen Fielding* 59; quoted in Ferriss and Young 1; quoted in Jacobson 3). These commentators criticize the lack of feminist politics and collectivity in 1990s depictions of the Singleton and they focus on – what they consider – her nostalgic and retrogressive pursuit of romance/marriage. Postfeminist texts are decried as "nothing more than the contemporary version of the 'How to Get Married Novel'", a "retro form that details the search for and nabbing of a husband, any husband" (Jacobson 3). The postfeminist Singleton is said to embrace a passive and disempowered image of womanhood that has simply been revamped for the postfeminist era but, in actual fact, rejects the feminist movement and its principles of communal social action. Postfeminism's "new woman" is seen to be almost identical to the old, firmly demarcated and determined by her quintessential femininity and her heterosexual appeal. Ultimately, Bridget and Co. are seen to be too feminine to be truly feminist, too preoccupied with their appearance and their desire to land a mate and neglectful of feminism's collective struggle and political agenda.

In this chapter, I resist unanimously dismissive accounts of the postfeminist Singleton that define her as an egocentric composite of frivolous neuroses and a pre-feminist nostalgist obsessed with male approval. Refusing the "narrow-minded description of the genre" as a reprisal of some well-worn clichés, advocates of chick lit insist that "these books don't trivialize women's problems" and can be designated as "coming-of-age stories, finding out who you are, where you want to go" (Jacobson 3).[5] Rather than locking the heroine in a vicious and immobilizing circle of introspection, postfeminism's personalized narratives depict the struggles and efforts of contemporary womanhood to blend and integrate her contradictory aspirations. The postfeminist Singleton endeavours to find a subject position that permits her to hang on to the material and social gains fostered by the women's movement as well as indulge in her romantic longings. As Bridget Jones proudly proclaims, "we are a pioneer generation daring to refuse to compromise in love and relying on our own economic power" (21). Instead of readily rejecting Bridget and her televised doppelgängers as spoiled princesses disrespectful of their mothers' feminist undertakings or as aspiring wives nostalgically searching for a role akin to that of a romance character, I want to discuss the postfeminist Singleton as a complex contemporary heroine, simultaneously bewildered and confident in her quest to "have it all". I propose that this postfeminist incarnation of the "new woman" epitomizes the divergent understandings and polysemy of postfeminism/postfemininity as she takes up paradoxical subject positions along a multi-focal postfeminist/postfeminine spectrum. In her most challenging depictions, the Singleton navigates an uncertain course on the postfeminist frontier, fluctuating between backlash pessimism and Girlie optimism in her attempt to displace a dualistic logic and hold together conflicting life components. She carves out a new subjective space that denies the possibility of a utopian, "Superwomanly" "having it all" in favour of a more complicated reconciliation of incongruity and paradox.

While critics have sought to categorize the 1990s figure of the Singleton in relation to either backlash or Girlie rhetoric, I maintain that she problematizes and depolarizes these standpoints in her open-ended negotiation of femaleness, femininity and feminism. Vacillating between anxiety and determination, she is simultaneously haunted by backlash images of the deviant and abject Singleton as well as elated by Girlie feminism's successful chick/chic achiever. The postfeminist Singleton recognizes the difficulties and tensions involved in her chaotic heterogeneity and, although she avoids reinforcing binary distinctions, she is unable to deny the existence of friction and struggle to combine her feminist and feminine, public and private desires. In this sense, her contradictory subjectivity causes her to be in a state of confusion and self-doubt and she is hopeful and disillusioned, enjoying and loathing her single life at once. Despite her happy ending in the arms of Mr Darcy, Bridget Jones provides a "terrifying picture . . . of a person at war with herself", "wracked with chronic body dysmorphia" and building her life around a set of imaginary rules and rituals (Whelehan, *Helen Fielding* 63, 45). At the same time, Bridget also celebrates the "joy of single life" that allows her to "seize power" in her job, spend "delicious night[s] of drunken feminist ranting" and forge "extended families in the form of networks of friends connected by telephone" (*Bridget Jones's Diary* 244, 133, 125, 245). These portrayals of the Singleton articulate the complexity of her in-between position and refuse to impose the idea of an appropriate and monolithic feminine/feminist identity. Rather than asserting the sheer impossibility or the effortless realization of a postfeminist nirvana where women can "have it all", the postfeminist Singleton expresses the pains and pleasures of her problematical quest for balance in a world where personal and professional, feminist and feminine traits are mutually pervasive.

While the Singleton has achieved a particular level of prominence in the 1990s, depictions of single, working women have appeared in popular culture ever since second wave feminism's fight for women's public empowerment drove housewives out of the kitchen and into the office. Prior to her late-twentieth-century heyday, the Singleton has been the subject of a range of investigations that explore the changing face of modern woman and her new social position in a feminist-inspired environment. Helen Gurley Brown's best-selling *Sex and the Single Girl* (1962) – republished in 2003 as a "cult classic" – offers a glamorized view of the possibilities available to "single girls" who head to metropolitan cities in their quest for careers, exciting affairs and – ultimately – marriage.[6] The opening sentences of the book set the tone for the rest: "I married for the first time at thirty-seven. I got the man I wanted. It *could* be construed as something of a miracle considering how old *I* was and how eligible *he* was" (3; emphasis in original). In essence, the book can be described as a self-help manual for plain and inexperienced working girls – Brown characterizes herself as a "mouseburger" from Arkansas – to transform themselves into sophisticated career women who prove to be irresistible to successful businessmen. Although much of the book seems to be geared towards marriage – the chapters comprise of a number of "how to" directives, from "where to meet" available men to "how to be sexy" and "how to" conduct an affair – Brown writes that it "is not a study on how to get married but how to stay single – in superlative style" (11). Her vision of the 1960s single girl provides a refreshing and compelling account of unmarried womanhood, removed from the negative and dreary connotations of the spinster:

> the single woman, far from being a creature to be pitied and patron-ized, is emerging as the newest glamour girl of our times. She is engaging because she lives by her wits. She supports herself. She has had to sharpen her personality and mental resources to a glitter in order to survive in a competitive world and the sharpening looks good. Economically she is a dream. She is not a parasite, a depen-dent, a scrounger, a sponger or a bum. She is a giver, not a taker, a winner and not a loser.
>
> (5–6)

Brown paints an attractive picture of single, urban career women with enviable, glamorous lifestyles, but she then admonishes her readers that "there is a catch to achieving single bliss. You have to work like a son of a bitch" (8). Her promise of success is premised on utter self-discipline and she prescribes an exhaustive programme, from strict dieting and exercise to more practical suggestions, like how to live on a budget, plan your wardrobe and what wall colours to choose. Brown is adamant that this is an all-encompassing, consuming task: "What you have to do is work with the raw material you have, namely you, and never let up. If you would like the good single life ... you can't afford to leave any facet of you unpolished" (9). One important element of this self-improvement regime is a conscious employment and promotion of femininity and sexuality. Brown expresses distinctly forthright views in her defence of pre-marital sex and women's right to a satisfying sexual relationship.

Those of her readers who might be "totally, horribly, hideously, irrevo-cably offended by this whole discussion of sex", she unapologetically advises to "skip the whole book" as it is "written for girls who may not marry but who are not necessarily planning to join a nunnery" (69). For Brown, a "sexy woman" is simply "a woman who enjoys sex" and that implies "accept[ing] yourself as a woman... with all the functions of a woman.... Being sexy means that you accept all the parts of your body as worthy and lovable" (65). Moreover, in Brown's opinion, sex should be used strategically as a bargaining tool and "powerful weapon for a single girl in getting what she wants from life, i.e., a husband or steady male companionship" (70). She even suggests that a woman should withhold intercourse in an act of sexual blackmail: "a single woman who doesn't deny her body regularly and often to get what she wants, i.e., married or more equitable treatment from her boy friend, is an idiot".

These final comments point towards the contradictions and/or limita-tions of Brown's argument: while she endorses a single woman's right to work and sexual freedom, she understands these developments as part of a tactical manoeuvre to increase the chances of marriage. Unlike other 1960s single women who have to marry in an act of social survival – or, as Marilyn French writes in *The Women's Room*, women have to arm themselves with "the title of *Mrs*, property of some men", to feel "stronger in the world" (52) – Brown's accomplished Singleton can make demands and marry "eligible" men – "single, reasonably attractive and introduceable to your friends" (17).[7] Marriage remains a primary goal on the single woman's agenda but it is no longer conceived as an enforced and self-denying patriarchal norm. As Brown notes in the introduction to the 2003 edition, "[a]mong single women I know, being with a man in a loving relationship is as natural as grape juice" (xiii). Moreover, she also reinforces her belief in sexuality as a route to female empowerment: "sex... is enjoyed by single women who participate not to please a man as might have been the case in olden times but to please *themselves*" (xiii; emphasis in original). In this way, Brown is not only, as has been suggested, "a child of the Sexual Revolution" but her ideas also hold relevance for contemporary Girlie feminists who revive the notion of femininity/sexuality as power (Whelehan, *Feminist Bestseller* 28).

Brown's important role in shaping the ideas and aspirations of young women from the mid-1960s through to the 1990s is exemplified by a later career move when she took over as Editor-in-Chief of *Cosmopoli-tan* magazine in 1965. As critics have observed, Brown's book already contains "the germs of the *Cosmopolitan* philosophy" that is designed "for young women who want to do better" (28). In the 32 years that she remained at the magazine, she introduced a similar emphasis on self-improvement and discipline, the use of first-person narratives and personal anecdotes,[8] and the idea of a hard won, commercial femininity dependent on perfectly applied make-up and appropriately styled clothing.[9] Imelda Whelehan has recently discussed the underlying principles and shortcomings of the *Cosmo* attitude:

> Brown is a pragmatist in her offered solutions to the palpable inequalities of men's and women's lives… [It] is based on an acceptance that it is a man's world and that men behave differently from women… it encourages women to fight their corner as individuals rather than encourage any more radical social challenges.
>
> (29–33)

Comparing Brown to her contemporary Betty Friedan, Whelehan describes two different trajectories for women in a post-war context: while Friedan argues for women's agency beyond the home, Brown is seen to "offer a more practical set of propositions around making the best of the feminine assets you have" (29–30).[10] Whereas Friedan rejects the mystique of feminine fulfilment, Brown encourages her readers to "practice your femininity", undermining the notion of feminine essence or nature (*Sex and the Single Girl* 61). In contrast to Friedan's bleak imagery of the "comfortable concentration camp", Brown's tone is characteristically optimistic, confident and light-hearted, indicative of her status as a self-help guru. As she spurs on her readers, "I'm counting on you to enjoy the good [days], make life special for people around you because you've got the love, compassion, the energy, the need inside of you to *do* that! Would you please get started!" (xix; emphasis in original).

Friedan's and Brown's outlooks have both been instrumental and influential in the construction of modern womanhood and the figure of the Singleton. Brown's core ideas – in particular, her belief in feminine/sexual power – are appealing to a late-twentieth-century female audience that celebrates the freedoms of single life and the material independence afforded by their jobs. However, these contemporary Singletons do not necessarily share Brown's self-confidence and discipline and, instead, they are characterized by a more Friedan-inspired sense of struggle. Earlier representations of the Singleton also engage variously with the problematics/joys of single life. Hailed as a breakthrough on American television, *The Mary Tyler Moore Show* (1970–1977) followed Brown's celebration of the single girl in its focus on an independent career woman as the central character. The series portrays the adventures of Mary Richards (Moore), a single woman in her thirties, who leaves her home town and moves to Minneapolis after breaking off a relationship with her boyfriend of 2 years. Importantly and innovatively for the time, Mary is not widowed/divorced or seeking a man to support her but she has chosen to pursue a career. The opening montage depicts Mary's journey to the city and is accompanied by the show's famous theme song (performed by Sonny Curtis) whose lyrics refer to the ending of her relationship and making a fresh start: "How will you make it on your own? This world is awfully big, and girl, this time you're all alone", concluding with words of encouragement to the newly single Mary, "you might just make it after all". Mary proves that she is more than capable of "making it" on her own when she applies for a secretarial job at TV station WJM-TV only to be offered the less well paid but more prestigious position of associate producer. Mary accepts the challenge, and for the next seven seasons that the show ran for, we witness her professional and private exploits and encounters, most notably with her tough-but-likeable boss Lou Grant (Edward Asner) and her neighbour Rhoda Morgenstern (Valerie Harper).

As Bonnie Dow has noted in her discussion of feminism and television, the series can easily be decoded in terms of a feminist equal-opportunity discourse with Mary as a representative of liberated womanhood (*Prime-Time Feminism* 30). Mary's rejection of the possibility of marriage in favour of an independent working life epitomizes the second wave's call for women's public empowerment. Yet, as Dow writes, Mary is only a "token woman" in the all-male enclave of the WJM-TV newsroom: "Mary's isolation as the sole female [at her workplace] and her portrayal as the only completely successful and fulfilled female in *Mary Tyler Moore* are evidence of her tokenism" (48). She gives up a bigger salary for the title of producer and – as we learn in a later episode – accepts the fact that she earns less than her male predecessor with her characteristic cheerfulness and good humour. As the likeable token woman, Mary "does not begin her job with the presumption of equality; rather, she will have to earn it" (31).[11] However, as Dow concludes, "in the end, Mary's no one's equal. She is inferior to other, specifically male, characters in the public realm...and she is superior to other female characters in the private realm, where her success and general happiness are a marked contrast to the other women" (48).

If the 1970s single woman was characterized by good-humoured tokenism, the backlash years of the 1980s produced a very different

Singleton who discarded traditionally "nice", feminine qualities and replaced them with masculine professionalism and aggression. While the narrative premise of *Mary Tyler Moore* revolved around the question of whether single girl Mary could make it on her own, the following decade gave rise to a number of Singletons who rose beyond such considerations. The eponymous main character of *Murphy Brown* (1988–1998) is no longer a struggling and underpaid assistant producer in local news but a powerful news anchor of prime-time magazine *FYI*. Unlike Mary, Murphy (Candice Bergen) is an award-winning media "star" and she has made it to the top of her profession by being abrasive and competitive. A recovering alcoholic who in the show's first episode returns to her job after a stay at the Betty Ford clinic, Murphy has none of Mary Richards's amiability and she is unashamedly difficult and outspoken – she is so relentless that she even causes one of her interviewees to die of a heart attack while being on air ("The Unshrinkable Murphy Brown"). With her characteristic deep voice, severe tailoring and androgynous name, Murphy has been described as "a male persona in female body" and an embodiment of liberal feminism's demands on women to adopt a male model of work (Japp 71). However – bearing in mind that these are backlash-ridden times – Murphy has supposedly taken this professional ambition too far, and in order to compete in a male world, she becomes "an extreme version of it, a caricature of the consequences of liberal feminism" (Dow, *Prime-Time Feminism* 142). Much of the comedy derives from the fact that, while rich and famous, Murphy is not a "real woman" – even her pregnancy during the 1991–1992 season and her later status as a single mother are used to reinforce Murphy's lack of femininity and her unsuitability for motherhood.[12] As Dow has suggested, *Murphy Brown* can be discussed at once as "an affirmation of women's progress" and "a reminder of the problems such progress has created" (139). The sitcom acts as a comment on the personal costs of professional success and the tensions between work and motherhood. A product of the 1980s backlash against women "having it all", "Murphy embodies the belated recognition that it is not possible all-at-once to do the deal, cook the dinner, give a man good lovin', and still flounce about with a chirpy Mary Tyler Moore bob and a smile" (quoted in Dow, *Prime-Time Feminism* 138). Yet, at the same time, *Murphy Brown* can also be said to leave "room for ambivalence": the show does not argue for the impossibility of combining careerism and motherhood but rather highlights the difficulties inherent in this choice; it makes some claims about women's supposed biological imperatives but it does not, in turn, make use of

Murphy's motherhood to further essentialist ideas about how becoming a mother might change a woman's thinking and behaviour (160).

While Murphy Brown's Singleton lifestyle offers some scope for interpretation, this is not necessarily the case with other, more one-dimensional backlash scenarios that encourage women to choose between "a womanly existence and an independent one" (Faludi 490). As we have seen in the previous chapter, 1980s representations of deranged single women were employed by the media to legitimize the repudiation of feminism and the return of women to their domestic roles as wives/mothers. In *Fatal Attraction* (1987), Alex Forrest (Glenn Close) is forcefully prevented from "having it all", and her joint desires to succeed in her career and have a child with her married lover are depicted as equivalent to madness and ultimately result in death. The backlash's demonization of the professional single woman continues to have a powerful deterring impact upon subsequent generations as the postfeminist Singleton is still troubled by Alex Forrest's caution-ary tale. However, there are also concerted efforts to deconstruct and subvert this negative and one-sided stereotype. Accordingly, the film adaptation of *Bridget Jones's Diary* (2001) opens with Bridget's realiza-tion that she is "about to turn into Glenn Close in *Fatal Attraction*" and her proactive decision "to take control of my life and start a diary to tell the truth about Bridget Jones". Similarly, in *Sex and the City* (1997), Candace Bushnell emphasizes that "there is nothing wrong" with the "smart, attractive, successful" single women in New York, insisting that "they're not crazy or neurotic. They're not *Fatal Attraction*" (25). Instead of readily accepting the backlash's pessimistic portrayals of unmarried career women, these postfeminist Singletons are also influenced by Brown's *Sex and the Single Girl*-style celebrations of female indepen-dence and sexuality that are revitalized in 1990s Girl discourse (see Chapter 4). Contemporary Girlies proclaim their "freedom" to adopt a sexualized/feminine image, conceptualizing a "new woman" who is self-assured and comfortable with her femininity and her sexual difference.

These 1990s depictions of the Singleton have been described as "pro-woman" but "anti-feminist", taking for granted women's right to educa-tion, career and wealth while repackaging these feminist principles into feminine issues. As L. S. Kim has argued in relation to *Ally McBeal* (1997–2002), this pro-woman/anti-feminist stance is illustrated by programmes that represent female protagonists in roles that are categorically strong and empowering but then deflate and feminize their feminist capaci-ties. Ally (Calista Flockhart) and her colleagues are Harvard Law School graduates, working in an up-and-coming Boston law firm and enjoying financial independence and social equality. As she notes, "I've got it great, really, good job, good friends, loving family, total freedom and long bubblebaths. What else could there be?" In Kim's framework, Ally's position as a liberated woman is sabotaged by her constant search for the missing element in her life – a man. Ally admits that, even though she is "a strong working woman", her existence "feels empty without a man" and, unlike her 1970s precursor Mary Richards, she "doesn't want to make it on her own". Kim objects that Ally remains trapped in "a state of pseudoliberation" as her education and professional credentials have not gained her personal fulfilment or self-understanding and her main strategy for success and happiness is "through sexuality" (321, 332). Following Kim's logic, Ally emerges as a "self-objectifying, schizophrenic woman" and a "falsely empowered image", too self-diminishing and indecisive to bear the feminist label (332, 323).

Rather than establishing an antithetical relationship between Ally's feminine and feminist, private and public traits, I maintain that her status as a contradictory feminist role model makes her an embodiment of postfeminist heterogeneity. Ally refuses to choose between her professional and personal, feminist and feminine aspirations and she unashamedly declares that she wants to "have it all" – marriage, children and partnership in the law firm. As she states,

> I had a plan. When I was 28, I was gonna be taking my little maternity leave, but I would still be on the partnership track. I would be home, at night, cuddled up with my husband reading "What to Expect When You're Nursing" and trying cases. Big home life, big professional life, and instead, I am going to bed with an inflatable doll, and I represent clients who suck toes. This was not the plan.
>
> (quoted in Moseley and Read 247)

The postfeminist Singleton is unwilling to compromise on her job and relationship ambitions and, despite discouraging setbacks, she perseveres in her attempt to realize her project. Armed with a feminist consciousness, she is alert to the tyranny of femininity that constructs the female subject as a passive object of male desire. Yet, simultaneously, she is also aware of her feminine power and its potential to be deployed in new and liberating ways. This Singleton inhabits an equivocal landscape that re-negotiates feminist, anti-feminist, feminine and patriarchal descriptions of womanhood. Importantly, she does not achieve an equilibrium between these competing forces but she is engaged in a persistent struggle to hold together her various components. As Ally McBeal asserts, "balance is overrated", "I don't want to be balanced", "I like being a mess. It's who I am". Similarly, Bridget Jones reveals that "confusion…is the price I must pay for becoming a modern woman" as she tries to combine her progressive feminist beliefs with her deeply entrenched views about gender and relationships (119). Bridget wants to promote "the Urban Singleton Family" as a "state…every bit as worthy of respect as Holy Wedlock" while simultaneously she is also determined to leave behind her "freakish" single life laden with "fearsome unattractiveness hang-up[s]", "an aching loneliness" and "a gaping emotional hole" (*Edge of Reason* 402; *Bridget Jones's Diary* 27, 244). Bridget's paradoxical outlook is encapsulated and summed up by her New Year's resolution to not "sulk about having no boyfriend, but develop inner poise and authority and sense of self as woman of substance, complete *without* boyfriend, as best way to obtain boyfriend" (2). This epitomizes the Singleton's inherent contradictoriness and illustrates the incoherence and inconsistencies of being feminist, feminine and female in the early twenty-first century.

In fact, postfeminist portrayals of the Singleton still feature backlash myths that record the perceived neuroses of the single, childless, thirty-something career woman. In *Sex and the City*, a fashionable urbanite laments that "the issue of unmarried, older women is conceivably the biggest problem in New York City" while Ally McBeal is reminded by her male colleague that, after the age of 30, she is statistically more likely to be "struck by lightning" than get married (Bushnell 28). Likewise, Bridget is acutely aware of her status as an "unmarried freak" and "love pariah" and she is whipped into high marital panic by the constant prompting and patronizing of her "Smug Married" friends that her "time's running out" and her biological clock is ticking away (*Bridget Jones's Diary* 132, 41; *Edge of Reason* 3). She reveals that "finding a relationship seems a dazzling, almost insurmountable goal" as she has reached her "female sell-by date" (*Bridget Jones's Diary* 144, 213). Bridget's mother condenses and summarizes the novel's backlash element by stating that the modern woman is "just so picky" and has "simply got too much choice" (195). Rather than "pretending to be superdooper whizz-kids" who will not compromise on "anybody unless he's James Bond", Bridget is instructed by her mother to embrace the traditional feminine doctrine to "expect little, forgive much" (*Edge of Reason* 373; *Bridget Jones's Diary* 196).

Bridget is reluctant to follow this old-fashioned feminine path and conform to Jerry Hall's famous adage that "a woman must be a cook in the kitchen and a whore in the sitting room" (*Edge of Reason* 18). Even though she sometimes wishes to be like her mother and she is envious of the preceding generation's "confidence in self", Bridget is unable to shed her doubts about the feminine trajectory to female empowerment and she acknowledges the unnaturalness and artificiality of femininity that is constructed through sheer hard work (*Edge of Reason* 371; *Bridget Jones's Diary* 66). As she puts it,

> being a woman is worse than being a farmer – there is so much harvesting and crop spraying to be done: legs to be waxed, underarms shaved, eyebrows plucked, feet pumiced, skin exfoliated and moisturized . . . The whole performance is so highly tuned you only need to neglect it for a few days for the whole thing to go to seed. Sometimes I wonder what I would be like if left to revert to nature – with a full beard . . . spots erupting, long curly fingernails like Struwelpeter . . . Is it any wonder girls have no confidence? (30)

Bridget is clearly familiar with feminist analyses that investigate the disciplinary practices of femininity that are part of an oppressive system of sexual subordination. Yet, she also admits that feminine discipline and performance provide her with a sense of identity and sexual power that "everyone is sensing" and "wanting a bit of" (66). As a "child of *Cosmopolitan*", she has been "traumatized by supermodels and too many quizzes" and she knows that "neither my personality nor my body is up to it if left to its own devices" (59). Bridget embodies a paradoxical position that combines censure with participation, denouncing as well as endorsing feminist and feminine values. The postfeminist Singleton's pluralistic stance has not only been condemned by critics as a "joke" at the expense of the feminist movement but Bridget's own love interest Mark Darcy also finds fault with, what he considers to be, her indecisiveness (Whelehan, *Helen Fielding*). As he notes, "a woman must know what she believes in, otherwise how can you believe in her yourself?" (*Edge of Reason* 253).

   In effect, Bridget's predicament is not related to her insecurity or inconclusiveness about her beliefs but it stems from her " 'Having It All' syndrome" and her unwillingness to sacrifice *either* her feminist *or* feminine, her public *or* private aspirations (*Bridget Jones's Diary* 71). She remains caught in a tension between her romantic longings, her feminist awareness, her feminine performance and her professional objectives. She is anxious that her feminist beliefs in equality and independence are incompatible with her femininity or, quite simply, that feminism has undermined and ruined her chances of having a meaningful heterosexual relationship. As she provocatively declares, "after all, there is nothing so unattractive to a man as strident feminism" (20). This statement's self-evident "truth" is reinforced by Bridget's later realization that her happy ending with Mark Darcy has been delayed by his misperception of her as a "radical feminist" and "literary whizzwoman" (236). While Mark's first impression of her relies on a flawed description by her smug married friends, Bridget herself has helped to create this image as during their first meeting she claims to be reading Susan Faludi's *Backlash* in order to give herself an aura of intellectual credibility.

Bridget and her Singleton friends have clearly inherited feminism's language of empowerment and agency that enables them to progress in their careers and renounce male "emotional fuckwittage" as "SHITTY, SMUG, SELF-INDULGENT BEHAVIOUR" (20, 127; emphasis in original). Bridget's feminist awareness allows her to turn down Daniel Cleaver's initial attempts to draw her into a sexual relationship without "getting involved" and she indignantly dismisses his overtures as "fraudulently flirtatious, cowardly and dysfunctional" (33). She seeks to advance the single woman's right to an earnest and lasting partnership and she refuses to be demeaned to a casual sexual liaison. Bridget wants to champion the unmarried state as a valuable identity and she aims to counter the mythologies of abject single femininity that proliferate in popular culture and among her smug married friends. In what amounts to a Singleton manifesto, Bridget's friend Shazzer proclaims,

> there's more than one bloody way to live: one in four households are single, most of the royal family are single, the nation's young men have been proved by surveys to be *completely unmarriageable*, and as a result there's a whole generation of single girls like me with their own incomes and homes who have lots of fun and don't need to wash anyone else's socks.
>
> (42; emphasis in original)

"Singletondom" thus asserts itself against "Middle-England propaganda" as "a normal state in the modern world", deserving of respect (*Edge of Reason* 402).

Bridget Jones's Diary emphasizes the difficulties of the almost quixotic project of "having it all", centring on the Singleton's persistent failure to live up to her ideals and her endeavour to combine her diverse longings. Critics have sought to polarize Bridget's inherent tension between the confident paragon she aspires to be and her striving, imperfect self as a feminist/feminine, public/personal dichotomy. Accordingly, the novel's "key contradiction" can be found in the gap between "the autonomous career women" who populate Singleton narratives and "the rather pathetic romantic idiots" they become in their relationships (Whelehan, *Helen Fielding* 42). This line of criticism relies on a perception of feminism/career as incompatible with femininity/romance and it presents Bridget as a divided, schizophrenic individual, torn between her image as an assertive and public feminist and a self-deprecating and private *femme*. Contrastingly, I maintain that Bridget's struggle is not so much to do with her choice between feminism and femininity, job and relationship, but it is associated with her determination to "have it all". The novel sets up a friction between Bridget's ideal, balanced persona and her chaotic, genuine self, depicting the Singleton's journey through self-doubt (aided by a vast amount of self-help books) to the understanding that "realness" is the only guarantee for happiness.

Ultimately, it is Mark Darcy's admiration for Bridget's genuineness that makes her appreciate her natural, messy identity in favour of the ideal and book-learned self she aspires to incarnate. It is Bridget's "realness" and gaucheness that apparently win Mark's heart, the fact that she is not "lacquered over" like "all the other girls" (237). Bridget is wanted and desired, not despite but because of her imperfections and her persistent failure to remake herself in another image, as thinner, more poised, more intellectual. The film adaptation translates this celebration of Bridget's chaotic self into Mark's revelation that he likes her "just as [she is]". Bridget's Singleton friends react to this statement with utter astonishment as it exposes their elaborate self-improvement schemes as futile and even reactionary. Bridget's lack of control proves to be her most loveable trait and thus she is rewarded for being chaotic, for being "no good at anything. Not men. Not social skills. Not work. Nothing" (224). Bridget's fallibility and haplessness come to be seen as the character's passport to happiness as she realizes that her "natural" self is infinitely preferable to a fictitious one and that being "real" and out of control is what makes her attractive (376). Importantly, the last entry in her diary is stripped of any weight and calorie updates and it confidently declares that she has "finally realized the secret of happiness with men" (307). Ironically, Bridget finds wisdom in the maternal advice to "do as your mother tells you" (307) – a point that is reinforced in Fielding's 1999 sequel when Mrs Jones meaningfully proclaims that "it doesn't make any difference what you look like...You just have to be real... You have to be brave and let the other person know who you are and what you feel" (376, 377).

In this sense, *Bridget Jones's Diary* discards the notion of a perfect feminine or feminist identity in its embrace of postfeminist/postfeminine "chaos" as the site of fulfilment. The book's optimistic and humorous ending reinforces the Singleton's unfailing belief in her right to heterogeneity and contradictoriness. Negotiating the conflicting demands of heterosexual romance and professional achievement, feminine embodiment and feminist agency, the contemporary version of the Singleton creates a new postfeminist/postfeminine subject position that complicates female identity rather than defining it. "Having it all" comes to be seen not only as a distinct possibility for twenty-first-century femaleness but also as an unavoidable dilemma that the postfeminist/postfeminine woman has to confront and struggle with.

8
Fighting It: The Supergirl

"Action heroines are a new breed of...female protagonists", Elizabeth Hills notes, emphasizing the transgressive and transformative nature of female characters who confound the masculine/feminine dualism (38). The modern-day action heroine does not adhere to the stereotypical "men act and women appear" polarization but she problematizes the critical framework that constructs the notions of passive femininity and active masculinity in terms of diametrical opposition and mutual exclusivity (Berger 46). As Yvonne Tasker reveals, at the most fundamental level, images of the active heroine disrupt "any clear set of critical distinctions between passivity, femininity and women on the one hand and activity, masculinity and men on the other" (77). This new type of heroine is far from being immobile and passive: she fights, she shoots, she kills, solves crimes and rescues herself and others from dangerous situations. She has been described as a "sheroe" who is "in full command of the narrative, carrying the action in ways that have normally been reserved for male protagonists" (Matrix 1; Brown 56). In effect, she adopts a number of characteristics and attitudes that have been deemed masculine or male and she challenges the essentialist dichotomy that denies women recourse to action and strength as means to empowerment. For that reason alone, "the very presence of the female action-adventure hero...is noteworthy" and it can be discussed as a symptom of and a response to feminist analyses that seek to undermine the binary systems of gendered identity (Helford 293). Elyce Rae Helford maintains that "we would not have female action-adventure heroes without a feminist...consciousness" and she defines the active heroine as "composed equally of her story, affirmative action, equal opportunity, and repudiation of gender essentialism and traditional feminine roles" (293).

Yet, at the same time as representing female force and activity, the action heroine has also been the target of critiques that interpret her as a compromised and even conservative figure. She is censured for her heroic/individualistic status that ultimately turns her into a token – an isolated symbol of empowered womanhood – far "stronger and faster than a typical woman" and displaying "new varieties of toughness that few real women can obtain" (Helford; Inness, *Tough Girls* 8, 179). While her individual greatness offers an alluring fantasy of transcendence and power in "a society where women are too commonly raped, assaulted, and murdered", her tokenism also works to secure the status quo as it glorifies the exception in order to "obscure the limits of mobility" and "the rules of the game of success" within this system (Inness 8; Cloud 122, 123). Moreover, the female action-adventure hero has also been criticized for her inability to shed and denounce all feminine signifiers and, as such, "the toughness of even the toughest women is limited, confined, reduced, and regulated" (Inness 178). Critics take issue with the fact that femininity remains a manifest component of the active heroine, as a visible sign of gender conformity or as a polar opposite that she wants to distance herself from by embracing a masculinized image. In this way, she is depicted as a "schizophrenic character", "split between traditionally feminine and masculine traits and sometimes strongly ambivalent about this division, suggesting that being tough is not 'normal' for women" (Inness 144, 149).

In this chapter, I want to complicate this notion of self-division and argue that the postfeminist/postfeminine action heroine inhabits a non-dualistic space characterized by the interaction of seemingly irreconcilable opposites. The action heroine's conflicting identifications involve a continuous play between passivity and activity, vulnerability and strength, feminism and femininity, individualism and communality. Each action heroine has diverse ways of bringing together these components and her negotiations can take the form of an apparently unproblematical alliance of contraries or, more interestingly, a painful and alienating struggle between binaries. I maintain that the contemporary action heroine has to be conceptualized from the outset as an intrinsically ambiguous persona who walks a tightrope to achieve an almost impossible balance. No portrayal of the action-adventure heroine is ever straightforward and unequivocal, allowing a definitive resolution of her inherent contradictions. As Sherrie Inness observes, "ambiguity" is "an essential element of tough women in the popular media" as "we are always confronted with a messy and contradictory message about women's toughness" (49). Inness reveals that female action heroes can "offer women new role models, but their toughness may also bind women more tightly to traditional feminine roles" (5). The action-adventure heroine is either portrayed as a semi-tough pretender to male power who is ultimately too feminine to be as effectual as her male counterpart; or depicted as a de-feminized male impersonator, reinforcing the link between masculinity and toughness. She performs a paradoxical cultural function as she both contests and reaffirms normative absolutes and stereotypes, simultaneously helping "to change how people perceive women's gender roles and to support mainstream notions about how women should act and look" (49).[1] In this sense, the action heroine embodies and projects contradictory values and meanings: she is both a feminist icon and a patriarchal token, comprising feminine and masculine, passive and active elements and encouraging women to adhere to traditional roles and also to challenge them.

Consequently, as Elizabeth Hills writes, "action heroines represent something of a methodological crisis": they "cannot easily be contained, or productively explained, within a theoretical model which denies the possibility of female subjectivity as active or full" (39). Hills is adamant that the transgressive potential of these female characters cannot be appreciated via binary frameworks and conventional theories that try to "impose a rigid and habituated explanation onto a new and alternative figure" and "claim to know in advance what female bodies are capable of doing" (39, 44). In effect, the assemblage of the terms "action" and "heroine" alters the nature of both structures to "become something beyond both" (46).[2] The action heroine thus epitomizes the multiple subject and agency positions that become available to women in a twenty-first-century context. The concepts of subject and object, man and woman (among others) are deconstructed and reinterpreted and it is this resignification of accepted terms and identities that can be witnessed through the figure of the action heroine. The male warrior-hero material is reconstituted in an attempt to fracture and reinvent the gendered identity of the action hero – in Tasker's words, we need to "re-examine the past" and find "there images whose meanings are less simple than they might once have appeared" (110). Accordingly, the female action hero has to be theorized outside a binary rationale that produces an overly simplistic and dualistic interpretation and cannot account for the changing representations of active women. Our critical discussions cannot be restricted to the polarizations that have framed images of female strength and activity but we now have to analyse the action heroine as a complex, multivalent figure that can be decoded in a number of ways.

I contend that postfeminism represents this new mode of conceptualizing the action-adventure heroine as a composite character who exceeds the logic of non-contradiction. As I have suggested in this book, the postfeminist frontier discourse is characterized by a double gesture that exploits in-between spaces in an attempt to undermine totalizing dichotomies. Postfeminism provides an alternative way of comprehending the figure of the action heroine as an "open image" that can be "interpreted, read and to an extent repopulated" (Macdonald, "Drawing the Lines" 22–3).[3] Within this postfeminist framework, the action-adventure heroine can be interpreted as a polysemic character who is engaged in a perpetual struggle that generates multiple meanings, readings and uses. Moreover, I propose that the new breed of action-adventure heroines finds its postfeminist/postfeminine expression in the "Supergirl" who emerges in 1990s popular culture and who not only destabilizes the hierarchal structure of dualistic constraints but crosses and transcends these binaries altogether. In particular, I argue that the postfeminist Supergirl reshapes and transforms the distinctions between masculinity and femininity, human and monster, good and evil, feminism and femininity, individualism and collectivity, conformity and resistance. The Supergirl displays a feminine body along with a feminist consciousness and a masculine assertiveness and power. She is set apart by her superhuman/supernatural abilities but, at the same time, she longs to be "normal" and part of a community. She fights the forces of evil and darkness (variously manifested by crime, terrorism, vampires and beauty queens) by internalizing them, understanding and tasting what she is supposed to battle and destroy. Paradoxically, she "protects the line which separates good from evil by crossing it, by becoming more and more other" (Petrova 10–11). The Supergirl can be discussed as a liminal or marginal character who evades categorization through her hybridization of conventional gender roles and human norms, her moral and ethical ambiguity and her interpretative potential. She combines qualities associated with masculinity and femininity, revealing the artifice of that opposition and undermining the boundaries that safeguard dualistic concepts. The Supergirl refuses to be contained within these simplistic and totalizing classifications as she sabotages and collapses the barrier between them, moving *across* binaries in order to establish an impure and ambiguous "in-betweenness".

This multifaceted and heterogeneous persona has been portrayed in contemporary popular culture both in cinema and fiction and she is exemplified by Stephanie Plum, a lingerie shop assistant cum bounty hunter; Olivia Joules, a beauty journalist cum spy; and Gracie Hart, a tough and tomboyish FBI agent who turns into a beauty queen.[4] These Supergirls proudly and confidently proclaim their intention to embrace a contradictory and pluralistic subjectivity that cannot be explained by a monological framework. As Helen Fielding's heroine Olivia Joules declares,

> I'm all I've got.... I'm going to be complete in myself. I'm not going to give a shit about anything anymore. I'm going to work out my own good and bad.... I'm going to search this shitty world for some beauty and excitement and I'm going to have a bloody good time.
>
> (14; emphasis in original)

In an act of self-transformation, she sheds her old identity and body – Rachel Pixley – and reinvents/renames herself as the glamorous Olivia Joules who has her own "Rules for Living" (93). As Olivia, she arms herself with "a great body as a useful tool in life" and sheds her "old plump self" for a "new thin self" (36). Olivia consciously manipulates her new image in order to achieve professionally and socially what may not have been available to her in her previous embodiment. At the same time, she insists that she has transgressed traditional binary gender codes that equate femininity with helplessness and passivity:

> she had painstakingly erased all womanly urges to question her shape, looks, role in life, or effect upon other people. She would watch, analyse and conform to codes as she observed them, without allowing them to affect or compromise her own identity.
>
> (12)

Olivia regards femininity as a means to empowerment and she deliberately "use[s] tears to get her own way" and extract information from the suspected Al-Qaeda terrorist Pierre Feramo (215). In a similar manner, she decides that, on her secret mission to track Osama Bin Laden, a "hairdryer is a more important tool than the nerve-agent dispenser" (263). Olivia's unashamed mix of femininity and power make her a "natural spy" and ultimately help her to avert a bomb attack that threatens the annual Oscar ceremony (249).

This Supergirl expresses and lives by the popular postfeminist/Girl Power belief that women can "handle the tools of patriarchy and don't need to be shielded from them" (Baumgardner and Richards 141). The postfeminist action heroine insists that the cultural and social weapons that have been identified by second wave feminists as instruments of subordination and objectification are no longer being exclusively wielded against women but are sometimes wielded by them. Her ability to be both beautiful and strong – a "perfectly accessorized and feminine killing machine" – makes the Supergirl an embodiment of "Girlie" feminism, the "intersection of culture and feminism" that claims femininity as a source of power (Karras 7, 4; Baumgardner and Richards 136). Accordingly, women can be successful and strong by "holding tight to that which once symbolized their oppression" and infusing the old and vilified signifiers of helpless femininity with new meanings of strength and agency (Baumgardner and Richards 137). As Helford writes, contemporary action heroines "are not just convinced [that] they can act out their 'choices' through individual (heroic) effort"; they also want to "recuperate the 'choice' of wearing high heels … and makeup to achieve their success" (296).

In the Hollywood film *Miss Congeniality* (2000), the tough and masculinized FBI agent Gracie Hart (Sandra Bullock) is forced to re-evaluate her dismissal of beauty queens as "air-head bimbos" and "performing monkeys in heels" who are "catering for some misogynistic Neanderthal mentality" when she goes undercover at the Miss United States Pageant to prevent a bomb attack. The film's central plot device resides in Gracie's Pygmalion-like transformation from "Dirty Harriet" – "a woman without a discernible smidgeon of oestrogen" – into a "unique" "lady" and "the nicest, sweetest, coolest girl at the pageant". Her initial rugged uncouthness and aggressiveness mark her as a "make-a-man of yourself" action heroine who believes that in order to function effectively within the threatening macho world of the action scenario (or, in this case, the FBI), she has to adopt masculine qualities (Stables 20). In Gracie's eyes, her refusal to dress and brush her hair is part of being a "real agent" who works "24/7" and in effect "[is] the job". She gradually comes to realize that her complete dedication to her masculine federal agent persona makes her an "incomplete" person who, "in place of friends and relationships", has "sarcasm and a gun". Her introduction to the world of feminine beauty proves to be an educational and psychological journey, "one of the most rewarding and liberating experiences of [her] life". In Girlie feminist terms, Gracie learns to accept and embrace her newly discovered femininity as a source of personal fulfilment and power. Sexualization and feminization come to be seen as important elements of female heroic representation – as Helford notes, there is an "increased emphasis on traditional femininity in looks and behaviour (in various combinations and to various degrees)" (296) – but, in this context, the action heroine's sexualized image is not understood as disempowering or denigrating as it is always combined with a demonstration of her agency, strength and self-reliance.

The postfeminist Supergirl does not assume a masculine identity in her active/heroic role but she remains garbed in the signifiers of stereotypical feminine attractiveness. In Jeffrey Brown's words, the notion of a "petite, pretty woman in a dress kicking ass" denies the narrative logic that allows viewers to "deride the heroine as a butch or as a woman trying to be a man" (63). In many ways, the feminine Supergirl is a reaction against the prevalence of the "hardbody, hardware, hard-as-nails heroine" who dominates the action scenarios of the 1980s and early 1990s and who is positioned as "phallic" or "figuratively male" (Brown 52; Hills 40). Famously embodied by the characters of Ripley (Sigourney Weaver) in the *Alien* films (1979, 1986, 1992, 1997) and Sarah Connor (Linda Hamilton) in *Terminator 2: Judgement Day* (1991), the hard-bodied heroine has been perceived as a man in a woman's body or a woman trying to be a man, as she rejects all feminine attributes to build up a muscular/masculine body and a macho posturing.[5] The postfeminist Supergirl confounds dualistic gender codes that assume that since the action role has always been conceived as male, to put a woman in it she too must, or wants to, be a man. She undermines the reasoning of a gendered binary that locks together the terms "masculine" and "strong", "feminine" and "weak". Importantly, the Supergirl combines femininity and strength, revising both concepts to create a new postfeminine signifying link between them. The traditional gender images and codes persist but they become dissociated from their previous significations and correlations to physical sex, so that they interrogate rather than support gender norms.

This postfeminist logic rejects previous understandings of the action heroine as either too tough or not tough enough, as butch "pseudo-males" who refuse and expunge femininity as a female weakness, or as "battling, lip-glossed Barbies" whose femininity ultimately compromises their feminist potential and active heroine status (Stables 20). The Supergirl resists dualistic formulations that seek to define her as either feminist or non-feminist/feminine, subversive or conservative, female or male. She blurs these distinctions as she opens up new, alternative ways to construct and depict female heroism and subjectivity. However, the Supergirl's contradictory status also ensures that, to a varying degree, she is engaged in a social and emotional struggle as she tries to accommodate her own ambiguity and complexity. In her most challenging incarnations, the Supergirl does not inhabit a harmonious space of plurality and pure difference, a utopia of choice where women can "have it all". Rather than celebrating an effortless alliance of opposites, the Supergirl endeavours to find a way to negotiate her inherent paradoxes. She seeks to come to terms with her own heterogeneity that ultimately leaves her ostracized from the very community she protects and without the security of fixed boundaries and standards.

The presence of this troubled and tormented Supergirl points to the more ambiguous and contradictory aspects of postfeminist discourse that ultimately does not dissolve conventional gender positions but rather hybridizes and resignifies them. We have to take into account the fact that "the images that the [action] form has generated are very far from being the transparent signifiers of a simplistic...hierarchy" and do not operate on "some blank page but within cultural contexts which are crowded with competing images and stereotypes" (Tasker 165, 152). The signifiers of strength and power that have traditionally been associated with masculinity cannot simply be written over onto the female/feminine body. As Sara Buttsworth suggests, the "tensions between exploring new character constructions and societal norms continue – even, or perhaps especially, in the figure of the female warrior hero" (190). Critics as well as characters are caught in a dilemma to apply a "both/and" logic and remain perplexed by the slippage between the action heroine as a self-reliant character and a sexual object, an empowered feminist role model and an agent employed by patriarchy. The postfeminist Supergirl contains and advances both readings/meanings, and in her most daring and provocative representations, she battles on the boundary between feminist transgression and patriarchal containment. She becomes the site of intense cultural negotiations where competing definitions of womanhood and power are tested and juxtaposed as well as personal crises that see her wrestle with her own "monstrous" impurities.

One of the best-known action-adventure heroines who emerged in late-twentieth-century popular culture and redefined the genre for a 1990s audience is Buffy Summers (Sarah Michelle Gellar), teenage girl and vampire-slaying champion. *Buffy the Vampire Slayer* (1997–2003) enacts in its title the foundational myth and the premise of the entire series, reflecting the chiastic relationship between the girly connotations of the name "Buffy" and the toughness inherent in the occupation "vampire slayer".[6] As the show's creator Joss Whedon reveals, "I made the title very specifically to say, 'This is what it is.' It wears itself on its sleeve.... It's all there in the title" (quoted in Siemann 129). The "joke" of the cheerleading demon hunter is not a "one-line throwaway gag" but encapsulates Buffy's ongoing struggle with her composite character as the "Chosen One" – who "alone will stand against the vampires, the demons and the forces of darkness" – and as a 16-year-old teenager who wants to do "girlie stuff" (Pender 42; *Welcome to the Hellmouth* 1001; *Faith, Hope and Trick* 3003).[7] Whedon sets up a deliberate contrast between Buffy's girlhood and her heroism and superhuman strength as he consciously (re)employs a number of preconceptions and clichés. As has been noted, "the name 'Buffy' suggests the lightest of lightweight girls of stereotypical limitation – thoughtless, materialistic, superficial" (Wilcox and Lavery xvii–xviii). Yet, this is the name of the heroine who will repeatedly risk and even give her life in her fight against evil demons and inhuman monsters. The show relies on the horror movie convention that sees a "bubblehead blonde" wandering into a dark alley and getting killed but it reverses and resignifies this scenario whereby – emulating second wave activist manoeuvres – the blonde "takes back the night", "takes care of herself and deploys her powers" (quoted in Bellafante, "Bewitching" 83; Chandler 1). Whedon points out that "the idea of Buffy was to…create someone who was a hero where she had always been a victim. That element of surprise, that element of genre busting is very much at the heart of…the series" (quoted in Thompson 4).[8] He admits that the image of the blonde victim has always been "more interesting to [him] than the other women. She was fun, she had sex, she was vivacious. But then she would get punished for it" (quoted in Vint 2). In effect, the blonde girl "keeps dying in horror movies" because "she has no skills" and "isn't expected to be anything but a bimbo" (quoted in Lippert 24).

Whedon is determined to "take that character and expect more from her", deconstructing the label of blonde (that is, dumb) femininity and linking it with notions of power and strength (quoted in Lippert 25). As he suggestively notes, "there are a lot of ways to break new ground without having original thoughts" (25). *Buffy the Vampire Slayer* relies on the resignification and re-visioning of a given script through the parody and reinterpretation of established cinematic concepts and identities. With her long blonde hair and thin, petite frame, Buffy is visibly coded by the conventional signifiers of attractive, helpless and (to some extent) unintelligent femininity. She is "the ultimate femme", "never disturbing the delicate definition of physical femininity" and "a girly girl through and through" (Fudge 3). On her first days in High School and later college, Buffy is described by onlookers as "a major league hottie", projecting a first impression of feminine prettiness rather than toughness and power (*The Initiative* 4007). Buffy herself repeatedly declares that she is "just a girl" but at the same time she constantly confounds and re-imagines

what "a girl" is capable of (*The Gift* 5022). The series foils both viewers' and characters' expectations as it portrays this cute cheerleader as
far from being anyone's victim but a "supremely confident kicker of
evil butt" (quoted in Krimmer and Raval 157). According to Whedon,
Buffy is intended both to be a feminist role model and to subvert the
non-feminine image of the "ironclad hero – 'I am woman, hear me
constantly roar'" (quoted in Harts 88).[9] He constructs Buffy as a feminine warrior whose girlhood is compatible with and even engenders her
empowerment and agency. Yet, he is also cautious to avoid an overly
optimistic alliance of femininity and heroism/power – propagated, for
example, by some forms of Girlie discourse – instead seeking to portray
"the weakness and the vanity and the foibles" of the modern-day action
heroine (88).

Faced with her fate as the "Chosen One" – "the one girl in all the
world... born with the strength and skill to hunt the vampires" – Buffy
reluctantly accepts the demands of her civic role that forces her out
of her natural terrain and community into her predestined place in
a long tradition of vampire slayers (*Welcome to the Hellmouth* 1001).
She is the temporary occupant of a firmly established position and
the present embodiment of a preternatural power that is automatically
transferred onto the next Slayer in line after Buffy's death(s). In her
slaying function, Buffy is supervised by the Watchers' Council, a hierarchical and patriarchal command structure that regards the Slayer as
"the instrument by which we fight" (*Checkpoint* 5012). As Buffy is told,
"the Council remains, the Slayers change. It's been that way from the
beginning" (*Checkpoint* 5012). In this sense, the figure of the Slayer is
ever-changing, ever-singular and forever incarnated by a teenage girl
who is supposed to blindly follow the Council's rules and accept her
"sacred duty" (*What's My Line, Part 1* 2009). Central to the law of the
Council is the proposition "kill vampires and demons", a rule that Buffy
questions from the start when she realizes that the vampire Angel (David
Boreanaz) has a soul and will not hurt her (*Angel* 1007). She refuses to be
moulded into the Council's image of the perfect Slayer as a regimental
soldier and she decides to disregard their orders and "do things my way"
(*What's My Line, Part 2* 2010).

Buffy is determined to maintain "a normal social life as a Slayer"
and does not want her "night job" to interfere with her teenage life
(*Never Kill a Boy on the First Date* 1005). Her girlhood and emotions are
depicted as inherent and empowering elements of her personality, as
"total assets" (*What's My Line, Part 2* 2010). This Supergirl's strength
is not only related to her supernatural and other-worldly power but

also resides to a large degree in her being-in-the-world as a middle-class, teenage American girl who can identify vampires instinctively by their lack of fashion sense (*Welcome to Hellmouth* 1001). As Buffy's Watcher Giles (Anthony S. Head) admits, she does not fit the Slayer profile and "the Slayer handbook" is of no use in her case (*What's My Line, Part 2* 2010). Her successful but unconventional approach to her slaying profession is due to her very "Buffy-ness", her involvement in adolescent life and girlie activities and her disregard for tradition. She fights as a girl in high-heeled boots and fashionable clothes, without ever assuming that this display of femininity jeopardizes her role as the Slayer and her ability as a warrior. Buffy never denigrates herself, nor is her girlhood ever depicted as a debilitating detraction or vulnerability. On the contrary, it is the very source of her empowerment, what differentiates her from other Slayers and helps her to survive and win where others failed and died. Without doubt, as Sherryl Vint notes, she is "more than a sex object, but she doesn't have to deny being sexy in order to be a strong woman" (2).

Buffy rejects her lonely and isolated Slayer position as she fights evil on her own terms and with the help of her teenage friends and her Watcher Giles. Her lasting success as a Slayer is directly attributable to her relationships with the "Scooby gang", her friends Willow (Alyson Hannigan) and Xander (Nicholas Brendon) (*The Witch* 1003). As Joelle Renstrom writes, one of the clearest lessons imparted on *Buffy the Vampire Slayer* is that "emotional connections...are necessary – not just for Buffy the person, but also for Buffy the Slayer" (1). Most problems and challenges are evaluated and solved through shared responsibility and cooperation, literally embodied in season 4 by the figure of the "Superslayer" who conjoins Buffy, Giles, Xander and Willow into a collective "we" in order to defeat the "kinematically redundant, biomechanical demonoid" Adam (*Primeval* 4021; *Goodbye Iowa* 4014). The group becomes a tightly knit and self-declared family that makes use of each member's special talents in their combined fight against the adversities of the Hellmouth (*Family* 5006). Buffy's extraordinary status as "a Slayer with family and friends" establishes narrative momentum towards collectivity and away from the individualist quest narrative typical of the action-adventure genre (*School Hard* 2003; Owen 27). Her attachment to a home and family reconstructs the stereotype of the action-adventure hero as a "tragic figure", "an outsider, often a lounger, a drifter", characterized by "loneliness, rootlessness, and homelessness" (Marchetti 194, 195). Buffy's friends represent an important emotional anchor that binds the Slayer to her humanity and life itself – as the vampire Spike (James Marsters) tells her, "the only reason you've lasted as long as you have is you've got ties to the world" (*Fool for Love* 5007).

Initially – much like a superhuman, adolescent version of the Superwoman – Buffy is confident that she can juggle her personal and professional lives, her slaying mission and her desire to "have a life" and "do something normal" (*The Witch* 1003). She conceptualizes her Slayerdom as something akin to a career choice – a "night job" – and she maintains an ironic distance to her warrior role and duties: "Destructo Girl, that's me", flippantly concluding that "I kill vampires, that's my job" (*Teacher's Pet* 1004; *Ted* 2011). Buffy believes that she can live up to her "superhero" identity and also pursue teenage pastimes like shopping, cheerleading and dating (*The Harvest* 1002; *The Witch* 1003). As she tells Giles, "this is the 90s...and I can do both. Clark Kent has a job. I just wanna go on a date" (*Never Kill a Boy on the First Date* 1005). She attempts to deal with her dual character as Buffy Summers – the archetypal California girl – and Buffy the vampire Slayer by separating these identities. Being "sixteen, and a girl, and the Slayer", she has "at least three lives to contend with, none of which really mesh" (*School Hard* 2003; *Reptile Boy* 2005).

The series becomes increasingly dark and the heroine increasingly disillusioned – again, resembling the fate of the Superwoman – when Buffy realizes that she cannot "take the Slayer out of the girl" as "the two halves can't exist without each other" (Pender 43; *The Replacement* 5003). Over the course of seven seasons, her fight is not only directed against an external danger that seeks to corrupt the order of the world but becomes more internalized when she is forced to admit the complex interactions between her heroic and girly components, the erosion of a "black and white space" and its replacement with a more threatening, potentially destructive ambiguity (*New Moon Rising* 4019). She has to accept that, although she tries to be like other girls, she sometimes is "just one of the troops" and "a real soldier" who thinks about ambush tactics and beheading instead of dates (*Enemies* 3017; *Halloween* 2006). Even though Buffy exists across binary distinctions between masculinity and femininity, toughness and weakness, human collectivity and supernatural singularity, she does not embrace her in-between position. Buffy's internal struggle between her Slayer and girly selves initially takes the form of a social crisis as the former cheerleader and Prom Princess has to relinquish her popularity and become the quintessential outsider in High School, a "crazed" "psycho loony" with whom "nobody cool wants to hang out" (*Homecoming* 3005; *The Pack* 1006).

Buffy's Slayer identity turns her into a "hideous dateless monster", a "freak" who will never have "a happy, normal relationship" (*Never Kill a Boy on the First Date* 1005; *I, Robot – You, Jane* 1008). She believes that her future is "sealed in fate" and "pretty much a non-issue" as she is "stuck in this deal" and "never going to get the chance to find out" what she could have achieved outside the dark alleys and graveyards (*What's My Line, Part 1* 2009).

On a number of occasions, Buffy seeks to escape her calling and looks for opportunities to rid herself of her Slayer persona and/or play out the fantasy of being a damsel in distress. For example, during Halloween, she becomes trapped in the image of helpless femininity when she is transformed by her costume into an eighteenth-century noblewoman (*Halloween* 2006). As she tells her vampiric boyfriend Angel, "I just wanted to be a real girl for once." In similar acts of evasion, Buffy leaves Sunnydale and assumes a new identity after her Slayer self is forced to kill Angel; in another episode, Buffy happily "tak[es] a vacation from me" during a brief spell of invisibility, noting that "for the first time" she is "free of rules and reports", "free of this life" (*Anne* 3001; *Gone* 6011). Buffy's dividedness is almost literalized when she faces a demon who can "split one person in half, distilling personality traits into two separate bodies" (*The Replacement* 5003). While Buffy does not experience the actual identity split (Xander is hit instead), she nonetheless reflects on her own internal contradictions and disunity, noting that there could be "two Buffys", "one with all the qualities inherent in Buffy Summers, and the other one with everything that belongs to the Slayer alone, the strength, the speed, the heritage" (*The Replacement* 5003).

Buffy's identity crisis reaches an existential turning point after her encounters with the First Slayer and Dracula who broaden her understanding of the Slayer's nature. When the First Slayer speaks to her in a vision, she presents a stark contrast to Buffy's own conception of Slayerdom: "I have no speech. No name. I live in the action of death, the blood cry, the penetrating wound. I am destruction. Absolute. Alone.... No friends. Just the kill. We are alone" (*Restless* 4022). Buffy learns from her forebear that her Slayer component, her "truest strength", is in part demonic and has been created at the expense of her humanity (*Get It Done* 7015). Both Dracula and Spike confirm the Slayer's inherent ambiguity, revealing that "every Slayer has a death wish" as her "power is rooted in darkness" (*Fool for Love* 5007; *Buffy vs. Dracula* 5001). Here, the Slayer is portrayed as an isolated warrior and a suicidal loner who "breeds" and "lives death" and for whom "the mission is what matters" (*Potential* 7012; *Lies My Parents Told Me* 7017). Buffy is confronted with her own irrational, dangerous and inhuman side when she recognizes that evil is an integral part of fighting evil. Her dark and supernatural roots make it impossible for her to connect and "be with someone who can take [her] into the light" (*The Prom* 3020). Buffy is attracted to "wicked energy" and, as she puts it, she needs "some monster in her man", and for her, "real love and passion have to go hand in hand with pain and fighting" (*First Date* 7014; *Into the Woods* 5010; *Hush* 4010). More disturbingly, her Slayer identity is also pulling her away from human contact and emotion and "is turning [her] into a stone" (*Intervention* 5018). Being the perfect Slayer means being "too hard to love at all", "being the Slayer ma[kes] [her] different" as it drives her to "cut [herself] off" and "just slip away" (*Intervention* 5018; *Touched* 7020). At the same time, Buffy's human ties – her friends and family – cause her to battle against this self-destructive personality trait and she continues to long for a stable and secure relationship. Importantly, Buffy's later affair with the vampire Spike leaves her unfulfilled and incomplete as she does not wholly "belong in the shadows" either and cannot be "at peace, in the dark" (*Dead Things* 6013; *Normal Again* 6017). As she tells her demon lover, "I could never be your girl....There is nothing good or clean in you. You are dead inside" (*Dead Things* 6013). By the time Buffy finds the strength to break up with him, she is not exaggerating when she says that the relationship is "killing" her, destroying her sense of self (*As You Were* 6015).

As a liminal character, Buffy is situated on the edge between light and dark, human and supernatural, girl and Slayer. As she declares, "nothing's ever simple anymore. I'm constantly trying to work it out. Who to love, or hate, who to trust. It's just like the more I know the more confused I get" (*Lie to Me* 2007). Buffy has to come to terms with the complexity of her role that positions her as not quite ordinary nor strictly human as well as the moral uncertainty of her world in which vampires are not necessarily evil and vampire Slayers inhabit an ambiguous space between binaries. Her discoveries lead her on a path of psychological and emotional isolation as she realizes the Slayer's burden and rejects the notion that she could have a normal life and be "a regular kid" (*What's My Line, Part 1* 2009). Buffy laments that once she "knew what was right. I don't have that anymore.... I don't know how to live in this world if these are the choices" (*The Gift* 5022). This sense of loss and confusion culminates in Buffy's most desperate escape from her clashing selves and the ultimate accomplishment of her Slayer duty when she kills herself in order to avoid the apocalypse. "The hardest thing in this world is to live in it", Buffy proclaims at the end of season

5 as she jumps to her death and surrenders her fight against her warring personae (*The Gift* 5022).

However, *Buffy the Vampire Slayer* does not conclude with this admission of defeat of a capitulated and beaten heroine, and in the following season Buffy is resurrected, "torn" out of heaven where she was "finished", "complete" and "at peace" and brought back to everyday "hell" where "everything … is hard, and bright, and violent" (*After Life* 6003). Buffy is unable to resume her second life and she can only deal with her regained identity crisis by turning into a "reckless general" who wants to win the final battle against the First Evil (*Lies My Parents Told Me* 7017). In order to shield herself from the pain of life, Buffy distances herself emotionally from her friends and family. To the newly resurrected Buffy, "making the hard decisions" means giving up part of her humanity and sacrificing the life of others to safeguard the mission (*Empty Places* 7019). Increasingly, Buffy claims a peremptory right to "draw the line" and decide that "human rules don't apply", "there's only me. I am the law" (*Selfless* 7005). In her egocentric quest, Buffy alienates her friends/family, and during the final season she finds herself expelled from her house and without her social support group (*Empty Spaces* 7019). Ultimately, however – reinforcing the series' focus on collective action and power – Buffy comes to realize that she cannot disallow her inherent contradictions if she wants to win her last battle. Acknowledging that she is the most effective Slayer only because she is also a girl who is connected to people with unique gifts and strengths, Buffy decides to "make some changes from the inside" (*This Year's Girl* 4015). She "redefin[es] the job" by questioning the heroic and patriarchal conventions that structure her universe and resignifying the position of Slayer (*Showtime* 7011). With the help of her friend and witch Willow, she "change[s] the rule" that was made by "a bunch of men who died thousands of years ago" and prescribes that "in every generation, one Slayer is born" (*Chosen* 7022). Buffy's Slayer strength is magically diffused and displaced onto "every girl who could have the power", so that "from now on, every girl in the world who might be a Slayer, will be a Slayer". Buffy actively manufactures a choice and future for herself that will no longer leave her isolated and she creates a collective of Slayers who will work together to fight the forces of evil. Thereby, she also recognizes and accepts her own heterogeneous and constantly changing self: "I'm cookie dough. I'm not done baking. I am not finished becoming to wherever … it is I'm gonna turn out to be…. Maybe one day I'll turn around and realize I am ready. I am cookies…. I am not really thinking that far ahead."

The humorous metaphor of unbaked "cookie dough" points towards the complexity of Buffy's character and highlights her refusal to compartmentalize and divide herself into disparate identities. The ingredients that make up the "Buffy recipe" give rise to a range of seemingly unimaginable mixtures: tough warrior and loyal friend, monster and human, lonely action heroine and loveable girl. The ending of *Buffy the Vampire Slayer* can be interpreted in terms of an acknowledgement of the multiple identity and agency positions that become available in contemporary society and culture while also integrating a message of the collective power of "misfits" that proves compelling to a teenage audience – often under peer pressure to "fit in" – and has clear echoes of other movements, like feminism, that sought social change through collectivist struggle. Buffy rejects the tokenism inherent in her unique position in favour of a community of Slayers who redefine the meaning of their task and restructure the power hierarchies in which they work. The series' conclusion does not necessarily make the point that contradictions can be resolved but it argues for an acceptance of the identity puzzles and entanglements that emerge in the context of changing social norms and conventions.

Commentators have criticized this "magic" creation of choice and they take issue with the suggestion that opposition and resistance can be transcended. In their search for the "real Buffy", critics seek to unravel "the ambivalent position Buffy occupies between authentic adolescent and supernatural Slayer" (Pender 36). They highlight the series' "mixed messages about feminism and femininity", upholding a dualistic logic that understands "Buffy's form and Buffy's content" as "distinct and incompatible categories" (Fudge 1; Pender 43). For example, Anne Millard Daughtery condemns the Slayer's feminine exterior on the grounds that "for all the efforts taken to negate the traditional male gaze, Buffy's physical attractiveness is, in itself, objectifying" (151). Buffy's "girl power" is seen as "a diluted imitation of female empowerment" that promotes "style over substance" and ultimately lacks a political agenda (Fudge 3). Buffy is censured for being a "hard candy-coated feminist heroine for the girl-power era" whose "pastel veneer" and "over-the-top girliness in the end compromise her feminist potential".[10] Many critics conclude that "replacing Barbie with Buffy is clearly not the victory that feminism hoped for" and, ultimately, "the series [only] plays at transgression" but "it remains to be seen whether transgressive play can challenge institutional relations of power" (Karras 6; Owen 31).

This line of reasoning relies on a binary framework that sets off feminine powerlessness/oppression against feminist power/critique. In this polarized reading, action heroines are defined by their adoption or their refusal of femininity whereby "Buffy cannot be a feminist because she has a cleavage" (Pender 43). *Buffy the Vampire Slayer* has been discussed as a contemporary version of the 1970s "pseudo-tough", "wanna be" action heroines exemplified by Wonder Woman and Charlie's Angels. As Sherrie Inness has argued, femininity was used in this context as a way to allay the heroine's toughness, tone down and compensate for her assertiveness and display of strength (*Tough Girls*). The threat that the tough woman poses to the patriarchal order is reduced by this connection between women, sexuality and femininity and by the suggestion that a woman's sexual availability and physical attractiveness are in no way diminished by her power. The heroine's actions are explained away and her toughness is undercut in an attempt to mitigate, if not resolve, the uncertainties posed by the strong and self-reliant woman. This mode of understanding establishes femininity as both anti-feminist and non-tough and thus it risks reaffirming essentialist stereotypes of female/feminine vulnerability and inaction. Toughness and strength remain associated with masculinity, and a strong, powerful woman ultimately has to be interpreted as masculine.[11] This construction of femininity and masculinity through a process of mutual exclusion upholds the connection between maleness and toughness and works to ensure male privilege and authority. The suggestion that action heroines are female "men in drag" represents an attempt to secure the masculine/feminine binary in a way that facilitates the dominance of gender absolutism and retains the notions of appropriate behaviour/appearance for men and women. As Jeffrey Brown writes, "rather than aggressiveness being deemed legitimate for women", the non-feminine hard-body is suspected of "transvestism" which reinforces the idea of mutually exclusive gender categories: "If a female character seen as kicking ass must be read as masculine, then women are systematically denied as a gender capable of behaving in any way other than passive" (60–3).

In my eyes, this coding of the action heroine leads to a reification of masculine power/feminine weakness and negates the transgressive potential of the action-adventure heroine who occupies an empowered and heroic position. In this chapter, I have argued for the legitimacy of the active heroine role, interpreting her as a liminal contemporary character who transcends binary formulations and subverts gender frameworks that underlie the concepts of masculine activity and feminine passivity. The postfeminist Supergirl severs the connections between femininity and victimization, negotiating a new, postfeminine stance that is characterized by agency as well as struggle. As I have suggested, Buffy does not resolve her own internal paradoxes but she makes a step towards a reconciliation of her inherent contradictions and heterogeneity. She learns to recognize and accept the complexity of her subject positions and her diverse roles that confront her with a world in which ambiguity is inevitable and "good" and "evil", "right" and "wrong" are slippery concepts. This late-twentieth- and early-twenty-first-century version of the action heroine endeavours to open up new subject spaces between previously antagonistic categories of identification that take into account the interplay between feminism and femininity, agency and passivity, critique and complicity. It is in this gap between dualities that the postfeminist/postfeminine possibilities are revealed for different, more complex and diverse understandings of modern-day womanhood, feminism and femininity.

Afterword

"Men like women. Don't act like a man, even if you are head of your own company. Let him open the door. Be feminine", authors Ellen Fein and Sherrie Schneider advise their readers in the bestselling book *The Rules* which, as its subtitle promises, uncovers the "time-tested secrets for capturing the heart of Mr. Right" (5). Given Fein's and Schneider's other recommendations for single women – which include, never initiating conversation with a man you are interested in, never calling him, never paying for dates, and never accepting a Saturday night date later in the week than Wednesday – one would be permitted the assumption that we are dealing here with an old-fashioned and antiquated advice manual for women, along the lines of Charles Contreras's booklet *How to Fascinate Men* (1953) or Helen Andelin's *Fascinating Womanhood* (1963) that counselled husband-searching women to be "childlike" and display the "spunk and sauciness of a little girl". However, *The Rules* reached the top of the *New York Times* best-seller list by the mid-1990s and its phenomenal success spawned the sequels *The Rules II* (1997) and *The Rules for Marriage* (2001), along with its own range of lipsticks which come in colours like "Felicity" (cocoa brown) and "Hush" (pink). The popularity of books like *The Rules* and *Fascinating Womanhood* – which incidentally was still in print at the turn of the twenty-first century – puts into doubt the suggestion that we have somehow progressed beyond stereotypical views of femininity as an inherently objectifying and victimizing female subject position. Indeed, if this is what modern-day femininity still represents, then we – as feminist cultural critics – should agree with Susan Brownmiller's assertion that "femininity in all respects is a matter of containment", built upon "a recognition of powerlessness" and necessitating a complete boycott of accepted forms of feminine behaviour and appearance (107, 6).

However, as I have sought to demonstrate in this book, for the past 40 years or so – since the advent of second-wave feminism – femininity has undergone a range of interrogations and reinterpretations that make it available for other readings and meanings of female empowerment and agency. I have tried to provide a different conceptualization and understanding of twenty-first-century femininity that accounts for the various and often-conflicting identifications and axes of power upon which modern women's lives are organized. Integral to this reappraisal of femininity has been my belief in the fundamental importance of feminism as a social movement for change. I have chartered the developments and interactions of feminism and femininity, both in popular culture and feminist writings, in relation to concepts of female victimization and power and I have put forward the notion of "post-femininity" to explore the possibilities and limitations of a paradoxical feminine stance that depolarizes the dichotomy between subject and object, victim and perpetrator, power and powerlessness. Importantly, I have not described postfemininity as a denial of a backlash against feminism – hence the existence and popularity of *The Rules* – but I have read the "post-ing" of femininity (and feminism) as a polysemic exercise that combines innovation and conservatism, progress and backlash. My aim here has been to emancipate femininity from a rhetoric of containment – employed by both patriarchal and feminist discourses – and release it into a more diverse future of multiple significations and associations.

In effect, this was also the desired goal of many earlier feminist analyses; Betty Friedan, for example, was adamant that "[w]e need a drastic reshaping of the cultural image of femininity" while Barbara Sichtermann maintained that "[o]ne of the logical tasks facing the feminist movement in its role as a consciousness-raising school was and still is to create a concept of 'femininity'" (*Feminine Mystique* 318; Sichtermann 105). Yet, as I have discussed, many of these second-wave investigations were designed to "surpass" femininity in "a radical and as yet unimagined transformation of the female body" – or, as Simone de Beauvoir puts it, to encourage woman to "escape from [her] past" (Bartky 78; Beauvoir 539). Later critics who were formulating their ideas in a feminist-inspired social and academic context were equally doubtful about the merits of femininity and – even while rejecting dichotomous perceptions – they still adhered to a split image of woman, divided between her feminist and feminine characteristics. As Susan Douglas concludes in *Where the Girls Are* (1995), "[w]e remain shattered into so many pieces, some of them imprinted by femininity, others by feminism. But they don't yet fit together into a coherent whole" (294). In many ways, I have argued against this notion of feminist/feminine wholeness and I have proposed the notion of a more fluid, ambiguous and contradictory postfemininity that does not aim for coherence and unity. As Deborah Siegel has recently noted, twenty-first-century women face the dilemma of a generation "wedged between old definitions of feminism that no longer work and new ones that have yet to be fully lived out" (*Sisterhood, Interrupted* 158). It is in this space between the "old" and the "new" that the aspirations and limits of a postfeminine/postfeminist present become apparent that both harks back to a past when women were subjugated and to a future when they might no longer be degraded. Maybe we have now reached a point in our examinations of the "woman question" when we are able to penetrate – what Beauvoir calls – the "shadows beyond that illuminated circle" of facts, when woman crosses the "threshold of reality", even if it is more perplexing and complex than she had hoped (719). I am tempted to finish on Beauvoir's words which still hold true after 60 years: "Woman is not a completed reality, but rather a becoming, and it is in her becoming that... her possibilities should be defined" (66; emphasis in original).

Notes

Introduction: the "f-Words"

1. On 29 June 1998, *Time* magazine's front cover featured a row of black-and-white photos of three famous white feminists (Susan B. Anthony, Betty Friedan and Gloria Steinem) and a colour portrait of fictional television lawyer Ally McBeal (Calista Flockhart), along with the caption "Is feminism dead?" In the accompanying article, journalist Ginia Bellafante bemoaned the state of contemporary feminism that is "wed to the culture of celebrity and self-obsession" (57). In fact, as *The Independent*'s columnist Joan Smith argues, obituaries for feminism appear so regularly in the press that they have come to constitute a specific genre:

   > "False feminist death syndrome," as it is known, has been around for a very long time, ever since the late Victorian press described campaigners for women's rights as "a herd of hysterical and irrational she-revolutionaries." ... We vividly recall *Newsweek* declaring "the failure of feminism" in 1990; *The New York Times* assuring its readers that the 'radical days of feminism are gone' in 1980; and *Harper's* magazine publishing a "requiem for the women's movement" as early as 1976.

2. On the "daughter" side of the debate, one finds a generation of young women for whom feminism is "no longer moving, no longer vital, no longer relevant" (Siegel, "Reading" 75). As Rebecca Walker notes in her introduction to the anthology *To Be Real: Telling the Truth and Changing the Face of Feminism* (1995),

   > Young women coming of age today wrestle with the term [feminist] because we have a very different vantage point on the world than that of our foremothers. ... For many of us it seems that to be a feminist in the way that we have seen and understood feminism is to conform to an identity and way of living that doesn't allow for individuality, complexity, or less than perfect personal histories.
   >
   > (xxxiii)

   In a similar manner, Rene Denfeld defines feminism as the "New Victorianism" that "has become as confining as what it pretends to combat" (2, 5). Denfeld's account of a demonized feminism relies on a narrative structure that, as Deborah L. Siegel notes, might be summarized as "Down with the 'bad' feminism and up with the good!" ("Reading" 67). In response, the feminist "foremothers" attacked their "daughters" for their historical amnesia and misappropriations of the feminist/familial legacy. According to Lynne

173

Segal, this new breed of feminists "were able to launch themselves and court media via scathing attacks on other feminists" – even worse, this kind of feminism has been "appropriated by a managerial elite" that works in the service of neoliberal values and is "eager to roll back welfare for workfare" (152).

3. As Joan Williams notes, on the work front, this is due to the "full-commodification model" that enshrines the ideal-worker woman as a model of what women should strive for and alienates those women whose lives are framed around caregiving. At the opposite end, women's maternal qualities and domestic duties are celebrated and pastoralized by conservative and "new traditionalist" rhetoric that holds that women "naturally" belong to the home (Probyn).

4. Hollows argues that some feminists have "produce[d] their own identity by projecting an image of an Other who lacks the same identity" (17). In this way, the "feminine anti-heroine" is constructed as an antithetical Other in an attempt to distinguish and demarcate a feminist consciousness and subject.

5. See also Judith Butler's *Bodies that Matter* (1993), in which she reformulates the materiality of bodies in order to construe sex as a cultural norm: " 'sex' is an ideal construct which is forcibly materialized through time.... 'Sex' is, thus, not simply what one has, or a static description of what one is: it will be one of the norms by which the 'one' becomes viable at all, that which qualifies a body for life within the domain of cultural intelligibility" (1–2).

6. In *Living Room Wars*, Ien Ang suggests that one of the most prominent features of living in the "postmodern world" is "living with a heightened sense of permanent and pervasive cultural contradiction" (1). As she notes, "uncertainty is a built-in feature", "a necessary and inevitable condition in contemporary culture" and any sense of order and security, of structure and progress, has to be recognized as provisional and circumstantial (163, 162).

7. For example, Harris (1999) describes "Woman" as a "questionable category (no graven image) that can never be fully described or defined" (183), while Teresa de Lauretis (1982) and Monique Wittig (1997) highlight the distinction between "Woman" (the "fictional construct") and "women" ("the real historical beings"). For more on feminist diversity and heterogeneity, see Whelehan (1995) and Brooks (1997). Michelene Wandor also expresses the need for a diversification of the feminist movement (that takes into account issues of race, class, age and sexuality), noting that "the political – and personal – struggle now needs a larger, more diverse 'we', who will combine in resistance to all the overlapping oppressions" (quoted in Thornham, "Second Wave Feminism" 42).

8. For more on how these different academic disciplines have contributed towards our understanding of the myths of femininity, see Macdonald (1995), 11–40.

9. Stone's analysis is based on Nietzsche's understanding of genealogy as a chain of historically overlapping phenomena.

10. Elsewhere I have described this internal echo as a Gothic presence that brings with it the threat of phallocentricity and the spectre of heterosexism. For more on this, see my article in *Postfeminist Gothic*.

11. Discussing the use of irony in "laddish" men's magazines like *FHM* and *Loaded*, Gauntlett argues that irony provides a "protective layer" between lifestyle information and the readers (168). He maintains that these magazines are fully aware that "women are as good as men, or better" and that "the put-downs of women ... are knowingly ridiculous, based on the assumption that it's silly to be sexist (and therefore is funny, in a silly way), and that men are usually just as rubbish as women" (168).

12. For example, Nick Stevenson, Peter Jackson and Kate Brooks argue that irony allows someone to express "an unpalatable truth in a disguised form, while claiming it is not what they actually meant" (quoted in Gill, *Gender and the Media* 40).

13. A particularly well-publicized example of such a return to a new (i.e. old) femininity was recently played out in the German press after Eva Herman published her contentious book *Das Eva Prinzip für eine neue Weiblichkeit* (The Eve Principle for a New Femininity) (2006). Herman, a popular television newsreader, argued that women had lost their feminine characteristics because of the excessive demands of feminists for sameness ("Gleichheit"). Under feminism's tutelage, women have been turned into "masculinized soldiers" ("vermännlichte 'Soldaten' " [181]), says Herman, and they have forgotten their feminine instincts and features: grace, purity, motherliness, considerateness, patience and faithfulness (220, 261). Herman's theses caused a public debate on the state of contemporary womanhood and were criticized by politicians, journalists and in particular feminists. Notably, the prominent German feminist Alice Schwarzer (who had been singled out in Herman's polemic) entitled her 2007 book simply *Die Antwort* (The Answer). Herman's downfall reached new lows when she was fired from her job as a newsreader after she commended Nazi Germany for its "family values" in her next book *Das Prinzip Arche Noah – Warum wir die Familie retten müssen* (The Principle of Noah's Ark – Why we have to save the Family).

14. As Butler writes, "the parodic repetition of 'the original' ... reveals the original to be nothing other than a parody of the *idea* of the natural and the original" (*Gender Trouble* 31). In this way, "gender parody reveals that the original identity after which gender fashions itself is an imitation without an origin" (138).

15. Butler emphasizes that performance is not a deliberate or volitional act by a free-willed agent:

> performativity must be understood not as a singular or deliberate "act", but, rather, as the reiterative and citational practice by which discourse produces the effects that it names.... [It] is neither free play nor theatrical self-presentation ... [but it] consists in a reiteration of norms which precede, constrain, and exceed the performer and in that sense cannot be taken as the fabrication of the performer's "will" or "choice." ... The reduction of performativity to performance would be a mistake.
>
> (*Bodies* 2, 95, 234)

16. The term "complicitous critique" is used by Linda Hutcheon to describe "a strange kind of critique, one bound up ... with its own complicity with power and domination, one that acknowledges that it cannot escape

implication in that which it nevertheless still wants to analyze and maybe even undermine" (*Politics of Postmodernism* 4). Terry Eagleton discusses "enlightened false consciousness" as a characteristic of "the new kind of ideological subject" who "is no hapless victim of false consciousness, but knows exactly what he is doing: it is just that he continues to do it even so" (39). To this extent, the contemporary subject seems "conveniently insulated against 'ideological critique' of the traditional kind, which presumes that agents are not fully in possession of their own motivations" (39).

17. Gill writes that contemporary femininity is "no longer associated with psychological characteristics and behaviours like demureness or passivity, or with homemaking and mothering skills"; instead, it is now defined "in advertising and elsewhere in the media as the possession of a young, able-bodied, heterosexual, 'sexy' body" (91).

18. In *Fire with Fire* (1993), Naomi Wolf distinguishes two traditions of feminism that she designates "victim feminism" and "power feminism": "One tradition is severe, morally superior and self-denying; the other is free-thinking, pleasure-loving and self-assertive" (180). According to Wolf, "victim feminism" is "when a woman seeks power through an identity of powerlessness" while "power feminism" is "unapologetically sexual" and "examines closely the forces arrayed against a woman so she can exert her power more effectively" (147, 149).

19. In *The Grounding of Modern Feminism* (1987), Nancy Cott notes that the term "postfeminist" appeared after the vote for women (over 30) had been gained by the suffrage movement:

> Already in 1919 a group of female literary radicals in Greenwich Village... had founded a new journal on the thinking, "we're interested in people now – not in men and women". They declared that moral, social, economic, and political standards "should not have anything to do with sex", promised to be "pro-woman without being anti-man", and called their stance "postfeminist".
>
> (282)

20. For an early 1980s account of postfeminism, see Bolotin's *New York Times Magazine* article that discusses young women's attitudes to feminism. One of Bolotin's interviewees is characteristic in her dismissal of feminism: "Look around and you'll see some happy women, and then you'll see these bitter, bitter women. The unhappy women are all feminists. You'll find very few happy, enthusiastic relaxed people who are ardent supporters of feminism. Feminists are really tortured people" (31).

21. See Rotislav Kocourek (1996) for more on the "programmatic indeterminacy" and "motivational ambiguity" of the prefix "post-".

22. For more on feminist differences, see Thornham's "Second Wave Feminism". Following Judith Butler, the feminist "we" can be recognized as a "phantasmatic construction" that denies "internal complexity and indeterminacy" and "constitutes itself only through the exclusion of some part of the constituency that it simultaneously seeks to represent" (*Gender Trouble* 142).

23. Given the statistical evidence, it is clear that such claims cannot be sustained. Women continue to earn less than their male counterparts (17%

less an hour if they work full-time; 36% if they work part-time). And 96% of executive directors of the United Kingdom's top 100 companies are men while only 20% of MPs are women. For more facts about gender inequality, visit http://www.fawcettsociety.org.uk (accessed 15 February 2008). As Vicki Coppock comments, "this is not to say that nothing has changed for women and some aspects of women's daily experiences can be defined as 'progressive.' ... While things may be different for women, this does not guarantee, nor translate into equality or liberation" (180).

24. Feminist critics take a unanimously negative view of this individualistic stance, arguing that "the political is personal" as "the distinction between feminist politics and feminist identity is in danger of completely disappearing" (Dow, *Prime-Time Feminism* 210, 209). The popular press provides the most explicit portrayal of the postfeminist utopia in which women can do whatever they please, provided they have sufficient will and enthusiasm. According to this optimistic formulation, women *choose* the life they want and they inhabit a world centred in, what Elspeth Probyn calls, *choiceoisie* that envisions all major life decisions as individual options rather than culturally determined or directed necessities. As Susan J. Douglas comments, "women's liberation metamorphosed into female narcissism unchained as political concepts and goals like liberation and equality were collapsed into distinctly personal, private desires" (246).

25. Similarly, Angela McRobbie uses the phrase "taken into accountness" to illustrate "the co-existence of feminism as at some level transformed into a form of Gramscian common sense, while also fiercely repudiated, indeed almost hated" ("Post-Feminism and Popular Culture" 256).

26. See, for example, Ann Brooks' *Postfeminisms* (1997), which defines postfeminism as "the intersection of feminism with a number of other anti-foundationalist movements including postmodernism, post-structuralism and post-colonialism" (1).

27. This is often accompanied by an attempt to impose a hierarchical structure that favours academic versions of postfeminism while deriding its popular manifestations. Indeed, reviews of media postfeminism almost invariably appear with an obligatory footnote on progressive academic postfeminism (see, for example, Ann Brooks' introduction in *Postfeminisms*).

28. For more on this, see my article "Third Way/ve: The Politics of Postfeminism".

29. For more on postfeminism as an interdiscursive and intercontextual movement, see my *Postfeminism: Cultural Texts and Theories*.

30. Here it is worth remembering that, as Nancy Whittier remarks, "the 'post-feminist generation' is not a homogeneous, unified group" (228).

31. Crucially, I do not want to write out of feminism women's struggles in other parts of the world, say the global South or the former Soviet bloc states, which would find it difficult to relate to postfeminism's consumerist, individualist notions of empowerment.

32. Postfeminism's "philosophical positioning of 'both at once'" (Harris 19) aligns it politically with New Labour's "Third Way", which steers a middle course between right and left ideologies. For more on this politicized interpretation of postfeminism, see my article "Third Way/ve: The Politics of Postfeminism" .

33. Rosalind Gill has recently discussed postfeminism in terms of a "sensibility" related to contemporary neoliberalism. As she argues, "citizens in the West today inhabit a postfeminist media culture in which women rather than men are constituted as the ideal neoliberal subjects" (249). She identifies a number of recurring themes and tropes that characterize gender representations in the media in the early twenty-first century, including the notion of femininity as a bodily property; the shift from objectification to subjectification; the emphasis on surveillance; a focus on individualism; the entanglement of feminist and anti-feminist ideas and an emphasis on consumerism (255).

34. British writer Natasha Walter entitled her 1998 book *The New Feminism*, in which she discusses the meaning and uses of contemporary feminism. Walter is characteristically optimistic in her belief that, as women, "we've never had it so good" (197). She insists that feminism has penetrated most bastions of power and women have achieved a "new freedom" that now makes it possible to "separate out the personal and the political" (5). While *The New Feminism* asserts the need for continuing political, social and economic reforms (exemplified by five concrete goals that conclude the book – the reorganization of the workplace, childcare, male inclusion in domestic life, the opening of the poverty trap and support for female victims of violence), the book's individualist and consumerist bias is encapsulated by the epilogue in which Walter celebrates the "ordinary freedoms" of sitting in a London café, wearing a trouser suit and paying for her drink "with my own money, that I earn from my own work" (256, 255).

35. The notion of resignifiability is important for my understanding of postfeminism and postfemininity as it opens up the process of meaning construction and allows for multiplicity without foreclosing any interpretations. Following Judith Butler, meaning can never be fully secured because "signification is not a founding act" but a site of contest and revision that accommodates the possibility of resignification, a citational slippage or deviation that creates new and unanticipated meanings (*Gender Trouble* 145).

36. Postfeminism can thus be aligned with "post-theory" that, as Fernando de Toro notes, implies "exploiting the in-between spaces ... a transitory space, a space other, a third space that is not here/there, but both" (20).

37. Marshment criticizes the beauty lure employed by patriarchal structures according to which

> women may themselves be seduced into accepting such images, both because patriarchal ideology has achieved a general hegemony, and because, however much they work against women's interests in the long term, in the short term they may offer what benefits are available to women in a patriarchal society.... [I]f definitions of femininity and heterosexuality demand that women wear make-up and high heels in order to be attractive to men, then not only might women wear them for this purpose, they may well come to feel more confident, more beautiful when wearing them. If, in this way, women come to be subordinated – even in their definitions of themselves and their desires – to the needs of patriarchy, it may be argued that this is because definitions of femininity appear to offer solutions to their material problems.
>
> (126)

1   The problem that has a name: the feminine concentration camp

1. Inspired by the Black Power Movement, feminists adapted CR strategies to encourage women to identify the social, psychological and political origins of their personal problems. One of the main second wave slogans ("the personal is political") illustrates this strategy: "the personal is political" implied that everyday interactions between men and women (sex, family life, household chores) were no longer simply private matters but implicated in the exercise of institutionalized power. Women were meant to become aware of this power through CR sessions which involved sharing experiences with a small group of other women and simultaneously learning about their experiences. It was hoped (and envisaged) that these personal acts of liberation would lead to a collective politics and activism. The strategic importance of collectivity is highlighted by another second wave motto: "sisterhood is powerful". Second wave feminists were adamant from the start that significant social change can only result from collective action. As the "Manifesto for Liberation of Women" (1974) proclaims, "Women cannot be individually liberated within a society that oppresses women. When you convince your husband that he should help with the washing-up, you have not made employers pay you an equal wage" (quoted in Whelehan, *Feminist Bestseller* 51).

2. The term "second wave" was coined by Marsha Weinman Lear in a 1968 article in the *New York Times Magazine* ("The Second Feminist Wave") and refers to an increased feminist activity in North America and Europe from the 1960s onwards. Linda Nicholson points out that "something important occurred in the 1960s.... That occurrence was a new intensity in many societies in the degree of reflection given to gender relations" (1). Nicholson continues to say that in the United States the beginnings of these changes can be seen in two, originally separate, political movements: The first was the Women's Rights Movement that emerged in the early 1960s and was composed largely of professional women who put pressure on government institutions to end discrimination against women as they entered the paid labour force; the second movement – the Women's Liberation Movement – grew out of the civil rights and New Left movements in the late 1960s. While the Women's Rights Movement has been more politically widespread, "expressing an ideology more in accord with that of the population as a whole", the Women's Liberation Movement has produced most of the theoretical works of the second wave (1–2). In her discussion of the feminist best-seller, Imelda Whelehan puts an end date on the second wave of "around 1975": "It wasn't that Second Wave feminism died in 1975...yet, nonetheless, the heady period of activism was on the wane and intra-feminist groupings were becoming more clearly demarcated than they had been" (*The Feminist Bestseller* 42).

3. Di Stefano distinguishes two more strategic positions: feminine anti-rationalism and feminist postrationalism. Feminine anti-rationalism is committed to a stronger version of difference and levels its protest against the rational/masculine and irrational/feminine construct. The anti-rationalist position attempts to revalorize (rather than overcome) traditional feminine experience, but as a result, it often fails to criticize the feminine and therefore

risks sliding into anti-feminism. On the other hand, feminist postrationalism argues that feminism must initiate a break with the rationalist paradigm and offer new, decentred narratives of opposition. While this strategy is theoretically appealing, di Stefano maintains that it is also complex and unnerving, inhabiting a constantly shifting ground of emerging and dissolving differences. With postrationalism, "she" dissolves into a perplexing plurality of differences, none of which can be theoretically or politically privileged over others (77).

4. For more on the effects of the Second World War on Western women's progress and the post-war backlash, see Faludi, *Backlash* 66–95.

5. Indeed, schizophrenia, hysteria and self-division have long been part of the feminist experience, even before feminism existed in its modern sense (the term was not coined until 1895). The burgeoning feminist – or the "emancipated woman" who "wants to be active, a taker" – is often represented as torn "between the desire to assert herself and the desire for self-effacement" (Beauvoir 727, 703). A fictional depiction of this internal split can be found in nineteenth-century women-centred narratives such as Charlotte Perkins Gilman's best-known piece *The Yellow Wallpaper* (1892), in which a woman is repressed, cut off from any intellectual pursuits and ultimately driven mad, specifically by her husband who insists on her confinement, but more generally by the violence of patriarchy. The narrator of *The Yellow Wallpaper* has been described as an example of, what Gilbert and Gubar have famously termed, "the madwoman in the attic" in an allusion to Charlotte Brontë's classic *Jane Eyre* (1847) and the unruly, "other" Bertha Mason.

6. This construction of the "woman question" has also been criticized as promoting an artificial boundary between "ordinary" women (who suffer from a "false consciousness") and feminist critics whose role is to "demythologis[e] the powerful and ever-changing myths about the female self and nature perpetuated in the mass media and other state apparatuses" (Whelehan, *Modern Feminist Thought* 229).

7. Wittig also reveals that

> "woman" does not exist for us: it is only an imaginary formation, while "women" is the product of a social relationship.... "Woman" is not each of us, but the political and ideological formation which negates "women."..."Woman" is there to confuse us, to hide the reality "women". In order to be aware of being a class and to become a class we first have to kill the myth of "woman" including its most seductive aspects.
>
> (313–14)

8. Beauvoir sets up a dichotomy between male/masculine transcendence and female/feminine immanence. As the accompanying endnote tells us, immanence is "the opposite or negation of transcendence, such as confinement or restriction to a narrow round of uncreative and repetitive duties"; it is in contrast to "the freedom to engage in projects of ever widening scope that marks the untrammelled existent" (94–5). Confined in immanence, woman is shut up within "the circle of herself" and she can propose to do nothing

more than "construct a life of stable equilibrium in which the present as a continuance of the past avoids the menaces of tomorrow" (467).

9. As Barbara Brook notes, this distinction is symptomatic of a mind/body split; that is, "while feminist critiques were being made of binarism, the general direction of much feminist theorising has itself been divided between the binaries of privileging either the mind and its transcendence, or the body and its immanence" (8).

10. There are clear overtones here of the Eve myth that sees woman as responsible for the seduction of Adam and consequently the Fall of Man.

11. In Beauvoir's eyes, this is the ultimate and sometimes pathetic effort of the imprisoned woman "to transform her prison into a heaven of glory" (639). Of course, this idea and imagery are not new: In her *Vindication* (1792), Mary Wollstonecraft also commented that "taught from infancy that beauty is woman's sceptre, the mind shapes itself to the body and roaming round its gilt cage, only seeks to adorn its prison" (113).

12. In her concluding chapter, Simone de Beauvoir also alludes to a Marxist perspective and model:

> A world where men and women would be equal is easy to visualize, for that precisely is what the Soviet Revolution *promised*: women reared and trained exactly like men were to work under the same conditions and for the same wages; Erotic liberty was to be recognised by custom, but the sexual act was not to be considered a 'service' to be paid for; woman was to be *obliged* to provide herself with other ways of earning a living.
>
> (733; emphasis in original)

13. Housewifery is thus ideologically repackaged as a skilled, highly technological industry of its own, with the homemaker acting more like an engineer and expert rather than an unskilled labourer. A contemporary example was General Electric's "Speedster" oven that allowed for "Push Button" cooking, along with other "de luxe features". For more on this, see Friedan 181–204.

14. In a similar manner, Beauvoir writes that "there is a contradiction between [a woman's] status as a real human being and her vocation as a female" and "as long as she still has to struggle to become a human being, she cannot become a creator" (359, 723).

15. Friedan also warns that "a job, any job" may not be the answer as it must be a profession that a woman can "take seriously as part of a life plan, work in which she can grow as part of society" (300).

16. In her critique of *The Feminine Mystique*, Joanne Hollows notes that this solution not only reproduces a masculine value system that sees feminine qualities as inferior qualities, but Friedan also depicts the character and experience of femininity in the 1950s as monolithic: she "presents the 1950s as a period of "conservatism and constraints", but this hides the complexity of the era and portrays women simply as victims" (12).

17. Beauvoir notes that "if woman seems to be the inessential which never becomes the essential, it is because she herself fails to bring about this change" (19); this is reiterated by Friedan's claim that, in the end, "a woman, as a man, has the power to choose, and to make her own heaven or hell" (12).

In a conference paper on the female identity crisis, she hints that women may be oppressing themselves: "It is not laws, nor great obstacles, nor the heels of men that are grinding women down in America today" (quoted in Siegel, *Sisterhood, Interrupted* 78).

18. In Beauvoir's text, men are represented as the beneficiaries of a patriarchal society, but they nonetheless suffer under its rule: "The truth is that just as – biologically – males and females are never victims of one another but both victims of the species, so man and wife together undergo the oppression of an institution they did not create" (500). She asserts that "the relation of man to woman is the most natural relation of human being to human being", so that in abolishing the slavery of woman, man will in effect "free himself in freeing her" (741, 500). In Beauvoir's mind, there is no doubt that both men and women will profit greatly from "the new situation" in which "the human couple will find its true form" and "genuine love" will be "founded on the mutual recognition of two liberties" (733, 741, 677).

19. As Joan Williams notes, the "ideal worker" is constructed in capitalist and much feminist rhetoric as "someone who works full time (and often overtime) and who can move if the job 'requires it'" (5). This "full-commodification model" privileges market work over family work and, by holding up a standard that is typically available only to men, alienates many women whose lives revolve around caregiving (56).

20. Deborah Siegel highlights the symbolic status of Friedan's home town: in the vaudeville era, comics and stage performers tried new productions in Peoria to measure audience acceptance: "If the show was a hit in Peoria, it was ready for Broadway. Hence the phrase 'If it plays in Peoria, it will play anywhere'" (*Sisterhood, Interrupted* 73). For Friedan, "playing in Peoria" thus had a special meaning.

21. For more on this haircutting episode, see Siegel, *Sisterhood, Interrupted* 85–86.

2   Burning the bra: second wave enemies of glamour

1. In *Gyn/Ecology* (1978), Mary Daly warns her readers of "the trap of confusing sisterhood with brotherhood" – "male comradeship/bonding depends upon energy drained from women" while "the bonding of Hags [Daly's "real" females] in friendship *for* women is not draining but rather energizing/gynergizing. It is the opposite of brotherhood" (319; emphasis in original).

2. Jo Freeman, the editor of the *Voice of the Women's Liberation Movement* (1968) – a newsletter dedicated to "radical women" – similarly writes that "Women's liberation does not mean equality with men. Mere equality is not enough. Equality in an unjust society is meaningless" (quoted in Whelehan, *Feminist Bestseller* 45).

3. Retrospectively, one can highlight a number of problems and risks associated with CR as a political strategy: not only could these analytical sessions be mistaken for self-help therapy (rather than a form of political action), but they also regularly antagonized women who did not agree with this perspective on female oppression. Radical feminist tracts implied that "dissenters" inevitably had to suffer from a "false consciousness" or actively collude in

their own domination. Moreover, the lack of structure and the smallness of the groups made it difficult to generalize about the activities and debates that took place during CR sessions. As Imelda Whelehan comments, "the clash between political agendas and the sum of the experiences which made up the grass-roots base of Women's Liberation in consciousness-raising was never likely to be easily resolved" (*Feminist Bestseller* 50).

4. Millett's usage of the term "patriarchy" to signify male domination has been criticized more recently for its ahistoricism and its tendency to obscure a more detailed examination of female subordination (Whelehan, *Modern Feminist Thought* 15–16).

5. Imelda Whelehan notes that "all radical feminists seemed to agree upon the need for separatism, but the scale of separatism varied considerably, ranging from political separatism (women-only discussion group, dealing purely with issues that affect women), to complete separatism (communes, etc.)" (*Modern Feminist Thought* 74).

6. Simone de Beauvoir expresses a similar point when she notes that "make-up, false hair, girdles, and 'reinforced' brassieres are all lies. The very face itself becomes a mask: spontaneous expressions are artfully induced, a wondering passivity is mimicked" (380). For Beauvoir, a woman who refuses objectification is defying society; "she is perhaps an anarchist" (546).

7. Other pictures taken on the day show young women standing behind a poster of a naked woman whose body is labelled like meat: Rump, Rib, Chuck, Round. Their banners proclaimed, "Welcome to the Miss America Cattle Auction"; "Atlantic City is a town with class – they raise your morals and they judge your ass!" (quoted in Siegel, *Sisterhood, Interrupted* 1).

8. For example, a contemporaneous article from the *Guardian* contrasts feminist protesters to the Miss World contestants under the headline "Beauty O'ershadowed by the Women's Lib" (21 November 1970). A *Times* article from 1971 similarly laments that

> some women's liberation girls decide against caring for their looks. The movement rejects the artificiality of bras, deodorants, depilatories and other wonders of twentieth-century technology which they feel exploit women commercially and debase them into sex objects.
>
> (quoted in Hinds and Stacey 161)

9. In this context, it is interesting to note that the 2003 study on men's and women's attitudes to equality in Britain (commissioned by the Equal Opportunities Commission [EOC]) found that feminism is regarded virtually unanimously in negative terms, from old-fashioned to "ball breaking". Other research also suggests that "the label 'feminism' operates as a negative cognitive frame" which might reduce women's support for the feminist movement in the future (Hall and Rodriguez 898). See www.equalityhumanrights.com/Documents/EOC/PDF/Research/talking_equality_report.pdf.

10. In many ways, the notion of the "zipless fuck" (sex without any emotional involvement or commitment) acts as a precursor to the chick lit–inspired, *Sex and the City*–style adventures of today.

11. Along the same lines, Ann Snitow writes of her early years in women's liberation: "Oppressed and depressed before the movement, I found sexual power unthinkable, the privilege of a very few women. Now angry and awake, I felt for the first time what the active eroticism of men might be like" (219).

12. Many radical feminists criticized heterosexual desire for being constructed exclusively around male needs, and in order to advance women's sexual pleasure and satisfaction, they turned to female anatomy and distinguished the different functions of clitoris and vagina: whereas the latter is an "organ of reproduction as well as sexuality" possessing little erogenous tissue, the clitoris – says Kate Millett – is "the only human organ which is specific to sexuality and to sexual pleasure" (117). See also Anne Koedt's influential essay "The Myth of Vaginal Orgasm" (1968), in which she argues that "[t]he vagina is not a highly sensitive area and is not physiologically constructed to achieve orgasm", concluding that vaginal intercourse and its associated sexual position and technique "should no longer be defined as standard" (quoted in Levy 54).

13. Steinem's exposé "I Was a Playboy Bunny" (reprinted in her collection *Outrageous Acts and Everyday Rebellions* 33–78) originally appeared as a two-part article, "A Bunny's Tale", in *Show* Magazine in 1963. This story not only established Steinem as a feminist writer but also received criticism from women who disagreed with what they saw as a victimizing characterization. In her book *The Bunny Years*, ex-Bunny Kathryn Leigh Scott chastises Steinem for her "women-as-victim mode", which depicts Bunnies as "forever young and dumb, the archetypal female sexual objects forced into positions of servitude toward men" (275). By contrast, Scott defines her "bunny years" as a willing exploitation of her "sexuality... intelligence, wit, upper arm strength, youthful exuberance and full range of survival instincts".

14. For more on these sex-critical stances and the "pornography wars", see Andrea Dworkin's *Pornography: Men Possessing Women* and Drucilla Cornell (ed.) *Feminism and Pornography*. With regard to "political lesbianism", Imelda Whelehan reveals that the sexual choices available to feminists were gradually presented as "more a decision about whether to choose lesbianism and invest in the love of one's sisters, despite one's sexual orientation, opt for celibacy, or simply keep silent about one's relationships with men" (*Feminist Bestseller* 132). Writing in 1973, Jill Johnston explains how the word "lesbian" expanded through political definition and became "a generic term signifying activism and resistance and the envisioned goal of a woman committed state" (quoted in Whelehan 133).

15. Dworkin continues, "It is the use of sex as the medium of oppression that makes the subordination of women so distinct from racism or prejudice against a group based on religion or national origin.... In the subordination of women, inequality itself is sexualized: made into the experience of sexual pleasure, essential to sexual desire. Pornography is the material means of sexualizing inequality; and that is why pornography is a central practice in the subordination of women" (30).

16. Daly notes that even feminists fall prey to patriarchal enculturation that turns them into "token feminists" whose hidden agenda includes "thinking like a man" while at the same time behaving according to feminine

stereotypes (334). As Daly comments, the token feminist is "the ultimate weapon in the hands of the boys" (335).

17. In her demand for sexual freedom and love, Firestone incorporates sexual interactions between adults and children, maintaining that "relations with children would include as much genital sex as the child was capable of" (215). Even more perturbing is Firestone's implicit acceptance of the possibility of incest: indeed, should a child choose to relate sexually to "his" own genetic mother – Firestone is careful to use the masculine pronoun here – then "there would be no *a priori* reasons for her to reject his sexual advances, because the incest taboo would have lost its function" (215). This suggestion is especially disturbing for a twenty-first-century reader, given that the social evil and spectre of paedophilia has come to dominate contemporary cultural fears and imagination. Rather short-sightedly and perhaps also worryingly, Firestone's critique of sex(ism) does not involve a consideration of the sexual dangers that children face.

18. There are clear echoes of Beauvoir in Firestone's assertion of a "love between two equals" that "would be an enrichment, each enlarging himself through the other" (115). This is reminiscent of Beauvoir's description of the "true" human couple: "mutually recognizing each other as subject, each will yet remain for the other an *other*" (740; emphasis in original).

19. Firestone gives another, more blunt, description of giving birth that, according to one of her friends, it is "like shitting a pumpkin" (181).

20. This can be compared to the four key demands (revised to seven in 1978) put forward by the first national Women's Liberation Conference held at Ruskin College, Oxford, in 1970: equal pay; equal opportunities and education; free contraception and abortion on demand; free 24-hour nurseries.

3 Boiling the bunny: the backlash and macho feminism

1. As Susan Faludi records, original screenings of the film were interrupted by moviegoers shouting verbal abuse at Glenn Close's character and encouraging Michael Douglas to "Beat that bitch! Kill her off now" (140). The audience's intensely violent feelings towards the single woman were also made explicit by the fact that the film's original ending (which sees Alex commit suicide in a white dress and Dan being arrested for her murder) was deemed too tame and not cathartic by preview audiences as Alex was not sufficiently brought to justice.

2. The term "bunny-boiler" has become part of our cultural knowledge and language to the extent that it is now defined in the Oxford Dictionary of English as "a woman who acts vengefully after having been spurned by her lover".

3. Alex Forrest fits this image: a liberated, independent businesswoman who is unashamedly assertive and "unladylike" in manner and speech, she caused audience outrage by calling Dan a "cocksucker" and insisting that he should be responsible for their unborn child – "I won't allow you to treat me like some slut you can just bang a couple of times and throw in the garbage", she tells him, "I'm gonna be the mother of your child. I want some respect."

4. In this sense, the bunny-boiler can be compared to the figure of the *femme fatale* whose sexuality represents a threat to the enthralled male. As Linda Dryden notes, the *femme fatale* is a "merciless, libidinous and murderous female monster whose prey is the male" (162).

5. The question of power within feminism became increasingly important as feminism was challenged from the inside by previously unheard voices of marginalized, colonized and indigenous women who objected to feminist theories that failed to address their needs. As a social and political movement that claims to embrace women's interests beneath the term "sisterhood", feminism is criticized for developing a methodology that uses as its paradigm white, heterosexual and middle-class female experience. Imelda Whelehan, for example, recognizes a dominant feminist stream of "white, heterosexual and bourgeois thought" that embodies the possible meanings and definitions ascribed to feminism, accompanied by a marked reluctance on the part of such "feminists to address the degrees of social acceptance and privilege that they enjoy at the expense of others" (*Modern Feminist Thought* 107–8). This "'mainstream' feminist analysis of female oppression" is denounced as "flawed and narrow in its focus" as it does not take into account that "a patriarchal ideology also supports a racist and heterosexist one" (110, 120). Black and lesbian feminists actively counter and reject these methodological boundaries of feminist discourse, refusing to be silenced by a "'hegemonic' feminism with its roots clearly located in the Anglo-American influences so powerful in the conceptualization of second wave feminism" (Brooks 4).

6. As Patricia Waugh argues,

> Certainly, for women in the 1960s and early 1970s, "unity" rather than dispersal seemed to offer more hope for political change. To believe that there might be a "natural" or "true" self which may be discovered through lifting the misrepresentations of an oppressive social system is to provide nurturance and fuel for revolutionary hope and practice.
>
> (13)

Feminism thus passed through "a *necessary* stage" of pursuing a unitary self, so that women "might fully understand the historical and social construction of gender and identity" (13; emphasis in original).

7. Critics argue that feminism has been diluted by its immersion in popular culture to the extent that feminism has become "a matter of identity or lifestyle, not politics" (Dow, "Ally McBeal" 259). As Dow writes, "[a] feminism driven by representational concerns and commodity logic, and that is willing to sacrifice specific political objectives in the quest for a more attractive image, is a feminism with little hope of making a material difference in the lives of all women" (*Prime-Time Feminism* 213). Hollows and Moseley explain in their introduction to *Feminism in Popular Culture* (2006) that the "idea of co-option is a central one in many debates about the relationship between feminism and popular culture, where it is frequently claimed that those elements of feminism that can be 'sold' – for example, ideas of liberation, independence and freedom – are appropriated by consumer culture but, in the process, become detached from the feminist discourses that anchored their radical meaning" (10). Yet, they also reveal that, from the 1980s onwards,

different ways of conceptualizing the connections between feminism and popular culture have emerged: "This debate is complex, because key concepts such as popular feminism, post-feminism and third-wave feminism are used in a range of different ways in different historical and national contexts" (7).

8. As Pat Brewer explains,

> [t]his shift was characterised by massive cuts to government, particularly in welfare and social provision, privatisation of state owned enterprises, attacks on union rights, greater emphasis on a free market, and the ideological dominance of individual responsibility and user-pays philosophy. In Britain and the US this was expressed more dramatically by the election of more right-wing neo-liberal governments under Thatcher and Reagan respectively.
>
> (8)

9. Whelehan also argues that the "backlash works by reassuring people that the 'old' values hold sway because they are undeniably true", adding that this "circular logic provides comfort to many, trapped as they are in the economy and vicissitudes of the old order" (18).

10. In this way, the backlash is not based on the assumption that, as Imelda Whelehan writes, "equality is incompatible with femininity and more particularly with motherhood, and women who attempt to take on a man's world will be effectively desexed" (*Overloaded* 17). Rather, the backlash makes a distinction between the women's movement on the one hand and women's social equality on the other. As Ann Braithwaite suggests, the backlash "works not by rejecting ideas about equality and women's 'rights,' but instead by acknowledging those at the same time as identifying feminism as the cause of women's current miseries" (22).

11. In her introduction, Faludi writes that the backlash is more than an antifeminist reaction – as would be indicated by a straightforward refusal to consider any social gains and transformations engendered by feminism on behalf of women – and it also incorporates a "celebration of women's victory" (1). As such, "the backlash is at once sophisticated and banal, deceptively 'progressive' and proudly backward" (12). Rather than being an overtly hostile response to the second wave, its persuasiveness lies in its ability to define itself as an ironic, pseudo-intellectual critique of the feminist movement.

12. As Friedan writes, "Alpha-style" is founded on "analytical, rational, quantitative thinking"; "the Alpha, or male, power is more 'direct' and 'aggressive,'" based on the experience of "abstracting one particular task or demand from its surroundings at a given time" (244). This is contrasted with the "Beta style", which is generally perceived to be more "feminine" and springs from "synthesizing, intuitive, qualitative thinking". Moreover, the Beta style is "more tuned to 'the subtleties of human interaction' than the direct style" and is able to "deal with change". Friedan contends that "we ourselves [as feminists] now must consciously transcend our own tendency to Alpha, masculine, win-lose, zero-sum, linear thinking" (248).

13. Friedan's liberal feminist view can be discussed as an extension of American democratic principles: repudiating "distorted sexual politics", she asserts that "our sexuality is a final frontier of privacy and autonomy any woman or man has the right, and need, to defend, according to personal values, in this invasive mass society where so little is left that we can control in our own lives" (206–7).

14. Friedan notes that women have different "set of needs": "woman's need for power, identity, status and security through her own work or action in society" and "the need for love and identity, status, security and generation through marriage, children, home, the family, which those feminists still locked in their own reaction deny. Both sets of needs are essential to women, and to the evolving human condition" (95).

15. For example, Greer makes a sharp distinction between the nuclear family she rejects and the capital letter Family she celebrates. The "notion of the Family with a capital F" strives to describe "an organic structure which can be shown in law, in genetic examination, in patterns of land ownership and parish records, but has its realm principally in hearts and minds" (265). The model from which Greer has developed this notion of the Family appears to be peasant communities that she has encountered in her travels around India and southern Italy. While these are primarily patriarchal orders, she admires the matriarchal possibilities they offer women. Thus, Marisa, a poor Italian woman, is described by Greer as "one of the most unequivocally successful women" she has ever met because "her sons-in-law and her grandchildren are firmly bound to her household rather than to her in-laws" (268).

16. Friedan is aware of the mediated, common-sensical position of feminism in popular culture that is in marked contrast to its distinct political identity: "there is a discrepancy between the power of the women's movement, as a fundamental change in the consciousness of and about women and their role in society, and the deadlocks and failures of the organized political movement" (201).

4   Going pink: postfeminism and girl power

1. According to Naomi Wolf, who coined the term, "power feminism" means identifying with other women through shared pleasures and strengths, rather than shared vulnerability and pain. In place of a sentimental "fantasy of cosmic sisterhood", power feminists make alliances based on economic self-interest and economic giving back (58). It is about "telling the difference between hating sexism and hating men". Although Wolf also discusses the need to harness the resources of the wealthy and mobilize the mass power of the poor, the most noticeable characteristic of power feminism that was picked up by the media is its implication of power through sex. The more sexed-up version of this position – "do-me feminism" – made its way into popular men's magazines in the early 1990s and refers to a "new" breed of feminists who are "untrammeled, assertive, exuberantly pro-sex, yet determined to hold [their] own in a man's world" (Shalit 27). Of course, as Deborah Siegel discusses, there is nothing inherently "new" about this sexualized feminist stance and it can be linked to pro-sex activism of the

1980s that emerged in reaction to the anti-pornography campaigns led by Catherine MacKinnon and Andrea Dworkin (*Sisterhood, Interrupted* 108).

2. As Joan Morgan puts it, we need to go beyond black-and-white binary thinking and be "brave enough to fuck with the grays" (quoted in Siegel, *Sisterhood, Interrupted* 142).

3. Butler's most famous example is of drag performances that "implicitly reveal the imitative structure of gender itself – as well as its contingency" (*Gender Trouble* 137). In response to some critical voices who (mis)interpreted her theories as promoting gender voluntarism – that is, gender is perceived to be "like clothes" that one can put on and take off at one's will – she later revisited and refined the notion of "gender-as-drag", arguing that "if drag is performative, that does not mean that all performativity is to be understood as drag" (*Bodies* 231). Moreover, she also reveals that "there is no necessary relation between drag and subversion" and "drag may well be used in the service of both the denaturalization and reidealization of hyperbolic heterosexual gender norms"; "[a]t best, it seems, drag is a site of a certain ambivalence" (125).

4. Butler acknowledges that her thinking has been influenced by the "New Gender Politics" that have emerged in recent years and combine movements concerned with transgender, transsexuality and intersex (*Undoing Gender* 4). As such, her discussion of femininity is part of an examination of "male-to-female (MTF) transsexuality":

> To understand gender as a historical category ... is to accept that gender ... is open to a continual remaking, and that 'anatomy' and 'sex' are not without cultural framing ... The very attribution of femininity to female bodies as if it were a natural or necessary property takes place within a normative framework in which the assignment of femininity to femaleness is one mechanism for the production of gender itself.
>
> (9–10)

5. The notion of "undoing gender" refers to Butler's 2004 essay collection of that title that focuses on "the question of what it might mean to undo restrictively normative connections of sexual and gendered life" (2). Equally, however, she adds, "the essays are about the experience of *becoming undone* in both good and bad ways" (1; emphasis in original). Angela McRobbie has focused on the negative aspects of this act of "undoing" in her recent article on postfeminism, arguing that contemporary popular culture is effective in the "undoing of feminism" by appearing to be engaging in "a well-informed and even well-intended response to feminism" but in actual fact "cast[ing] it in the shadows" where it is made to seem redundant (255).

6. Again, Butler is instructive here in her description of signification – the process of meaning construction – as "at once a reenactment and reexperiencing of a set of meanings already socially established" (*Gender Trouble* 140). The "resignification of norms" can thus be discussed as "a function of their *inefficacy*, and so the question of subversion, of *working the weakness in the norm*, becomes a matter of inhabiting the practices of its rearticulation" (*Bodies* 237; emphasis in original).

7. We can rephrase this idea employing Betty Friedan's terminology whereby postfemininity can be said to present a challenge both to the "feminine mystique" and to the equally constraining "feminist mystique". In a postfeminine framework, femininity is not opposed to feminism but is rather constitutive of its understanding of agency, empowerment and resistance.

8. Beauvoir herself is dismissive of the kind of woman who "play[s] on both sides, demanding old-fashioned respect and modern esteem, banking on [her] old magic and [her] new rights" (727). Her sympathies lie with the man who, "understandabl[y]", "becomes irritated" and "feels tricked". For her, there is "no doubt [that] this procedure is unfair tactics". Beauvoir – relying on an unchanging definition of feminine passivity – can interpret the actively feminine woman only as "an object paradoxically endued with subjectivity".

9. Whelehan discusses feminism's refusal to play the media game whereby "the Movement went into defensive retreat" and "feminists weren't beyond expelling people summarily if they were felt to have betrayed the central principles of feminism" (*Feminist Bestseller* 138). Rosalind Miles clearly expressed this anti-media, anti-consumerist attitude in *The Fiction of Sex* (1974): "there are always the commercially-minded who are quite ready to climb up on their sisters' backs to make their impact (and their fortunes)" (quoted in Whelehan 138).

10. Consider, for example, this statement by the prominent grrrl heroine Courtney Love that neatly entwines an ideology of sexual agency and confidence with an embrace of feminine paraphernalia and consumerist brand culture: "we like our dark Nars lipstick and LaPerla panties, but we hate sexism, even if we do fuck your husbands/boyfriends" (quoted in Gillis and Munford, "Genealogies and Generations" 173). Another example of the commercial appeal of Girlie culture is the publishing industry's reliance on candy-coloured book covers as a marketing tool to create a generic category of "chick lit". Elisa Sheffield has criticized this use of colour (in particular, the "blatant little-girl color" pink) as "an affront to the mature feminist, to all the women who have struggled over the decades to be taken seriously. And one could say that the title, Chick-Lit, only deepens the insult, that it's like snapping gum in your mother's face" (par. 1).

11. On a political level, this can be linked to a neo-liberal framework, prevalent in late-twentieth- and early-twenty-first-century capitalist societies in the West. Neo-liberalism is generally understood in political economy terms as the dismantling of the welfare state and the expansion of the global free trade. Its importance for cultural analysis lies in its extension of market values and rationality to other areas of life, including its construction of the individual as an "entrepreneur" and consumer-citizen who should self-regulate and self-care. This resonates with postfeminism's individualist and commoditized understanding of empowerment and agency that is at odds with second wave notions of collective politics and community activism. For more on the connections between postfeminism and neo-liberalism/Third Way, see my article "Third Way/ve: The Politics of Postfeminism".

12. Similarly, Angela McRobbie argues that postfeminism shifts not just feminist ideas and values into the past but also its community-based, activist politics. Within postfeminist work, there is, as she says, a "double

failure": "In its over-emphasis on agency and the apparent capacity to choose in a more individualized society, it has no way of showing how subject formation occurs by means of notions of choice *and* assumed gender equality coming together to actually ensure adherence to new unfolding norms of femininity" ("Notes on Post-feminism" 10–11; emphasis in original).

13. This DIY philosophy is perhaps best encapsulated by the large number of Internet webzines: "We believe zine-making embodies the phrase 'the personal is political' by encouraging active participation in the creation of one's own culture... It is a truly democratic form of media, everyone who reads a zine can create one" (www.grrrlzines.net).

14. Sarah Projansky has recently examined the interconnections between postfeminism and the emergence of girl discourse in the 1990s, which, she suggests, can be analysed in five ways: first, "both postfeminism and girlness can be seen as part of a focus on youthful femininity"; second, the cultural obsession with girlhood can be read as a response to postfeminism, a kind of 'backlash' against the 1980s postfeminist woman who is "unhappy with how career has displaced family"; third, girlness epitomizes postfeminism whereby "the postfeminist woman is quintessentially adolescent", no matter what her age; fourth, the emphasis on girls can be interpreted as a way to "keep postfeminism fresh in the context of corporate commodity culture"; lastly, the fifth explanation portrays late 1980s and 1990s girls as the daughters of an earlier postfeminism and postfeminist women, "produced by and raised in a postfeminist milieu" (45).

15. Similarly, Rosalind Coward describes how the Spice Girls "coined the phrase [Girl Power] as a bit of promotional fun but it passed quickly into the wider culture as a good label to use in any situation in which girls might be putting themselves forward in new, brash, and 'unfeminine' ways" (122).

16. As Angela McRobbie notes, the definition of feminism as "out of date" depends on girlness and youth. One strategy to disempower feminism includes it being "historicised and generationalised": "the new female subject is, despite her freedom, called upon to be silent, to withhold critique, [in order] to count as a modern sophisticated girl" ("Post-Feminism and Popular Culture" 258, 260). Girl Power thus presents itself as youthful and energetic while installing an image of feminism as "old". At the same time, in its celebration of young femininity and its application of the term "girl" to adult women, Girl Power is seen to infantilize and belittle women of all ages by treating them as children or adolescents. As Yvonne Tasker and Diane Negra have argued, in these circumstances, girlhood is imagined as "being for everyone; that is, girlhood offers a fantasy of transcendence and evasion, a respite from other areas of experience" (18).

17. The term "third wave" was brought to public attention by activist and writer Rebecca Walker (daughter of Alice, the author of *The Color Purple*) in a *Ms.* magazine article in 1995. Previous usages include a 1987 essay in which Deborah Rosenfelt and Judith Stacey reflect on the ebbs and flows of feminism throughout the 1970s and 1980s, suggesting that "what some are calling a third wave of feminism [is] already taking shape" (359). By the mid-1990s, third wave feminists produced a number of, largely non-academic, publications – *Listen Up: Voices from the Next Feminist Generation* (1995), *To Be Real: Telling the Truth and Changing the Face of Feminism* (1995) and

Manifesta: Young Women, Feminism, and the Future (2000) – that provide personal accounts of feminist awakenings and are meant as guides to feminism for a popular audience.

18. As Heywood and Drake assert, "it is this edge, where critique and participation meet, that third wave activists must work to further contentious public dialogue" (52). The third wave contests a politics of purity that separates political activism from cultural production; it asks us "to re-imagine the disparate spaces constructed as 'inside' and 'outside' the academy…as mutually informing and intersecting spheres of theory and practice" (Siegel, "The Legacy of the Personal" 70).

19. This exemplifies the third wave's politics of ambiguity and their rejection of a black-and-white binary model. According to the third wave agenda, "there is no one right way to be: no role, no model" (Reed 124). In fact, "contradiction…marks the desires and strategies of third wave feminists" who "have trouble formulating and perpetuating theories that compartmentalize and divide according to race and gender and all the other signifiers" (Heywood and Drake 2; Walker xxxiii). As Walker writes, "we find ourselves seeking to create identities that accommodate ambiguity and our multiple positionalities: including more than excluding, exploring more than defining, searching more than arriving" (xxxiii).

20. Deborah Siegel explains the difference between the two:

> "Grrl" [*sic*] was "girl" with a healthy dose of youthful female rage, minus the sugar and spice. The word entered the lexicon sometime around 1991, along with the Riot Grrl movement – a loosely connected network of all-girl punk bands and their fans that started in Olympia, Washington, and Washington, D.C.…Described by the *New York Times*…as girl "with an angry grrrowl," "grrl" was also a derivation and a repossession of "girl"…its self-affirming undertones akin to the reclamation of the words "queer" by the gay and lesbian community and "nigger" by some African Americans.…Not to be confused with…"Girl Power" (a marketing ploy that deployed empowerment rhetoric to sell products), grrl was a grassroots popular expression engendered and disseminated by girls and young women themselves.
>
> (*Sisterhood, Interrupted* 146)

21. In a similar vein, Deborah Siegel notes that "the 'third wave' is a response to what one might call the cultural dominance of postfeminism", "a welcome voice of contention for many second wave feminists, for whom the threat of 'postfeminism'…is particularly resonant" ("The Legacy of the Personal" 52). In *Sisterhood, Interrupted* (2007), she explains the difference as follows: the third wave can be described as "the ironic embodiment of their mothers' failure" to achieve their goals while postfeminism exists on "the presumption that feminists ha[ve] effectively changed the world" (139).

22. Yvonne Tasker and Diane Negra characterize the third wave as "a more scholarly category" and "self-identification" while postfeminism is described as a "popular idiom" (19).

23. Adopting Patricia Mann's terminology, I have described postfeminism in terms of a feminized/sexualized "micro-politics" that engages with multiple agency positions (Genz, "Third Way/ve"). As Mann writes, in today's political

climate, "[e]ach engaged individual must attempt to integrate and reconcile a confusingly varied set of motivations, obligations, and desires for recognition or reward on a day-to-day basis, and over time" (171).

24. Lemish's study of 12-year-old Israeli girls' talk about the Spice Girls seems to reinforce the fact that the band provided positive role models for pre-teen girls. One of them expressed her understanding of the pop group: "They are not afraid. They say everything they've got. They don't care what people will say. They are kind of independent and they don't need anyone to help them" (153). Another interviewee defined Girl Power as "equality... that girls are strong, each one in her own way".

25. Gillis and Munford describe Girlies as "an older group of young women, focused on popular culture, similarly forging a space of social agency and resistance through zines such as *Bitch* and *BUST*" ("Genealogies" 171).

26. Debbie Stoller, editor of *BUST* magazine, expresses her feminine feminism in a similar manner, arguing for a creative re-imagining of femininity that positions it at the heart of feminist resistance: "We love our lipstick, have a passion for polish, and, basically, adore this armor that we call 'fashion'. To us, it's fun, it's feminine, and, in the particular way we flaunt it, it's *definitely* feminist" (47; emphasis in original).

27. Delombard's discusses "femmenism" as part of an examination of butch-femme identities in queer theory: "Femmenism is looking like a straight woman and living like a dyke...Femmenism is playing up your femininity even when you know it can and will be used against you...Femmenism is political but not correct" (21–2). Delombard is adamant that this display of femininity is not a symptom of her internalized heterosexism but it has developed despite and in resistance to a context of prohibition: "no one force-fed me femininity. Quite the contrary: I had to fight for it tooth and nail.... my female socialization was countered by feminism, a critical apparatus that enabled me, indeed forced me, to question every step I made along the long and winding road of gender-role identification" (33).

28. The process of *assujetissement* is not exclusive to postfeminism/postfemininity but also characterizes, for example, radical feminism and liberal feminism, which attempt to subject women to certain discourses at the same time as those discourses provide the resources for their action. See my article "Third Way/ve: The Politics of Postfeminism" for a more politicized discussion of this.

29. With regard to Girl Power (as a predominantly white phenomenon), one yet unexplored area of analysis relates to the question of race, and more work needs to be done on how brands of new femininities function for women/girls of different ethnicities.

5 The (un)happy housewife heroine

* Some of the ideas expressed in this chapter have appeared in *Feminism, Domesticity and Popular Culture* (2009).

1. In her instant classic "The Housewife's Moment of Truth" (1972), Jane O'Reilly describes such a "click" moment as the precise occasion when a

woman, "suddenly and shockingly", perceives "the basic disorder in what has been believed to be the natural order of things". The "blinding click" is thus a moment of truth, the instant when a woman realizes that her private anxieties and frustrations are not her personal failings but the inevitable response to patriarchal expectations of womanhood.

2. Henrik Ibsen's play *A Doll's House* (1879) has often been credited as one of the first fictional explorations of the housewife state and a critical assessment of nineteenth-century marriage norms. In it, the proto-feminist character Nora struggles to break free from a suffocating marriage that she experiences as a violation of her personality. As she tells her husband Torvald, "[I have] my duties to myself ... I believe that before everything else I'm a human being – just as you are ... or at any rate I shall try to become one ... I was simply your little songbird, your doll ... I can't bear to think of it – I could tear myself to little pieces" (228–30). Ibsen himself dismissed the idea that he had "worked for women's rights", emphasizing that for him "it [writing the play] has been a question of human rights".

3. Barnes's parting line that she "didn't want to miss another birthday party" has often been quoted by new traditionalists who see the workplace as a source of female frustration and uphold the joys of home and motherhood as an antidote to work-related stresses (quoted in Kingston 96).

4. For more on domestic nostalgia, see Stephanie Coontz's *The Way We Never Were: American Families and the Nostalgia Trap* (1992), in which she discusses the happy 1950s household (represented, for example, by Ozzie and Harriet or the Cleavers) as a cover-up that is neither traditional nor accurate.

5. As Joan Williams notes, Friedan's emphasis on market (or paid) work is exemplary of feminism's "full-commodification strategy" whereby women's equality is directly linked to full-time work, with childcare delegated to the market (40–5).

6. Friedan makes a number of problematic and potentially misogynist claims by comparing housewives to concentration camp victims, psychiatric patients who have "portions of their brain shot away" (270), "schizophrenics" who have "forfeited their ability to relate to the real world," and "mentally retarded" inmates who are used by their institutions as houseworkers (224). As Friedan notes, housework can hardly "use the abilities of a woman of normal human intelligence" and, as such, constitutes an "appalling waste of woman-power" (224).

7. Beauvoir makes allowances for the "enchantment" and magic of some aspects of housewifery, like cooking: woman becomes a "sorceress" in the kitchen, "effect[ing] the transmutation of substances" and "there is poetry in making preserves" as the housewife "has enclosed life in jars" (472). Cooking can thus be "revelation and creation; and a woman can find special satisfaction in a successful cake or a flaky pastry, for not everyone can do it: one must have the gift". Ultimately however, Beauvoir concedes, "as with other housework, repetition soon spoils these pleasures", and as women cannot "quickly escape" into the public world (like men), they end up being doomed to "the general and the inessential" (473).

8. In *Housewife* (1974), Oakley describes how women's domestic identity does not allow for creativity and individuality: " 'Housewife' is a political label after all, a shorthand symbol for the convenience to a male-oriented society

of women's continued captivity in a world of domestic affairs – a one-word reference to those myths of woman's place which chart their presence in the home as a natural and universal necessity" (240).

9. Admittedly, the power relations between Bettina and her husband slightly change as Jonathan admits that he has lost his money on the stock market, has had an affair and been in analysis. However, his confession does not propel any major changes as Bettina does not confess in return and the reader is left with an enigmatic final image of a cockroach on the kitchen clock.

10. Tellingly, towards the end of the novel, Mira rebukes herself for indulging in the joys of homemaking and taking pleasure in her "humming happy" home and "the fresh liquid green smell of the string beans" (493) – interestingly, in marked contrast to the earlier image of "the shit and string beans" that had characterized her life as a young housewife/mother (103). As she tells herself off for her domestic happiness, "My God! She dropped the string beans, dried her hands, sank into a chair, and lighted a cigarette. It was the American Dream, female version. Was she still buying it? She didn't even like to cook, she resented marketing . . . But she still believed in it: the dream stood of the happy humming house" (493). Here, the domestic is still experienced as a source of female oppression and a form of indoctrination that one should be wary of, and no attempt is made to redefine the relationship between women and the home.

11. The term "Stepford Wife" has entered popular vocabulary and consciousness where it refers to "someone who is robotically conformist or obedient" (*Oxford Dictionary of English*).

12. This highlights another aspect of Friedan's critique of suburban domesticity that is linked to consumerism and materialism. As Friedan asks pointedly, "[w]hy is it never said that the really crucial function, the really important role that women serve as housewives is *to buy more things for the house?*" (181; emphasis in original). "Properly manipulated", Friedan writes, American women become "*victims* of that ghastly gift, that power at the point of purchase" (182; emphasis in original).

13. Interestingly, the 2004 remake of *The Stepford Wives* differs from its predecessor in a number of ways, most importantly the ending. Here, the new Joanna (with the help of her husband) survives and fakes her mechanical transformation, reverses those of the other Stepford wives and unmasks the real brain behind Stepford's domestic utopia: a female scientist who killed her cheating husband, turned him into a robot and then set up the community of Stepford in an attempt to recreate old-fashioned sex roles. As Anne Williams has recently discussed, this comic optimism reflects a postfeminist perspective and sensibility that takes into account women's changed roles and cultural status in contemporary society. For a detailed analysis of both *Stepford* films, see Anne Williams's article in *Postfeminist Gothic* (2007).

14. As Joanne Hollows has discussed, the figure of the housewife has been particularly resistant to such attempts at re-interpretation. Critics have focused on new femininities that have appeared between non-domestic and feminist identities – particularly younger femininities, such as the Girlie – but no corresponding move was made to investigate "what emerges between the feminist and the housewife" ("Feeling like a Domestic Goddess" 180).

15. The refrain "I'm not a feminist, but…" has often been cited by critics as indicative of a popular disavowal of and moratorium on feminism. Susan Douglas examines the motto:

> the comma…is the fulcrum of the whole statement, which marks the divisions – and, more important, the profound connections – between the disavowal of feminism in the first part of the phrase and its embrace at the end. The comma says that the speaker is ambivalent, that she is torn between a philosophy that seeks to improve her lot in life and a desire not to have to pay too dearly for endorsing that philosophy…. This conversational gambit [means] that the speaker probably supports some combination of equal pay for equal work…. It also means that the speaker shaves her legs, bathes regularly, does not want to be thought of as a man-hater, a ball-buster, a witch, or a shrew…. Most of all, it means that the possibility of having, inside you a unified, coherent self that always believes the same things at the same time is virtually zero.
>
> (270–3)

16. One interesting example is provided by the "Feminist Housewives" website, which acts as an Internet forum for highly educated stay-at-home mothers. The website slogan ("we're housewives, not housebroken") points towards a new conception of domesticity: "we were the guinea pigs of this new era. We're the latchkey, daycare generation and we want something different for our families…. This isn't backsliding – we're socially conscious and making our own decisions" (www.feministhousewives.com/).

17. One particularly pertinent example of this withdrawal is the "mummy wars" that are fought out in the media between stay-at-home mums and working mothers. The January 2007 edition of *Marie Claire* pointedly puts forward the question in its review article "Modern Mothers: Who's Doing It Best?" According to the author, the conflict between working and non-working women has reached crisis point with both camps attacking each other and forcing mothers to take sides. While the article mainly discusses privileged women who can afford to choose between staying at home and going out to work – featuring statements from TV presenter Sophie Raworth, who has "a good work/life balance"; TV executive Sam Morley, who gave up her job as head of research to be with her two children; as well as famous stay-at-home mums such as actresses Calista Flockhart and Vanessa Paradis – it also makes the important point that for most mothers work is an unavoidable economic necessity: "There's a very narrow band of upper-middle class women who exercise choice. The rest of us simply try to make the best of it" (Moore 242).

18. This deconstruction of domesticity will necessarily also involve a restructuring of work, including changing the definition of what an "ideal worker" is. Following Joan Williams, the ideal worker is "someone who works full time (and often overtime) and who can move if the job 'requires it'" (5). In *Unbending Gender* (2000), Williams argues for a shift in feminist strategy that eliminates the ideal-worker norm and moves away from the "full-commodification model", which privileges market work over family work. Williams' goal is a "reconstructive feminism" (or "family humanism") that

no longer separates home and work but instead reflects family values and "the norm of parental care".

6 Having it all: the superwoman

1. As Friedan notes, "community work often expands in a kind of self-serving structure of committees and red tape... until its real purpose seems to be just to keep women busy" (300).
2. A contemporary TV jingle aptly summarizes the mood of the era:

> I can put the wash on the line
> Feed the kids, get dressed, pass out the kisses
> And get to work by five to nine
> 'Cause I'm a woman. (quoted in Williams 46)

3. Here we have a clear indication of Friedan's anti-radicalism and her rejection of "sexual politics". The image of the short-haired, non-maternal woman corresponds to the stereotype of the radical feminist who is politically opposed to cookie-baking and other feminine tasks.
4. The second stage of the struggle for equality is thus characterized by a convergence of women's and men's needs. Friedan argues that women by themselves did not have enough power to bring about an all-encompassing social transformation: "women tried to solve these problems by taking it all on themselves as superwomen" but "[they] did not and will not have [the power] to change the structure of jobs by and for themselves alone.... there will be a new, and sufficient, *combined* force for the second stage" (160; emphasis in original).
5. Friedan writes that "the real question, the basic question, has still to be asked":

> Must – can – women now meet a standard of perfection in the workplace set in the past by and for men who had wives to take care of all the details of living and – *at the same time* – meet a standard of performance at home and as mothers that was set in the past by women whose whole sense of worth, power and mastery had to come from being perfect, all-controlling housewives and mothers?
>
> (80; emphasis in original)

6. Katie Roiphe shot to notoriety in the early 1990s when her first book *The Morning After: Sex, Fear and Feminism* (1993) controversially argued that second wave feminism was responsible for a particular form of "victim feminism" and a "date rape hysteria" that, she claimed, was overrunning American campuses. She suggested that feminist anti-rape initiatives (like "Take Back the Night" marches) are self-defeating as they celebrate women's vulnerability instead of bolstering their strength. According to Roiphe, feminism's preoccupation with women's victim status was fuelled by an outdated model of sexuality, "one in which men want sex and women

don't" (Siegel, *Sisterhood, Interrupted* 99). As Deborah Siegel has commented, Roiphe's case is notable "not so much for what she argued...but because it sparked a war between – and also among – generations of feminists" (100).

7. This tendency to blame feminism for the work/family conundrum continues well beyond the 1980s. A *Redbook* survey in the mid-1990s found that nearly 40% of women polled believed that feminism had worsened the work/family conflict, while another 32% felt that it made no difference. As Joan Williams recounts, "younger women no longer praised the [feminist] movement for giving them access to jobs, but blamed 'feminists' for longer hours and job insecurity" (47). One stressed-out mother of two reportedly asked Gloria Steinem, "Why didn't you tell us that it was going to be like this?", to which Steinem replied, "Well, we didn't know" (47).

8. As Williams writes, "[w]omen's entrance into the workforce without the changes to either the structure of market work or the gendered allocation of family work means that women with full-time jobs work much longer hours than women at home" (47).

9. This characterizes the so-called "macho feminism" that, as Susan Faludi describes, "has deceived women in that it convinced them that they would be happy only if they were treated like men, and that included treating themselves like men" (278).

10. As Susan Faludi has suggested, in 1980s cinema "there's only room for one woman at a time. Female solidarity in this film is just a straw man to knock down" (158). While Katherine betrays Tess's trust at the first opportunity – the advertisement for the film called her "the boss from hell" – Tess achieves her goals by "playing the daffy and dependent girl" and she "succeeds in love Sleeping Beauty-style, by passing out in a man's arms".

11. The film de-emphasizes the fact that Dan instigates the key events by asking Alex out for a drink, trying to cover up his affair by suggesting an abortion, threatening to kill her and physically attacking her.

12. This dichotomy is undermined by the film's undercurrent that constantly hints at a breakdown in differences between the two principle women. As Kerstin Westerlund-Shands suggests, Alex and Beth, businesswoman and housewife, can be discussed in terms of their closeness and overlap: "they inhabit different spaces. But the borderline between those spaces is precarious: the two women also mirror each other and can be seen as two sides of the same woman, or as two sides of Woman" (114).

13. Obviously, the downshifting solution is not readily available to everyone and the rural idyll remains out of reach for the majority of city-dwelling mothers. As Hollows rightly points out, the downshifting narrative is "profoundly classed" and "thoroughly commodified" centring around "choices for those who inhabit specific middle-class femininities" (110–11). Faludi makes a similar point in connection to *Baby Boom* when she criticizes the Tiger Lady's retreat to "an obscenely expensive farmhouse that she can afford only because of her prior Wall Street pay cheques" (161).

14. Susan Faludi has criticized the film's ending and, in particular, the Tiger Lady's failure to rebuke her former colleagues: "Her speech might have been an opportunity to take the firm to task for expelling its most valuable employee simply because she had a child. She could have spoken up for the

rights of working mothers" (161). Instead, Faludi comments, the character "dribbles off into a dewy-eyed reverie about the joys of rural living".

15. In *Unbending Gender*, Joan Williams argues for a "reconstructive feminism" (or "family humanism") that "encourages the development of new ways of organizing work as well as family, emotional, and political life. The guiding principles are that society needs not only market work but also family work, and that adults who do family work should not be marginalized" (4). This involves a restructuring of market employment and masculine work norms that discriminate against women and particularly mothers, as well as a self-conscious use of domesticity (199).

16. A 2008 study carried out by the women's magazine *Brigitte* found that 80% of the over 1000 women interviewed wanted to earn their own money and have a family (Thelen 164). Instead of living up to a "Miss Perfect" image at home and work, women are now asking for pragmatic solutions and deciding for themselves what their life plans should be. They are distancing themselves from the idea of the 1980s career woman and slowly changing the structure of society and the employment market: "Tschüss, Miss Makellos, hallo, Miss Risiko" (168).

7 Making it on her own: the singleton

*A version of this chapter will appear in *The Journal of Popular Culture* (2009).

1. Lee writes that the media image of the "new woman" is often contradictory, propagating diverse forms of *in vogue* femaleness and femininity that reflect the transient and changing definitions of modernity and liberation:

> during the Second World War the propaganda machine got women to work by celebrating the 'new woman' as one who could labour and love in perfect unison. And when the war was over, that very same 'new woman' was the one who preferred housework to paid work. Similarly, in the sixties, the enjoyment of sex was presented as yet another role for women. The advent of 'the Pill' meant that women were suddenly being encouraged from almost every direction to have more sex.
>
> (168)

2. Interviewed on the BBC's Bookworm programme, Fielding also observed that "single women today, sort of in their thirties, are perhaps a new type of woman that hasn't really got an identity. And that's all very worrying. Women have said to me: it [*Bridget Jones's Diary*] makes us feel that we're part of a club and we're not the only ones that feel stupid" (quoted in Whelehan, *Feminist Bestseller* 187). As Imelda Whelehan has commented, "this acknowledgment of some form of identity crisis clearly echoes the feelings of women in the 1960s and 1970s...and the idea that reading *Bridget Jones's Diary* makes them feel part of a community suggests a longing for an inclusive female sphere of experience" (177).

3. Similarly, Imelda Whelehan notes the differences between the two: in the case of 1960s and 1970s feminist writings, "the central protagonists are

trying to look beyond the space traditionally designated for the female into the worlds of education and creativity which represent the opportunity for self-definition" (*Feminist Bestseller* 181). Conversely, the 1990s heroines are portrayed as "located firmly – and lazily – in the home, regardless of their career identity". Whelehan is pessimistic about the potential and value of this kind of narratives, concluding that "[u]nfortunately, this revival of confessional writing...is not likely to prompt a heady renaissance of feminism along the lines of 1970s politics" (188).

4. In line with a "pre-feminist" agenda, Bridget has been discussed as a post-feminist embodiment and reinvention of Jane Austen's nineteenth-century character Elizabeth Bennet. Helen Fielding admitted in an interview introducing the film DVD that "the plot of *Bridget Jones's Diary* was actually stolen from *Pride and Prejudice*". Fielding's novel acknowledges its 1813 predecessor in a number of ironic allusions, exemplified by Bridget's observation on her first meeting with Mark that "it struck me as pretty ridiculous to be called Mr. Darcy and stand on your own looking snooty at a party" (13). Commentators have criticized *Bridget Jones's Diary*'s romance element, noting that "as Bridget gets her Darcy at the end of the book, we are not only given a narrative with some structural similarities to Jane Austen's work, but some of its dominant values as well" (Whelehan, *Overloaded* 138). Fielding takes up the Jane Austen connection in her sequel *Bridget Jones: The Edge of Reason* (1999), which mirrors elements of Austen's later work *Persuasion* (1818) and which sees Bridget and Mark pulled apart by misunderstandings and flawed advice.

5. *Bridget Jones's Diary* has often been described as the urtext of "chick lit". As Suzanne Ferriss and Mallory Young note, "[t]he entire chick lit phenomenon is invariably traced back to this single novel" (4). They describe chick lit as a form of women's fiction that "features single women in their twenties and thirties navigating their generation's challenges of balancing demanding careers with personal relationships" (3). Scarlett Thomas is more condescending in her definition of chick lit as "a 'fun' pastel-covered novel with a young, female, city-based protagonist, who has a kooky best friend, an evil boss, romantic troubles and a desire to find the One – the apparently unavailable man who is good-looking, can cook and is both passionate and considerate in bed" (quoted in Whelehan, *Feminist Bestseller* 201). By the early 2000s, chick lit had established itself as a profitable literary genre and market, earning more than $71 million in 2002 and prompting publishers such as Harlequin and Broadway to create separate imprints dedicated to it (Ferriss and Young 2).

6. In the introduction to the 2003 edition of the book, Brown defends her usage of the term "girl": "Forgive my continuing to call women girls but I think in many ways we continue to *be* girls all our lives.... I think the basic *girl* is still in there whooshing around – loving fun, being spontaneous, mainlining on enthusiasm, don't you?" (xii; emphasis in original).

7. Brown confesses that "I'm not beautiful or even pretty...Yet I managed to sink into the consciousness and subconsciousness of an advertising tycoon, a motivational research wizard, two generals, a brewer, a publisher, a millionaire real estate developer and two extremely attractive men who were younger than I" (13).

8. As Brown writes, the original *Sex and the Single Girl* was based on personal experiences and dealt with "what was happening to my girlfriends and me" (xii).

9. In the case of *Cosmopolitan*, this focus on cosmetic tools and procedures was vital: "the magazine's commercial success depended on a more disingenuous promotion of feminine wiles with its dependence for advertising revenue on the beauty and fashion industries" (Whelehan, *Feminist Bestseller* 29).

10. Brown clearly regards herself as a feminist, asserting that "I was there before Betty Friedan and *The Feminine Mystique*. I was there saying, 'You're your own person, go out there and be somebody...' You don't have to get your identity from being somebody's appendage" (quoted in Whelehan, *Feminist Bestseller* 30).

11. As Dow notes, Mary is "a woman sophisticated enough to recognize sexism when she sees it, but she is not necessarily assertive enough to do anything about it" (31).

12. Murphy's decision to become a single mother caused a political stir in the 1992 presidential elections when Vice-President Dan Quayle criticized the character for ignoring the importance of fathers and rearing a child alone. Quayle's remarks provoked a public discussion on family values and structures that raged across the media and culminated in the 1992–1993 season when the show featured a special episode of *FYI* celebrating the diversity of the American family.

8 Fighting it: the supergirl

1. As Inness notes, the tough heroine exemplifies the contradictions inherent in popular culture: "the popular media are never feeding their audience a single message about women's roles; instead, the media convey countless different messages, with some contradicting others" (49).

2. A similar point has been made with regard to Girl Power where we have been asked to interrogate the connections between "the 'power' and the 'girl'" (Gillis and Munford, "Genealogies" 173).

3. Sharon Macdonald uses the notion of "open/closed images" to argue that imagery is not a purely superficial phenomenon but rather the means through which we articulate and define the social order and nature. She identifies closed images as analogous to symbols and ideals that appear fixed in public consciousness, whereas open images expose coded symbols and chart new meanings for stereotypes (22–3).

4. These are the respective heroines of Janet Evanovich's *One for the Money* (1994), Helen Fielding's *Olivia Joules and the Overactive Imagination* (2003) and the Hollywood film *Miss Congeniality* (2000).

5. This is in line with 1980s backlash portrayals of "macho feminists", the "hard-faced women who were bound and determined to carve their place in their world, no matter whose bodies they have to climb over to do it" (Faludi 277–8). In the case of the hard-bodied action heroine, the body that she has to "climb over" and "carve" is her own. As Sherrie Inness writes, "Ripley demonstrated that women did not have to look as though they stepped directly from a beauty parlor when they battled foes" while the buff

figure of Sarah Connor in the second *Terminator* film "showed that women could compete with men as action-adventure heroes" ("Boxing Gloves and Bustiers" 3). Earlier representations of "tough women" include the 1960s television show *The Avengers*, which featured Mrs Emma Peel (Diana Rigg) as a British spy who was more than capable of taking on any man – although she did have a male partner. In the 1970s, *Charlie's Angels* and *The Bionic Woman* also proved that there was an audience for tough women, albeit beautiful and heterosexually desirable ones (3).

6. The television series was preceded by a moderately successful film of the same title (1992) which adopts the same premise – a cheerleader chosen by fate to fight and kill vampires – but is less "dark" than the series and more compromised by commercial success. As screenwriter Joss Whedon has often observed, the TV series is a much closer rendering of his original vision than the movie.

7. All dialogue is taken from the website http://uk.geocities.com/slayermagic/Scripts.html. The episode numbering system I employ indicates season and episode. Thus, 1002 means first season, second episode.

8. Whedon reveals that *Buffy the Vampire Slayer* is his "response to all the horror movies [he has] ever seen where some girl walks into a dark room and gets killed" (quoted in Early 13). As he states,

> I saw so many horror movies where there was that blonde girl who would always get herself killed, and I started feeling bad for her. I thought, you know, it's time she had a chance to take back the night. The idea of Buffy came from just the very simple thought of a beautiful blonde girl walks into an alley, a monster attacks her, and she's not only ready for him, she trounces him.
>
> (quoted in Chandler 1)

9. Whedon wants to avoid preachiness and "coming off as dramatized infomercials of the National Organization for Women": "if I can make teenage boys comfortable with a girl who takes charge of a situation without their knowing that's what's happening, it's better than sitting down and selling them on feminism" (quoted in Bellafante, "Bewitching" 83).

10. The conflict surrounding Buffy's femininity and feminism was further intensified by actress Sarah Michelle Gellar, who, in an interview with *Detour* Magazine, controversially proclaimed that she is not a feminist, reinforcing in this way popular (mis)understandings of postfeminism as anti-feminist: "I hate the word 'feminist'. It has a bad connotation of women who don't shave their legs or under their arms…. There's no femininity in feminism, which is really weird because it's technically the same word" (quoted in Woodlock 1).

11. In effect, the figure of the hard-bodied, butch action heroine of the 1980s and early 1990s represents the flip side of the same critical attitude that depicts the feminine heroine as a masquerader who plays at being tough. This polarized logic can only conceive of physically strong and powerful female protagonists as "pseudo males" who are really "boys" in "girls' clothing" (Brown 53).

Bibliography

Acker, Kathy. "All Girls Together." *Guardian Weekend* 3 May 1997: 12–19.

Adkins, Lisa. "Passing on Feminism: From Consciousness to Reflexivity?" *European Journal of Women's Studies* 11.4 (2004): 427–44.

Albury, Kath. *Yes Means Yes: Getting Explicit about Heterosex.* Crows Nest, Australia: Allen & Unwin, 2002.

Alexander, Priscilla. "Introduction: Why This Book?" *Sex Work: Writings by Women in the Sex Industry.* Ed. Frédérique Delacoste and Priscilla Alexander. Pittsburgh: Cleis, 1987. 14–18.

Alice, Lynne. "What is Postfeminism? or, Having it Both Ways." *Proceedings of the Feminism/Postmodernism/Postfeminism Conference, November 17–19, 1995: Working Papers in Women's Studies.* Albany, NZ: Massey University, 1995. 7–35.

Allyn, David. *Make Love, Not War: The Sexual Revolution, an Unfettered History.* New York: Routledge, 2001.

Andelin, Helen B. *Fascinating Womanhood.* 1963. New York: Bantam Books, 2007.

Ang, Ien. *Living Room Wars: Rethinking Media Audiences for a Postmodern World.* London and New York: Routledge, 1996.

Apter, Emily. "Reflections on Gynophobia." *Coming out of Feminism.* Ed. Mandy Merck et al. Oxford: Blackwell, 1998. 102–22.

Baby Boom. Dir. Charles Shyer. Perf. Diane Keaton, Sam Shepard, and Harold Ramis. MGM, 1987.

Ballantyne, Sheila. *Norma Jean the Termite Queen.* 1975. Harmondsworth: Penguin, 1983.

Banet-Weiser, Sarah. "What's Your Flava? Race and Postfeminism in Media Culture." *Interrogating Postfeminism: Gender and The Politics of Popular Culture.* Ed. Yvonne Tasker and Diane Negra. Durham and London: Duke University Press, 2007. 201–26.

Barrett, Michèle. "Feminism's 'Turn to Culture.'" *Woman: A Cultural Review* 1 (1990): 22–24.

Bartky, Sandra Lee. *Femininity and Domination: Studies in the Phenomenology of Oppression.* London and New York: Routledge, 1990.

Baumgardner, Jennifer, and Amy Richards. *Manifesta: Young Women, Feminism, and the Future.* New York: Farrar, Straus and Giroux, 2000.

Beal, Frances. "Double Jeopardy: To be Black and Female." *Sisterhood is Powerful.* Ed. Robin Morgan. New York: Random House, 1970. 382–404.

Beauvoir, Simone de. *The Second Sex.* 1953. Trans. of *Le Deuxième Sexe.* 1949. London: Vintage, 1997.

Bellafante, Ginia. "Bewitching Teen Heroines: They're all over the Deal, Speaking Out, Cracking Wise and Casting Spells." *Time* 5 May 1997: 82–84.

– – –. "Who Put the 'Me' in Feminism?" *Time* 29 June 1998: 54–60.

Berger, John. *Ways of Seeing.* London: British Broadcasting Corporation, 1972.

Bolotin, Susan. "Voices from the Post-feminist Generation." *New York Times Magazine* 17 Oct. 1982: 31.

Braithwaite, Ann. "Politics and/of Backlash." *Journal of International Women's Studies* 5.5 (2004): 18–33.

Brewer, Pat. "Has Identity Politics Shifted Feminism to the Right?" *Papers from the Jubilee Conference of the Australasian Political Studies Association.* Canberra: Australian National University, 2002. 1–25.

Bridget Jones's Diary. Dir. Sharon Maguire. Perf. Renée Zellweger, Hugh Grant, and Colin Firth. Working Title, 2001.

Bromley, Susan, and Pamela Hewitt. "Fatal Attraction: The Sinister Side of Women's Conflict about Career and Family." *Journal of Popular Culture* 26.3 (1992): 17–23.

Brontë, Charlotte. *Jane Eyre.* 1847. Harmondsworth: Penguin, 2006.

Brook, Barbara. *Feminist Perspectives on the Body.* London and New York: Longman, 1999.

Brooks, Ann. *Postfeminisms: Feminism, Cultural Theory and Cultural Forms.* London and New York: Routledge, 1997.

Brown, Jeffrey A. "Gender and the Action Heroine: Hardbodies and the *Point of No Return.*" *Cinema Journal* 35.3 (1996): 52–71.

Brownmiller, Susan. *Against our Will: Men, Women and Rape.* New York: Simon and Schuster, 1975.

---. *Femininity.* London: Paladin, 1986.Brunsdon, Charlotte. *Screen Tastes: Soap Opera to Satellite Dishes.* London: Routledge, 1997.

---. *The Feminist, the Housewife, and the Soap Opera.* Oxford: Oxford University Press, 2000.

Budgeon, Shelley. "Fashion Magazine Advertising Constructing Femininity in the 'Postfeminist' Era." *Gender & Utopia in Advertising: A Critical Reader.* Ed. Luigi and Alessandra Manca. Lisle, IL: Procopian Press, 1994. 55–70.

---. "Emergent Feminist (?) Identities: Young Women and the Practice of Micropolitics." *The European Journal of Women's Studies* 8.1 (2001): 7–28.

Bushnell, Candace. *Sex and the City.* London: Abacus, 1997.

Butler, Judith. "Variations on Sex and Gender: Beauvoir, Wittig and Foucault." *Feminism as Critique.* Ed. Seyla Benhabib and Drucilla Cornell. Minneapolis: Minnesota University Press, 1988. 128–42.

---. *Gender Trouble: Feminism and the Subversion of Identity.* London and New York: Routledge, 1990.

---. "Lana's 'Imitation': Melodramatic Repetition and the Gender Performative." *Genders* 9 (1990): 1–18.

---. *Bodies that Matter: On the Discursive Limits of "Sex."* London and New York: Routledge, 1993.

---. "Imitation and Gender Insubordination." *The Lesbian and Gay Studies Reader.* Ed. H. Abelove, M. A. Barale, and D. M. Halperin. London and New York: Routledge, 1993. 307–20.

---. *Excitable Speech: A Politics of the Performative.* London and New York: Routledge, 1997.

---. *The Psychic Life of Power: Theories in Subjection.* Stanford, CA: Stanford University Press, 1997.

---. "Performative Acts and Gender Constitution: An Essay in Phenomenology and Feminist Theory." *Writing on the Body: Female Embodiment and Feminist Theory.* Ed. Katie Conboy, Nadia Medina, and Sarah Stanbury. New York: Columbia University Press, 1997. 401–17.

---. *Undoing Gender.* New York and London: Routledge, 2004.

Butler, Judith et al. "For a Careful Reading." *Feminist Contentions: A Philosophical Exchange.* New York and London: Routledge, 1995. 127–43.

Buttsworth, Sara. " 'Bite Me': Buffy and the Penetration of the Gendered Warrior-Hero." *Continuum: Journal of Media & Cultural Studies* 16.2 (2002): 185–99.

Chandler, Holly. "Slaying the Patriarchy: Transfusions of the Vampire Metaphor in *Buffy the Vampire Slayer.*" *Slayage: The On-Line International Journal of Buffy Studies* 9. 24 Jan. 2004 <http://www.slayage.tv/essays/slayage9/Chandler.htm>.

Chick Lit USA. 2004. 14 June 2004 <http://www.chicklit.us/whatiscl.htm>.

Cloud, Dana L. "Hegemony or Concordance? The Rhetoric of Tokenism in 'Oprah' Winfrey's Rags-to-Riches Biography." *Critical Studies in Mass Communication* 13.2 (1996): 115–37.

Conran, Shirley. *Superwoman: Everywoman's Book of Household Management.* 1975. Harmondsworth: Penguin, 1977.

Contreras, Charles. *How to Fascinate Men.* Hollywood: Chesterfield Publishing Company, 1953.

Coontz, Stephanie. *The Way We Never Were: American Families and the Nostalgia Trap.* New York: HarperCollins, 1992.

Coote, Anna, and Beatrix Campbell. *Sweet Freedom: The Struggle for Women's Liberation.* Oxford: Basil Blackwell, 1987.

Coppock, Vicki, Deena Haydon, and Ingrid Richter. *The Illusions of "Post-Feminism": New Women, Old Myths.* London: Taylor & Francis, 1995.

Cornell, Drucilla, ed. *Feminism and Pornography.* Oxford: Oxford University Press, 2000.

Cott, Nancy F. *The Grounding of Modern Feminism.* New Haven and London: Yale University Press, 1987.

Coward, Rosalind. *Sacred Cows: Is Feminism Relevant to the New Millennium?* London: HarperCollins, 1999.

Daly, Mary. *Gyn/Ecology: The Metaethics of Radical Feminism.* 1978. London: The Women's Press, 1995.

Daniele, Daniela. "Locations: Notes on (Post) Feminism and Personal Criticism." *Critical Studies on the Feminist Subject.* Ed. Giovanna Covi. Trento: Dipartimento di Scienze Filologiche e Storiche, 1997. 79–99.

Daughtery, Anne Millard. "Just a Girl: Buffy as Icon." *Reading the Vampire Slayer.* Ed. R. Kaveney. New York: Tauris Parke, 2002.

Delmar, Rosalind. "What is Feminism?" *What is Feminism?* Ed. Juliet Mitchell and Ann Oakley. Oxford: Basil Blackwell, 1986. 8–33.

Delombard, Jeannine. "Femmenism." *To Be Real: Telling the Truth and Changing the Face of Feminism.* Ed. Rebecca Walker. London: Anchor Books, 1995. 21–33.

Denfeld, Rene. *The New Victorians: A Young Woman's Challenge to the Old Feminist Order.* New York: Warner Books, 1995.

Dickerson, Victoria C. "Young Women Struggling for an Identity." *Family Process* 43.3 (2004): 337–48.

Doane, Mary Ann. *Femmes Fatales: Feminism, Film Theory, Psychoanalysis.* London and New York: Routledge, 1991.

---. "Film and the Masquerade: Theorizing the Female Spectator." *The Sexual Subject: A Screen Reader in Sexuality.* London and New York: Routledge, 1992. 227–43.

Douglas, Mary Vavrus. "Putting Ally on Trial: Contesting Postfeminism in Popular Culture." *Women's Studies in Communication* 23.3 (2000): 413–28.

Douglas, Susan J. *Where the Girls Are: Growing Up Female with the Mass Media*. London: Penguin, 1995.

Dow, Bonnie J. *Prime-Time Feminism: Television, Media Culture, and the Women's Movement since the 1970s*. Philadelphia: University of Pennsylvania Press, 1996.

---. "*Ally McBeal*, Lifestyle Feminism, and the Politics of Personal Happiness." *The Communication Review* 5 (2002): 259–64.

Dryden, Linda. "*She*: Gothic Reverberations in *Star Trek: First Contact*." *Postfeminist Gothic: Critical Interventions in Contemporary Culture*. Ed. Benjamin A. Brabon and Stéphanie Genz. Houndmills: Palgrave Macmillan, 2007. 154–69.

Dubrofsky, Rachel. "Ally McBeal as Postfeminist Icon: The Aestheticizing and Fetishizing of the Independent Working Woman." *The Communication Review* 5 (2002): 265–84.

Dutton, Judy. "Meet the New Housewife Wannabes." *Cosmopolitan* June 2000: 164–67.

Dworkin, Andrea. *Pornography: Men Possessing Women*. 1979. London: The Women's Press, 1992.

---. "Against the Male Flood: Censorship, Pornography, and Equality." *Feminism and Pornography*. Ed. Drucilla Cornell. Oxford: Oxford University Press, 2000. 19–38.

Eagleton, Terry. *Ideology: An Introduction*. New York: Verso, 1991.

Early, Frances. "Staking her Claim: Buffy the Vampire Slayer as Transgressive Woman Warrior." *Journal of Popular Culture* 35.3 (2001): 11–27.

Elam, Diane. "Sisters are Doing it to Themselves." *Generations: Academic Feminists in Dialogue*. Ed. Devoney Looser and Ann E. Kaplan. Minneapolis: University of Minnesota Press, 1997. 55–68.

Evanovich, Janet. *One for the Money*. Harmondsworth: Penguin, 1994.

Faludi, Susan. *Backlash: The Undeclared War against Women*. London: Vintage, 1992.

Fatal Attraction. Dir. Adrian Lyne. Perf. Michael Douglas, Glenn Close, and Anne Archer. Paramount, 1987.

"Fearless Dotty." *Scarecrow and Mrs. King*. Writ. Timothy Burns. Dir. Christian I. Nyby II. CBS. 26 Mar. 1984.

Feigenbaum, Anna. "Remapping the Resonances of Riot Grrrl: Feminisms, Postfeminisms, and 'Processes' of Punk." *Interrogating Postfeminism: Gender and The Politics of Popular Culture*. Ed. Yvonne Tasker and Diane Negra. Durham and London: Duke University Press, 2007. 132–52.

Fein, Ellen, and Sherrie Schneider. *The Rules: Time-tested Secrets for Capturing the Heart of Mr. Right*. New York: Warner Books, 1995.

---. *The Rules II: More Rules to Live and Love by*. New York: Warner Books, 1997.

---. *The Rules for Marriage: Time-Tested Secrets for Making your Marriage Work*. 2001. New York: Warner Books, 2002.

Fekete, John. "Introductory Notes for a Postmodern Value Agenda." *Life after Postmodernism*. Ed. John Fekete. New York: St. Martin's Press, 1987.

Ferriss, Suzanne, and Mallory Young, ed. *Chick-Lit: The New Woman's Fiction*. New York and London: Routledge, 2006.

Fielding, Helen. *Bridget Jones's Diary*. London: Picador, 1996.

- - -. *Bridget Jones: The Edge of Reason*. London: Picador, 1999.
- - -. *Olivia Joules and the Overactive Imagination*. London: Picador, 2003.
"Filming Raul." *Scarecrow and Mrs. King*. Writ. Rudolph Borchert. Dir. Oz Scott. CBS. 19 Mar. 1984.
Findlen, Barbara, ed. *Listen Up: Voices from the Next Feminist Generation*. Berkeley, California: Seal Press, 1995.
Firestone, Shulamith. *The Dialectic of Sex: The Case for Feminist Revolution*. 1970. New York: Farrar, Straus and Giroux, 2003.
French, Marilyn. *The Women's Room*. 1977. London: Warner, 1993.
Freud, Sigmund. "Three Essays on the Theory of Sexuality." 1905. *The Standard Edition of the Complete Psychological Works of Sigmund Freud*. Ed. James Strachey. Vol. 7. London: Hogarth Press, 1953–86. 125–245.
- - -. "Femininity." 1933. *The Standard Edition of the Complete Psychological Works of Sigmund Freud*. Vol. 22. London: Hogarth Press, 1964. 112–35.
Friedan, Betty. *The Feminine Mystique*. 1963. London: Penguin, 1992.
- - -. "An Open Letter to the Women's Movement." *It Changed My Life: Writings on the Women's Movement*. New York: Random House, 1976. 370–88.
- - -. *The Second Stage*. 1981. London: Abacus, 1983.
Fudge, Rachel. "The Buffy Effect: A Tale of Cleavage and Marketing." *Bitch: Feminist Response to Pop Culture* 10 (1999). 10 Dec. 2000 <http://daringivens. home.mindspring.com/buffyeffect.html>.
Gallop, Jane. *Feminist Accused of Sexual Harassment*. Durham, N.C.: Duke University Press, 1997.
Gamble, Sarah. "Postfeminism." *The Routledge Companion to Feminism and Postfeminism*. Ed. Sarah Gamble. London: Routledge, 2001. 43–54.
Gauntlett, David. *Media, Gender and Identity: An Introduction*. 2002. London and New York: Routledge, 2007.
Genz, Stéphanie. "Third Way/ve: The Politics of Postfeminism." *Feminist Theory* 7.3 (2006): 333–53.
- - -. "(Re)Making the Body Beautiful: Postfeminist Cinderellas and Gothic Tales of Transformation." *Postfeminist Gothic: Critical Interventions in Contemporary Culture*. Ed. Benjamin A. Brabon and Stéphanie Genz. Houndmills: Palgrave Macmillan, 2007. 68–84.
- - -. " 'I am not a Housewife, but ...' Postfeminism and the Revival of Domesticity." *Feminism, Domesticity and Popular Culture*. Ed. Stacy Gillis and Joanne Hollows. New York and London: Routledge, 2009. 49–62.
- - -. "Singled Out: Postfeminism's 'New Woman' and the Dilemma of 'Having It All.' " *The Journal of Popular Culture* 42.1 (2009), forthcoming.
Genz, Stéphanie, and Benjamin Brabon. *Postfeminism: Cultural Texts and Theories*. Edinburgh: Edinburgh University Press, 2009.
Gilbert, Sandra M. and Susan Gubar. *The Madwoman in the Attic: The Woman Writer and the Nineteenth-Century Literary Imagination*. New Haven: Yale University Press, 1979.
Giles, Judy. *The Parlour and the Suburb: Domestic Identities, Class, Femininity and Modernity*. Oxford: Berg, 2004.
Gill, Rosalind. "From Sexual Objectification to Sexual Subjectification: The Resexualisation of Women's Bodies in the Media." *Feminist Media Studies* 3.1 (2003): 100–06.
- - -. *Gender and the Media*. Cambridge: Polity, 2007.

Gill, Rosalind, and Jane Arthurs. "New Femininities?" *Feminist Media Studies* 6.4 (2006): 443–51.

Gill, Rosalind, and Elena Herdieckerhoff. "Rewriting the Romance: New Femininities in Chick Lit?" *Feminist Media Studies* 6.4 (2006): 487–504.

Gillis, Stacy, and Rebecca Munford. "Harvesting our Strengths: Third Wave Feminism and Women's Studies." *Journal of International Women's Studies* 4.2 (2003): 1–6.

---. "Genealogies and Generations: The Politics and Praxis of Third Wave Feminism." *Women's History Review* 13.2 (2004): 165–82.

Gillis, Stacy, and Joanne Hollows. "Introduction." *Feminism, Domesticity and Popular Culture.* Ed. Stacy Gillis and Joanne Hollows. New York and London: Routledge, 2009. 1–14.

Gilman, Charlotte Perkins. *The Yellow Wallpaper.* 1892. London: Virago, 1981.

Gould, Lois. *Such Good Friends.* 1970. London: Corgi, 1972.

Greer, Germaine. *The Female Eunuch.* 1970. London: Flamingo, 1999.

---. *Sex and Destiny: The Politics of Human Fertility.* New York: Harper and Row, 1984.

---. *The Whole Woman.* 1999. London: Anchor, 2000.

Grrrl Zine Network. Ed. Elke Zobl. 2008. 10 June 2008. <http://www.grrrlzines.net/about.htm>.

Gurley, Helen Brown. *Sex and the Single Girl.* 1962. Fort Lee, New Jersey: Barricade, 2003.

Hall, Elaine J., and Marnie Salupo Rodriguez. "The Myth of Postfeminism." *Gender and Society* 17.6 (2003): 878–902.

Haran, Maeve. *Having It All.* London: Signet, 1991.

Harris, Geraldine. *Staging Femininities: Performance and Performativity.* Manchester and New York: Manchester University Press, 1999.

Harts, Kate. "Deconstructing Buffy: *Buffy the Vampire Slayer*'s Contribution to the Discourse on Gender Construction." *Popular Culture Review* 12.1 (2001): 79–98.

Hawkesworth, Mary. "The Semiotics of Premature Burial: Feminism in a Postfeminist Age." *Signs: Journal of Women in Culture and Society* 29.4 (2004): 961–85.

Helford, Elyce Rae. "Postfeminism and the Female Action-Adventure Hero: Positioning *Tank Girl.*" *Future Females, the Next Generation: New Voices and Velocities in Feminist Science Fiction.* Ed. Marleen S. Barr. Lanham, Boulder, New York, Oxford: Rowman & Littlefield, 2000. 291–308.

Herman, Eva. *Das Eva Prinzip für eine neue Weiblichkeit.* Munich and Zurich: Pendo, 2006.

---. *Das Prinzip Arche Noah – Warum wir die Familie retten müssen.* Munich and Zurich: Pendo, 2007.

Heywood, Leslie, and Jennifer Drake. "Introduction." *Third Wave Agenda: Being Feminist Doing Feminism.* Ed. Leslie Heywood and Jennifer Drake. Minneapolis and London: University of Minnesota Press, 1997. 1–20.

---. "We Learn America Like a Script: Activism in the Third Wave; or, Enough Phantoms of Nothing." *Third Wave Agenda: Being Feminist Doing Feminism.* Ed. Leslie Heywood and Jennifer Drake. Minneapolis and London: University of Minnesota Press, 1997. 40–54.

---. "The Third Wave and Representation." *Third Wave Agenda: Being Feminist Doing Feminism.* Ed. Leslie Heywood and Jennifer Drake. Minneapolis and London: University of Minnesota Press, 1997. 101–02.

Hills, Elizabeth. "From 'Figurative Males' to Action Heroines: Further Thoughts on Active Women in the Cinema." *Screen* 40.1 (1999): 38–50.

Hinds, Hilary, and Jackie Stacey. "Imaging Feminism, Imaging Femininity: The Bra-Burner, Diana, and the Woman Who Kills." *Feminist Media Studies* 1.2 (2001): 153–77.

Hollows, Joanne. *Feminism, Femininity and Popular Culture*. Manchester and New York: Manchester University Press, 2000.

---. "Feeling Like a Domestic Goddess: Postfeminism and Cooking." *European Journal of Cultural Studies* 6.2 (2003): 179–202.

---. "Can I Go Home Yet? Feminism, Post-Feminism and Domesticity." *Feminism in Popular Culture*. Ed. Joanne Hollows and Rachel Moseley. Oxford: Berg, 2006. 97–118.

Hollows, Joanne, and Rachel Moseley. "Popularity Contests: The Meanings of Popular Feminism." *Feminism in Popular Culture*. Ed. Joanne Hollows and Rachel Moseley. Oxford: Berg, 2006. 1–22.

Hutcheon, Linda. *A Poetics of Postmodernism: History, Theory, Fiction*. London and New York: Routledge, 1988.

---. *The Politics of Postmodernism*. London and New York: Routledge, 1989.

---. "An Epilogue: Postmodern Parody: History, Subjectivity, and Ideology." *Quarterly Review of Film and Video* 12 (1990): 125–33.

Ibsen, Henrik. *A Doll's House and Other Plays*. 1879. Harmondsworth: Penguin, 1987.

Inness, Sherrie A. *Tough Girls: Women Warriors and Wonder Women in Popular Culture*. Philadelphia: University of Pennsylvania Press, 1999.

---. "Pretty Tough: The Cult of Femininity in Women's Magazines." *Critical Readings: Media and Gender*. Ed. Cynthia Carter and Linda Steiner. Maidenhead: Open University Press, 2004. 123–42.

---. " 'Introduction: Boxing Gloves and Bustiers': New Images of Tough Women." *Action Chicks: New Images of Tough Women in Popular Culture*. Ed. Sherrie A. Inness. Houndmills, Basingstoke: Palgrave Macmillan, 2004. 1–17.

Jackson, Sue. " 'Street Girl': 'New' Sexual Subjectivity in a NZ Soap Drama?" *Feminist Media Studies* 6.4 (2006): 469–86.

Jacobson, Aileen. "Books and the Single Girl." *NYNewsday.com*. 2004. 14 June 2004 <http://www.nynewsday.com/features/booksmags/ny-p2two>.

Japp, Phyllis. "Gender and Work in the 1980s: Television's Working Women as Displaced Persons." *Women's Studies in Communication* 14 (1991): 49–74.

Jones, Amelia. " 'Post-Feminism' – A Remasculinization of Culture." *M/E/A/N/I/N/G: An Anthology of Artists' Writing, Theory and Criticism* 7 (1990): 7–23.

Jong, Erica. *Fear of Flying*. 1973. London: Vintage, 1998.

Kalbfleisch, Jane. "When Feminism Met Postfeminism: The Rhetoric of a Relationship." *Generations: Academic Feminists in Dialogue*. Ed. Devoney Looser and Ann E. Kaplan. Minneapolis: University of Minnesota Press, 1997. 250–66.

Karras, Irene. "The Third Wave's Final Girl: *Buffy the Vampire Slayer*." *Thirdspace*. 23 June 2002 <http: //www.thirdspace.ca/articles/pr_kar.htm>.

Kastelein, Barbara. "Popular/Post-Feminism and Popular Literature." Diss. U of Warwick, 1994.

Kaufman, Sue. *Diary of a Mad Housewife*. 1967. London: Serpent's Tail, 2002.

Kavka, Misha. "Feminism, Ethics, and History, or What is the 'Post' in Postfeminism." *Tulsa Studies in Women's Literature* 21.1 (2002): 29–44.

Kim, L. S. " 'Sex and the Single Girl' in Postfeminism: The *F Word* on Television." *Television & New Media*. 2.4 (2001): 319–34.

Kingston, Anne. *The Meaning of Wife*. London: Piatkus, 2004.

Kinsella, Sophie. *The Undomestic Goddess*. London: Bantam Press, 2005.

Klein, Melissa. "Duality and Redefinition: Young Feminism and the Alternative Music Community." *Third Wave Agenda: Being Feminist Doing Feminism*. Ed. Leslie Heywood and Jennifer Drake. Minneapolis and London: University of Minnesota Press, 1997. 207–25.

Klein, Naomi. *No Logo: No Space, No Choice, No Jobs*. New York: Picador, 2002.

Kocourek, Rotislav. "The Prefix Post- in Contemporary English Terminology: Morphology, Meaning, and Productivity of Derivations." *Terminology: International Journal of Theoretical and Applied Issues in Specialized Communication* 3.1 (1996): 85–110.

Krimmer, Elisabeth, and Shilpa Raval. "'Digging the Undead' Death and Desire in *Buffy*." *Fighting the Forces: What's at Stake in* Buffy the Vampire Slayer. Ed. Rhonda V. Wilcox and David Lavery. Lanham, Boulder, New York, Oxford: Rowman & Littlefield, 2002. 153–64.

Lauretis, Teresa de. *Alice Doesn't. Feminism, Semiotics, Cinema*. London: Bloomington, 1982.

Lear, Marsha Weinman. "What Do these Women Want?: The Second Feminist Wave." *New York Times Magazine* 10 March 1968: 24–25, 50–62.

Lee, Janet. "Care to Join Me in an Upwardly Mobile Tango? Postmodernism and the 'New Woman.' " *The Female Gaze: Women as Viewers of Popular Culture*. Ed. Lorraine Gamman and Margaret Marshment. London: The Women's Press, 1988. 166–72.

Lemish, Deborah. "Spice Girls' Talk: A Case Study in Development of Gendered Identity." *Millennium Girls. Today's Girls Around the World*. Ed. Sherrie Inness. Lanham: Rowman & Littlefield, 1998. 145–67.

Levin, Ira. *The Stepford Wives*. 1972. London: HarperCollins, 2002.

Levy, Ariel. *Female Chauvinist Pigs: Women and the Rise of Raunch Culture*. London: Pocket Books, 2006.

"Life of the Party." *Scarecrow and Mrs. King*. Writ. Steve Hattman. Dir. Will Mackenzie. CBS. 18 Feb. 1985.

Lippert, Barbara. "Hey There, Warrior Grrrl." *New York* 15 Dec. 1997: 24–25.

Lloyd, Justine, and Lesley Johnson. "The Three Faces of Eve: The Post-war Housewife, Melodrama, and Home." *Feminist Media Studies* 3.1 (2003): 7–25.

Lockford, Lesa. *Performing Femininity: Rewriting Gender Identity*. Walnut Creek, CA: Altamira Press, 2004.

The Long Kiss Goodnight. Dir. Renny Harlin. Perf. Geena Davis, Samuel L. Jackson, Brian Cox, and Yvonne Zima. New Line Cinema, 1996.

Lorde, Audre. *Sister Outsider: Essays and Speeches by Audre Lorde*. Freedom, CA: The Crossing Press, 1984.

Macdonald, Myra. *Representing Women: Myths of Femininity in Popular Media*. London: Edward Arnold, 1995.

Macdonald, Sharon. "Drawing the Lines – Gender, Peace and War: An Introduction." *Images of Women in Peace & War: Cross-Cultural and Historical Perspectives*. Ed. S. Macdonald, P. Holden, and S. Ardener. Madison: University of Wisconsin Press, 1987. 1–26.

Machelidon, Véronique. "Masquerade: A Feminine or Feminist Strategy?" *Psycho-analyses/Feminisms*. Ed. P. L. Rudnytsky and A. M. Gordon. New York: State University of New York Press, 2000. 103–20.

Mann, Patricia S. *Micro-Politics: Agency in a Postfeminist Era*. Minneapolis and London: University of Minnesota Press, 1994.

Marchetti, Gina. "Action-Adventure as Ideology." *Cultural Politics in Contemporary America*. Ed. Ian Angus and Sut Jhally. London and New York: Routledge, 1989. 182–97.

Marshment, Margaret. "The Picture is Political: Representation of Women in Contemporary Popular Culture." *Thinking Feminist: Key Concepts in Wom en's Studies*. Ed. Diane Richardson and Victoria Robinson. New York: Guilford Press, 1993. 125–51.

Matrix, Sidney Eve. "Badgirls, Cyberchicks, and Postfeminists in US Pop Culture." 31 May 2001 <http://www.tc.umn.edu/~matri001/wost3306/Description.htm>.

McNay, Lois. *Gender and Agency: Refiguring the Subject in Feminist and Social Theory*. Oxford: Polity, 2000.

McRobbie, Angela. *Postmodernism and Popular Culture*. London and New York: Routledge, 1994.

---. "More!: New Sexualities in Girls' and Women's Magazines." *Cultural Studies and Communications*. Ed. James Curran, David Morley, and Valerie Walkerdine. London: Edward Arnold, 1996.

---. "Notes on Postfeminism and Popular Culture: Bridget Jones and the New Gender Regime." *All about the Girl: Culture, Power, and Identity*. Ed. Anita Harris. London: Routledge, 2004.

---. "Post-Feminism and Popular Culture." *Feminist Media Studies* 4.3 (2004): 255–64.

Millett, Kate. *Sexual Politics*. 1970. London: Virago, 1989.

Miss Congeniality. Dir. Donald Petrie. Perf. Sandra Bullock, Michael Caine, and Benjamin Bratt. Warner Bros, 2000.

Modleski, Tania. *Feminism without Women: Culture and Criticism in a "Postfeminist" Age*. London and New York: Routledge, 1991.

Moore, Anna. "Modern Mothers: Who's Doing it Best?" *Marie Claire* Jan. 2007.

Morgan, Robin. *Sisterhood is Powerful: An Anthology of Writings from the Women's Liberation Movement*. New York: Vintage Books, 1970.

Moseley, Rachel, and Jacinda Read. " 'Having it *Ally*': Popular Television (Post-) Feminism." *Feminist Media Studies* 2.2 (2002): 231–49.

Munford, Rebecca. " 'Wake Up and Smell the Lipgloss': Gender, Generation and the (A)politics of Girl Power." *Third Wave Feminism: A Critical Exploration*. Ed. Stacy Gillis, Gillian Howie, and Rebecca Munford. Houndmills, Basingstoke: Palgrave Macmillan, 2004. 142–53.

Neustatter, Angela. *Hyenas in Petticoats: A Look at Twenty Years of Feminism*. London: Harrop, 1989.

Nicholson, Linda, ed. *The Second Wave: A Reader in Feminist Theory*. New York and London: Routledge, 1997.

Oakley, Ann. *The Sociology of Housework*. London: Martin Robertson, 1974.

---. *Housewife*. 1974. Harmondsworth: Penguin, 1976.

O'Faolain, Nuala. "You've Come a Long Way, Baby." *The Guardian* 13 Sept. 2003.

O'Reilly, Jane. "The Housewife's Moment of Truth." *Ms*. Spring 1972.

Ouellette, Laurie. "Victims No More: Postfeminism, Television, and *Ally McBeal*." *The Communication Review* 5 (2002): 315–37.

Overholser, Geneva. "What 'Post-Feminism' Really Means." *The New York Times* 19 Sept. 1986: 30.

Owen, Susan A. "Vampires, Postmodernity, and Postfeminism: *Buffy the Vampire Slayer*." *Journal of Popular Film and Television* 27.2 (1999): 24–31.

Pearson, Allison. *I Don't Know How She Does It*. London: Vintage, 2003.

Pender, Patricia. " '*I'm Buffy and You're…History*' The Postmodern Politics of *Buffy*." *Fighting the Forces: What's at Stake in* Buffy the Vampire Slayer. Ed. Rhonda V. Wilcox and David Lavery. Lanham, Boulder, New York, Oxford: Rowman & Littlefield, 2002. 35–44.

Petrova, Erma. " 'You Cannot Run from your Own Darkness'/'Who says I'm Running?': Buffy and the Ownership of Evil." *Refractory: A Journal of Entertainment Media*. 2003. 21 Feb. 2004 <http://www.refractory.unimelb. edu.au/journalissues/vol2/ermapetrova.htm>.

Probyn, Elspeth. "New Traditionalism and Post-Feminism: TV does the Home." *Screen* 31.2 (1990): 147–59.

Projansky, Sarah. "Mass Magazine Cover Girls: Some Reflections on Postfeminist Girls and Postfeminism's Daughters." *Interrogating Postfeminism: Gender and The Politics of Popular Culture*. Ed. Yvonne Tasker and Diane Negra. Durham and London: Duke University Press, 2007. 40–72.

Railla, Jean. "Feminism and the New Domesticity." 30 November 2005 <http://getcrafty.com/blogs.php?user=jean&entry=598>.

Reed, Jennifer. "Roseanne: A 'Killer Bitch' for Generation X." *Third Wave Agenda: Being Feminist, Doing Feminism*. Ed. Leslie Heywood and Jennifer Drake. Minneapolis and London: University of Minnesota Press, 1997. 122–33.

Renstrom, Joelle. "Is the Slayer Destined to be Alone? Is the Mission All that Matters?" *the buzz: an entertainment e-zine*. 2003. 20 February 2004 <http://www. the-buzz.com/b_7_19a.html>.

Riviere, Joan. "Womanliness as a Masquerade." 1929. *Formations of Fantasy*. Ed. Victor Burgin, James Donald, and Cora Kaplan. London and New York: Methuen, 1986. 35–44.

Roberts, Chadwick. "The Politics of Farrah's Body: The Female Icon as Cultural Embodiment." *The Journal of Popular Culture* 37.1 (2003): 83–104.

Roiphe, Anne. *Loving Kindness*. New York: Simon and Schuster, 1987.

Rosenfelt, Deborah, and Judith Stacey. "Second Thoughts on the Second Wave." *Feminist Studies* 13 (1987): 341–61.

Rowe, Aimee Carillo, and Samantha Lindsey. "Reckoning Loyalties: White Femininity as 'Crisis.' " *Feminist Media Studies* 3.2 (2003): 173–91.

Rutland, Barry. "The Other of Theory." *Explorations on Post-Theory: Toward a Third Space*. Ed. Fernando de Toro. Frankfurt am Main: Vervuert; Madrid: Iberoamericana, 1999. 71–83.

Sanders, Lise Shapiro. " 'Feminists Love a Utopia': Collaboration, Conflict, and the Futures of Feminism." *Third Wave Feminism: A Critical Exploration*. Ed. Stacy Gillis, Gillian Howie, and Rebecca Munford. Houndmills, Basingstoke: Palgrave Macmillan, 2004. 49–59.

---. "Consuming Nigella." *Feminism, Domesticity and Popular Culture*. Ed. Stacy Gillis and Joanne Hollows. New York and London: Routledge, 2009. 151–63.

Schwarzer, Alice. *Die Antwort*. Cologne: Kiepenheuer & Witsch, 2007.

Scott, Kathryn Leigh. *The Bunny Years*. Los Angeles: Pomegranate Press, 1998.
Segal, Lynne. "Theoretical Affiliations: Poor Rich White Folk Play the Blues." *New Formations* 50 (2003): 142–56.
Shalit, Ruth. "Canny and Lacy: Ally, Dharma, Ronnie, and the Betrayal of Postfeminism." *The New Republic* 6 Apr. 1998: 27–32.
Sheffield, Eliza. "Postfeminist Fiction." *Electronic Book Review* 9 Jan. 1996, Writing (Post) Feminism. 16 Jan. 2006. <http:www.electronicbookreview.com/thread/writingpostfeminism/denotative>.
Sichtermann, Barbara. *Femininity: The Politics of the Personal*. 1983. Cambridge: Polity, 1986.
Siegel, Deborah L. "Reading Between the Waves: Feminist Historiography in a 'Postfeminist' Moment." *Third Wave Agenda: Being Feminist, Doing Feminism*. Ed. Leslie Heywood and Jennifer Drake. Minneapolis and London: University of Minnesota Press, 1997. 55–82.
---. "The Legacy of the Personal: Generating Theory in Feminism's Third Wave." *Hypatia* 12.3 (1997): 46–75.
Siegel, Deborah. *Sisterhood, Interrupted: From Radical Women to Grrls Gone Wild*. Houndmills and New York: Palgrave Macmillan, 2007.
Siemann, Catherine. "Darkness Falls on the Endless Summer: Buffy as Gidget for the Fin de Siècle." *Fighting the Forces: What's at Stake in* Buffy the Vampire Slayer. Ed. Rhonda V. Wilcox and David Lavery. Oxford: Rowman & Littlefield, 2002. 120–29.
Skeggs, Beverley. *Formations of Class and Gender*. London: Sage, 1997.
Smith, Joan. "I'm a Feminist, so I suppose I Must be Dead." *The Independent* 6 July 2003.
Snitow, Ann. "Pages from a Gender Diary: Basic Divisions in Feminism." *Dissent* 36.2 (1989): 205–24.
Sonnet, Esther. "'Erotic Fiction by Women for Women': The Pleasure of Postfeminist Heterosexuality." *Sexualities* 2.2 (1999): 167–87.
The Spice Girls. *Girl Power!* London: Zone/Chameleon Books, 1997.
Stables, Kate. "Run Lara Run." *Sight and Sound* 11.8 (2001): 18–20.
Stacey, Judith. "Are Feminists Afraid to Leave Home? The Challenge of Conservative Pro-Family Feminism." *What is Feminism?* Ed. Juliet Mitchell and Ann Oakley. Oxford: Basil Blackwell, 1986. 219–48.
Stefano, Christine di. "Dilemmas of Difference: Feminism, Modernity, and Postmodernism." *Feminism/Postmodernism*. Ed. Linda J. Nicholson. New York and London: Routledge, 1990. 63–81.
Steinem, Gloria. *Outrageous Acts and Everyday Rebellions*. New York: Signet, 1983.
The Stepford Wives. Dir. Bryan Forbes. Perf. Katherine Ross, Paula Prentiss, and Peter Masterson. Palomar, 1975.
The Stepford Wives. Dir. Frank Oz. Paramount Pictures, 2004.
Stoller, Debbie. "Introduction: Feminists Fatale: Bust-ing the Beauty Myth." *The BUST Guide to the New Girl Order*. Ed. Marcelle Karp and Debbie Stoller. New York: Penguin, 1999. 42–47.
Stone, Alison. "On the Genealogy of Women: A Defence of Anti-Essentialism." *Third Wave Feminism: A Critical Exploration*. Ed. Stacy Gillis, Gillian Howie, and Rebecca Munford. Houndmills, Basingstoke: Palgrave Macmillan, 2004. 85–96.
Tasker, Yvonne. *Spectacular Bodies: Gender, Genre and the Action Cinema*. London and New York: Routledge, 1993.

Thelen, Christa. "Kind? Beruf? Beides! Warum junge Frauen darauf pfeifen, perfekt zu sein. Wann Schluss ist mit dem Entweder-Oder. Und warum wir in Zukunft alle anders leben werden." *Brigitte* 7 May 2008: 164–70.

"There Goes the Neighborhood." *Scarecrow and Mrs. King.* Writ. Brad Buckner and Eugenie Ross-Leming. Dir. Rod Holcomb. CBS. 10 Oct. 1983.

Thompson, Jim. " 'Just a Girl' – Feminism, Postmodernism and *Buffy the Vampire Slayer.*" *Refractory: A Journal of Entertainment Media.* 2003. 21 Feb. 2004 <http://www.refractory.unimelb.edu.au/journalissues/vol2/jimthompson.htm>.

Thornham, Sue. "Second Wave Feminism." *The Routledge Companion to Feminism and Postfeminism.* Ed. Sarah Gamble. London and New York: Routledge, 2001. 29–42.

---. *Women, Feminism and Media.* Edinburgh: Edinburgh University Press, 2007.

Tincknell, Estella, et al. "Begging for It: 'New Femininities,' Social Agency, and Moral Discourse in Contemporary Teenage and Men's Magazines." *Feminist Media Studies* 3.1 (2003): 47–63.

Tasker, Yvonne. *Spectacular Bodies: Gender, Genre and the Action Cinema.* London and New York: Routledge, 1993.

Tasker, Yvonne, and Diane Negra. "Introduction: Feminist Politics and Postfeminist Culture." *Interrogating Postfeminism: Gender and The Politics of Popular Culture.* Ed. Yvonne Tasker and Diane Negra. Durham and London: Duke University Press, 2007. 1–25.

Tong, Rosemarie. *Feminist Thought: A Comprehensive Introduction.* London: Routledge, 1989.

Toro, Fernando de. "Explorations on Post-Theory: New Times." *Explorations on Post-Theory: Toward a Third Space.* Ed. Fernando de Toro. Frankfurt am Main: Vervuert; Madrid: Iberoamericana, 1999. 9–23.

Unger, Irwin, and Debi Unger. *The Times Were a Changin': The Sixties Reader.* New York: Three Rivers Press, 1998.

Vint, Sherryl. " 'Killing Us Softly'? A Feminist Search for the 'Real' Buffy." *Slayage: The On-line International Journal of Buffy Studies* 5. 24 Jan. 2004 <http://www.slayage.tv/essays/slayage5/vint.htm>.

Walker, Rebecca. "Being Real: An Introduction." *To Be Real: Telling the Truth and Changing the Face of Feminism.* Ed. Rebecca Walker. London: Anchor Books, 1995. xxix–xl.

---. "Becoming the Third Wave." *Ms.* Jan.–Feb. 1995: 39–41.

Walter, Natasha. *The New Feminism.* 1998. London: Virago, 2006.

Wallis, Claudia. "Onward, Women!" *Time* 4 Dec. 1989: 80–81.

Walters, Suzanna Danuta. *Material Girls: Making Sense of Feminist Cultural Theory.* Berkeley: University of California Press, 1995.

Waugh, Patricia. *Feminine Fictions: Revisiting the Postmodern.* London and New York: Routledge, 1989.

"Welcome to America, Mr. Brand." *Scarecrow and Mrs. King.* Dir. Winrich Kolbe. CBS. 21 Oct. 1985.

Westerlund-Shands, Kerstin. "Female Fatality in the Movies." *Moderna Språk* 87.2 (1993): 113–120.

Whelehan, Imelda. *Modern Feminist Thought: From the Second Wave to "Post-Feminism.*" Edinburgh: Edinburgh University Press, 1995.

---. *Overloaded: Popular Culture and the Future of Feminism.* London: The Women's Press, 2000.

---. *Helen Fielding's* Bridget Jones's Diary: *A Reader's Guide*. London and New York: Continuum, 2002.

---. *The Feminist Bestseller: From* Sex and the Single Girl *to* Sex and the City. Houndmills, Basingstoke: Palgrave Macmillan, 2005.

Whiteley, Sheila. *Women and Popular Music: Sexuality, Identity and Subjectivity*. London: Routledge, 2000.

Whittier, Nancy. *Feminist Generations: The Persistence of the Radical Women's Movement*. Philadelphia: Temple University Press, 1995.

Wilcox, Rhonda V. "Bite-Size Pieces: Disassembling the Gothic Villain in *Witchblade*." *Postfeminist Gothic: Critical Interventions in Contemporary Culture*. Ed. Benjamin A. Brabon and Stéphanie Genz. Basingstoke: Palgrave Macmillan, 2007. 43–55.

Wilcox, Rhonda, V., and David Lavery. "Introduction." *Fighting the Forces: What's at Stake in* Buffy the Vampire Slayer. Ed. Rhonda V. Wilcox and David Lavery. Lanham, Boulder, New York, Oxford: Rowman & Littlefield, 2002. xvii–xxix.

Williams, Anne. "*The Stepford Wives*: What's a Living Doll to Do in a Postfeminist World?" *Postfeminist Gothic: Critical Interventions in Contemporary Culture*. Ed. Benjamin A. Brabon and Stéphanie Genz. Basingstoke: Palgrave Macmillan, 2007. 85–98.

Williams, Joan. *Unbending Gender: Why Family and Work Conflict and What To Do About It*. Oxford: Oxford University Press, 2000.

Wittig, Monique. "One Is Not Born a Woman." *Writing on the Body: Female Embodiment and Feminist Theory*. Ed. Katie Conboy, Nadia Medina, and Sarah Stanbury. New York: Columbia University Press, 1997. 309–17.

Wolf, Naomi. *Fire with Fire: The New Female Power and How it Will Change the 21st Century*. 1993. London: Vintage, 1994.

Wollstonecraft, Mary. *A Vindication of the Rights of Woman*. 1792. Vol. 5 of *The Works of Mary Wollstonecraft*. Ed. J. Todd and M. Butler. London: Pickering and Chatto, 1958.

Woodlock, Delanie. "A Call for Young Women to Get Mad!" *Feminista* 4.2 (2000). 25 July 2001 <http://feminista.com/v4n2/woodlock.html>.

Working Girl. Dir. Mike Nichols. Perf. Melanie Griffith, Sigourney Weaver, Harrison Ford, and Joan Cusack. 20th Century Fox, 1988.

Zeisler, Andi. "Marketing Miss Right." *Bitch Magazine* 12 (1999). 19 Feb. 2001 <http://www.bitchmagazine.com/archives/12_99missr/miss.htm>.

Index

action heroine, 32–3, 152–8, 168n11
Ally McBeal, 32, 134–5, 145–7

Baby Boom, 32, 124, 127–9, 198n13–14
backlash, 30, 32, 69–75, 79, 80, 99,
    111, 123–5, 127, 139, 143–4,
    147n9–10
Beauvoir, Simone de, 29, 37, 39–43,
    46, 50, 85, 101–2, 170n8,
    181n11–12, 181n14, 181n17,
    182n18, 183n6, 185n18, 190n8,
    194n7
bra-burner, 29, 53–6, 66, 93
Bridget Jones's Diary, 32, 135–9, 145,
    147–51
Brown, Helen Gurley, 139–43,
    200–201n6–8, 201n10
Buffy the Vampire Slayer, 33, 159–69,
    202n6, 202n8–10
bunny boiler, 65–7, 73n2,
    185n4
Butler, Judith, 5–6, 13–15, 17, 31,
    84–5, 96n6, 175n14–15,
    189n3–6

chick lit, 1, 83n10
choice, 3, 9, 10, 15–16, 20–1, 25, 28–9,
    31–3, 85–6
consciousness-raising, 38, 50–1,
    137n1, 182–183n3
consumerism, 24, 45, 82, 85–6, 88,
    93n10, 195n12
Cosmopolitan, 141–2, 148n9

Daly, Mary, 30, 59–60, 63, 77, 102n1,
    184n16
Denfeld, Rene, 173
Diary of a Mad Housewife, 31, 103–5,
    194n8
Doane, Mary Ann, 12–13
domesticity, 32, 67, 72–4, 76, 78,
    99–117, 127n10, 196n18
downshifting, 128–9, 132n13

Faludi, Susan, 21, 30, 65, 71–5, 79,
    111, 149
Fatal Attraction, 32, 65–6, 73, 125–7,
    145n1–3, 198n11–12
Fear of Flying, 57–8
The Feminine Mystique, 29, 43–7, 77,
    100–1, 118–20, 181n16
femininity, 5–18, 25–8, 31, 33, 37–8,
    40, 69–70, 83–5, 95–6, 153, 160,
    162
  and class, 41–3, 48–9
  and feminism, 9, 16, 33, 39, 48–9,
    53–6, 59, 61, 63, 70, 72, 75–6,
    78, 81, 83–4, 87, 93–6, 109, 148,
    167n8, 193n26–7, 202n10
  genealogical approach to, 7–8, 85
  new forms of, 8–9, 17, 33, 56, 76,
    78–9, 85, 92–5, 160, 162
  as performance, 9–11, 13–15,
    148
feminism
  liberal, 38–50
  and popular culture, 28–9, 54–5, 67,
    69, 82, 85–6, 186–187n7,
    189n5
  and postfeminism, 20–2
  radical, 29, 38, 42, 49, 50–64
  second wave, 1–2, 4, 10, 20, 23,
    26, 28–30, 35, 37–40, 53, 85,
    100–3, 109–10, 118–20, 139,
    143n2
feminist mystique, 30, 35,
    78n7
Fielding, Helen, 136, 199n2, 200n4
Firestone, Shulamith, 30, 53, 57–8,
    60–2, 185n17–20
Friedan, Betty, 7, 29–31, 38, 43–9,
    67–8, 75–81, 100–1, 118–20,
    121–3, 142n15, 181–182n17,
    187–188n12–14, 188n16, 190n17,
    194n6, 194n12, 197n1, 197n3–5,
    201n10